AF291437

PERFECT ORGANISM

With thanks to the patrons of
Perfect Organism:

Tim Atkins
Michael Bailey
Philip Bak
John Bower
Gareth Coker
Drewin Cottren
Luc De Brouwer
Michael Douse
(Gonzo850) Edgard Gonzalez Summers
Tim Heaton
Marc Laidlaw
Brian Mattucci
Ryan Meikle
Jamie Moorcroft-Sharp
David Morris
Conor O'Donovan
Thomas Painter
Sam Rickman
Travis Roesner – @Teqonix
Harvey Smith
Neil Stuchbury
Liam Tart
Stu 'Stoonami' Taylor
David Wilson
Catherine Woolley

PERFECT ORGANISM

AN ALIEN: ISOLATION COMPANION

ANDY KELLY

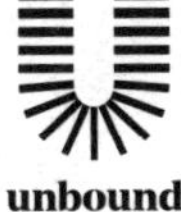

unbound

First published in 2024

Unbound
c/o TC Group, 6th Floor King's House,
9–10 Haymarket, London SW1Y 4BP

www.unbound.com

While every effort has been made to trace the owners of
copyright material reproduced herein, the publisher would like
to apologise for any omissions and will be pleased to incorporate
missing acknowledgements in any further editions.

Typeset by Jouve (UK), Milton Keynes

A CIP record for this book is available from the British Library

ISBN 978-1-80018-351-3 (hardback)
ISBN 978-1-80018-353-7 (ebook)

Printed in Great Britain by Bell and Bain Ltd, Glasgow

1 3 5 7 9 10 8 6 4

Contents

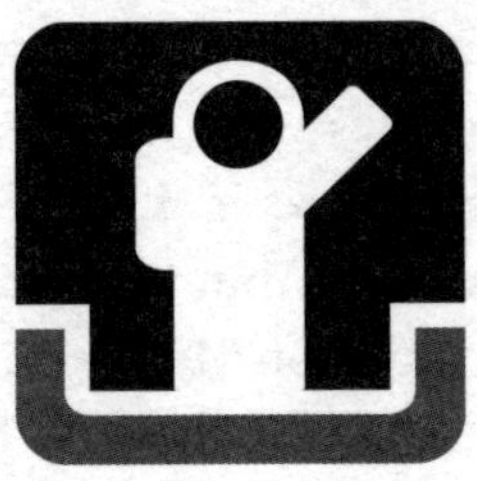

Introduction

An obsession is born.

I remember the first time I heard about *Alien: Isolation*. It was 2014 – a cold January afternoon – and I was in the PC Gamer office in Bath, England. A colleague, Chris Thursten, had just been to a press event organised by Sega to see a new *Alien* game. Almost exactly a year earlier Sega had published Gearbox's staggeringly poor *Aliens: Colonial Marines*, so I wasn't too excited to hear about another bad video game based on my favourite sci-fi series.

But it was clear from the moment Chris started talking about this new game from, bizarrely, the creators of the *Total War* series – breathlessly describing its retro-futuristic aesthetic, clever systems-driven design and dynamic alien adversary – that this was a different beast altogether.

It sounded like the *Alien* game I always dreamed someone would make, taking inspiration from Ridley Scott's original 1979 movie rather than James Cameron's sequel. An *Alien* game where H. R. Giger's famous creature wasn't just cannon fodder waiting to be mowed down with a pulse rifle, but an intelligent, formidable and unpredictable foe. A perfect organism.

When you work in the games media you attend a *lot* of preview events, and at a certain point they all start to blur into one another. But there have been a handful over the years that I remember creating a palpable buzz in the shared offices where all of Future Publishing's games magazines were made.

One was a demo of *Fallout 3*, in which developers Bethesda showed journalists a mission that gives the player the choice to either save or nuke the town of Megaton. The people who saw it were, appropriately enough, blown away by the magnitude of this decision and its impact on the world.

Another was the aforementioned media preview event for *Alien: Isolation* – because no one knew what the game *was*. They were led into a dark room, given headphones and a controller, and suddenly thrown into a nightmare with this creature that could out-smart them, adapt to their playing habits and intelligently hunt them down. A lot of nerves were shattered that day, and word of mouth began to spread through the media like wildfire.

In an interview with PCGamesN, lead designer Gary Napper recalls a journalist at this event stuffing Ripley into a locker to hide from the alien, taking his headphones off, turning to the developers, exhaling, and saying: I'm safe here. 'A second later, the alien ripped into the locker and killed him!'

Alien: Isolation featured on the cover of *PC Gamer* later that month, and Chris's hands-on preview – the cover feature – was glowing to say the least. I read it and re-read it, thinking it sounded too good to be true. But I knew, looking at the screenshots pro-vided by developers Creative Assembly to illustrate the feature, that this was a studio that just *got Alien*.

When publishers or developers send screenshots to the press, they're usually so-called *bullshots* – carefully staged to make a game look as flattering and exciting as possible, even if it doesn't reflect the experience of actually playing it. But for *Isolation*, most of the screenshots were of empty environments. A desk with a glowing CRT monitor and a chunky IBM-style keyboard, revealing the game's retro-futuristic art design. An industrial, submarine-like corridor, just like the ones in which the crew of the *Nostromo* were hunted down. A table scattered with junk, including one of those drinking birds from the movie.

There were a few shots of the alien itself, but in all of them the creature was obscured in some way. Lurking in the shadows, moving behind a piece of scenery or out of focus in the distance as Amanda Ripley stared fearfully at a motion tracker. Even the artwork on the cover of the magazine made a point of hiding the alien, with it looming menacingly over the shoulder of Ripley's pressure suit rather than being front and centre for all to see.

As an *Alien* fan, this tasteful, considered choice of images spoke volumes. It told me that Creative Assembly was going to great lengths to recreate the movie's 1970s vision of the future, from the architecture down to the environmental clutter that made the *Nostromo* feel so convincingly lived-in. A screenshot of a close-up of a computer monitor might seem like a weird thing to send to journalists to print in a magazine, but in the case of *Isolation* it was a statement about how this developer was building its world.

The reluctance to show the alien was telling too. You barely see the xenomorph in *Alien*, which only makes it scarier. It's done this way because Ridley Scott had to use shadows, close-ups and quick cuts to hide the fact that his 'alien' was, in fact, a tall man in a rubber suit. But this limitation worked in his favour, and *Alien: Isolation* carries the tradition on. In both the game and the movie, the alien is scarier when you *can't* see it. Just the suggestion of it being there, your mind filling in the terrible blanks, is enough.

All of this was evidence for me that Creative Assembly understood the source material on a deeper level than any developer that had come before. After years of first-person shooters that reduced Giger's creature to a cardboard pop-up at a funfair shooting gallery, *Alien: Isolation* was a breath of fresh air.

Later in 2014, in late September, a review code arrived in my inbox. My editor, Samuel Roberts, had assigned me *Alien: Isolation* to review, and I remember the excitement of redeeming the code in Steam, thinking: this is it. It's *here*. A week later, after having spent far too long playing the game (especially up against a tight print deadline), I started writing the review.

The game was everything I hoped it would be and more. I scored it 93/100, which is incredibly high for PC Gamer – an outlet that historically never scores anything above 96. Why? I'm not sure; it's just one of those traditions that sticks and is passed down through each generation of UK writers. I didn't quite go to the top, despite my obvious love for the game. I had some issues with the narrative, which felt like the weak link in an otherwise exceptional game. But in hindsight I wish I'd gone for the 96. I mean, here I am writing an entire book about the thing. Surely that alone is worth PCG's highest honour.

'*Alien: Isolation* is a taut, confident, and electrifying horror game that perfectly captures the essence of Ridley Scott's legendary film,' I wrote. 'This is the game the *Alien* series has always deserved.' I also wrote a five-star review for the *Guardian*, in which I described it as 'a passionate homage to a horror classic and an unusually clever and subversive triple-A game.'

Alien: Isolation as of early 2024, sits at a respectable 81 on review aggregator website Metacritic. Most journalists loved (or at least *liked*) it, with Rock Paper Shotgun, Eurogamer, The Escapist, Destructoid and others all rightly singing its praises. But a handful of high-profile outlets were not as enthusiastic, with IGN – one of the biggest and most influential gaming websites in the world – slapping a 5.9 on it. I don't even want to think about all the people who didn't play the game because of that review. But that's all I'll say for now.

I even wrote a defensive rebuttal to the negative reviews in a *PC Gamer* article, which is kinda embarrassing to read back. But what can I say: I loved this game, and I still do. After I filed my reviews, I thought that would be the end of it. But *Alien: Isolation* was never far from my mind, and throughout the next decade I wrote countless articles about it. I've interviewed dozens of developers, on and off the record, online and in person, penned thousands of words about every aspect of the game, appeared on numerous podcasts to talk about it, argued about it with another critic who didn't like it on BBC radio. And I've continued to play it in my free time. It just won't leave me, even after all these years, and this enduring obsession is what led to me pitching this book.

But an important disclaimer: I wasn't there for the development of the game. I don't know the full story of its creation, and nobody except the people who worked on it ever will. Everything in this book has been sourced from on-the-record interviews conducted by me and other journos, books, articles, YouTube documentaries, forums and wikis, as well as my own analysis and knowledge of the game. *Perfect Organism* is more of a tribute to the finished product than a deep dive into the nitty gritty of its development. Hopefully that story will be told one day, if a journalist manages to navigate all those NDAs.

Also, special thanks to Matt Filer, the only person I know who loves *Alien: Isolation* more than me. A lot of the information in *Perfect Organism* concerning cut content, deleted scenes and development insights – and a lot more besides – comes from him digging deep into the game's data files.

Anyway, I hope you enjoy reading this highly niche book. *Alien: Isolation* is a video game like no other, and this is my ode to both the game and its developers. I don't know why it took so long for someone to make a game like this, but I'm glad Creative Assembly were the ones to realise the potential of an *Alien* game in which the creature was every bit the merciless, fearsome killing machine Ash so gleefully, chillingly described in Ridley Scott's horror classic.

Why *Alien: Isolation* Matters

The new standard for horror video games.

Why write an entire book about *Alien: Isolation*? I get asked that a lot – and even ask myself it sometimes. The simplest answer, but by no means the only one, is that this is a special, singular video game whose existence I think deserves to be immortalised in the pages of a book. I grew up reading games magazines and spent a good chunk of my adult life writing for them, so I have an enduring, admittedly increasingly outdated, fondness for the printed page. I've written more articles about the game than I can count, for many fantastic websites, but for me a book was the best way to pay tribute to the game. Seeing these words printed on a page, instead of just being slotted into a generic article template, just feels more meaningful. I'm old school like that.

It took a ridiculously long time for someone to make a great *Alien* game. There were plenty of good ones, but none that even came close to the tense, spine-chilling magic of that original movie. Until *Alien: Isolation* changed everything, the best *Alien* games were all about the action: chopping through heaving swarms of xenomorphs with heavy-duty weaponry, usually as a space marine – or even occasionally playing *as* a xenomorph, ripping marines to shreds. Then, suddenly, here's this game that eases its foot off the gas, takes the high-powered arsenal away, and decides playtime is over. Forget this empowering, all-out, guns-blazing sci-fi jarhead fantasy: it's time to get *scared*.

Alien: Isolation is, and I feel completely confident in making this claim, the scariest horror game ever made. There really is no contest. It baffles me that, since it launched in 2014, nothing has come close. Creative Assembly set a new standard for the genre, but it seems it was too high a standard. As I write this, no developer, no matter how talented, has managed to match it in terms of pure, mind-terrorising horror – and I don't think anyone ever will. *Isolation* increasingly feels like a true one-off. A rare moment in video games that will never truly be replicated. But why?

The art direction and sound design are a big part of it. By obsessively, painstakingly back-engineering the grimy, realistic production design of Ridley Scott's 1979 movie, Creative Assembly's artists built a setting – the decrepit space station Sevastopol – that feeds directly into the horror. Every small space, low ceiling, snaking air vent and labyrinthine network of narrow corridors has been specifically designed to make you feel oppressed and unsettled. There's no space worse to share with an alien killing machine.

Sound is, like in the movie, a crucial piece of the puzzle too. In every corner of the station, you hear computers chirping, boilers hissing, reel-to-reel tapes whirring and other ambient sounds that combine to create a disorientating, quietly overwhelming sonic landscape. There's no silence to help you listen out for distant movements of the xenomorph or a malfunctioning android marching in your direction. Occasionally an alarm will sound, or jets of steam will spew violently from overhead pipes, adding to the confusion: a trick borrowed from the final scenes of *Alien* where Ellen Ripley is trying desperately to trigger the *Nostromo*'s self-destruct sequence as the creature stalks her. Everything in *Isolation*, even the station itself, conspires against you. This is a video game that revels in – and is worryingly good at – making you feel uncomfortable. Playing in the dark with headphones is a challenge all of its own. I've lost count of how many people who've told me they physically can't play the game because of how relentlessly scary it is.

Then there's the fact that traditional weapons – usually a source of comfort in horror games – are essentially useless because, no matter how hard you try, the alien can never be killed. A revolver or shotgun might feel reassuring to hold in front of you as you creep through a dark corridor, but bullets won't even scratch the alien. You can scare it away with a flamethrower, but it won't be gone for long. All you'll do is piss it off. Firearms will do some damage to Working Joes and are effective against human enemies, but they make such a racket, alerting the alien to your presence, that using them is generally ill-advised. Guns will not save you here. The *Alien* universe may be set in a distant, hyper-advanced vision of a space-faring future, but this is not a utopian sci-fi universe like, say, *Star Trek*, where every problem can be solved through an ingenious, bafflingly termed use of technology. Synchronise the transporter's annular confinement beam to the frequency of the warp core? Sure, why not.

Alien: Isolation is also a rare AAA game – especially one based on an established intellectual property (IP) – whose gameplay has actual systemic depth. Although its depth might not reach the heights of something like *Deus Ex* or *System Shock*, there are still plenty of ways to toy with the AI and make creative use of Ripley's gadgets. It's not strictly an immersive sim, but it has the soul of one. For instance, if a group of trigger-happy human survivors are blocking the path ahead, throw a noisemaker at them. The high-pitched shrieking will alert the alien to their presence and they'll be torn to shreds without you having to lift a finger. The game doesn't tell you to do this: it's a tactic that emerges naturally through the game's interlocking systems and the reactions of the enemy AI.

But all of this would be nothing without the alien itself, the real star of the game. *Alien: Isolation* is the only horror game I've played where the malevolent force sent to kill you seems like it's *thinking*. A lot of clever stuff goes on behind the scenes, including an AI 'director' that measures how pressured the player is feeling in the moment and responds accordingly by increasing the aggression of the beast as this pressure increases. Even if you know all this, it doesn't matter one bit, because in the heat of the moment you don't feel like you're trying to outsmart a machine; you feel like you're facing off against an intelligent, reactive and horrifyingly driven creature with a devilish, implacable mind of its own.

This is the main thing that sets *Alien: Isolation* apart from other horror games. Monsters are rarely interesting in this genre. They'll usually follow a prescribed route through the world, springing to life if you make a sound or cross their line of sight. There are some exceptions, like *Dead Space 2*'s swift, tricksy Stalkers, but even their IQ is low compared to *Isolation*'s xeno. Creative Assembly's creation is jarringly, thrillingly unpredictable, even going so far as to *learn* from your habits and change its behaviour in response. It's an animal – a predator – not a code-brained automaton. This, and all of the above, is what makes *Isolation*, still, the undisputed master of the horror genre.

Alien: Isolation has a lot of fans, and fiercely passionate ones at that, but it's still very much a cult game. It's not a household name (even if the movie is) like *Half-Life*, *Grand Theft Auto*, *Bio-Shock*, or *Call of Duty*. But to me it's as important, worthy and medium-defining as any of those games. *Perfect Organism*, then, is me laying out a case for why I think that is so. You might not agree with me now, but hopefully by the end of this book, you'll realise why it deserves a spot in this pantheon of legendary video games – even if its audience is, in comparison, much smaller. More simply: *Alien: Isolation* is one of the best video games ever made, and this is my tribute to it.

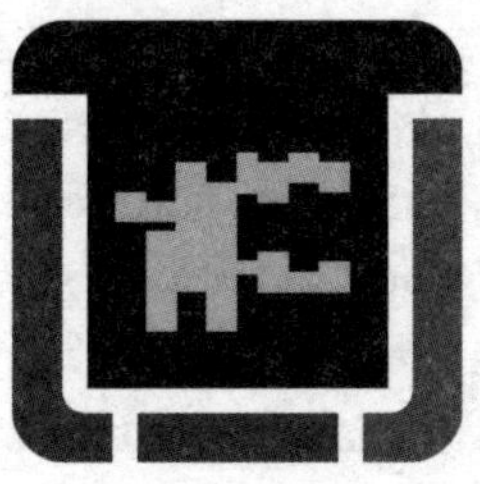

A Brief History of *Alien* Video Games

The good, the bad, the terrible.

Alien: Isolation may be the most authentic *Alien* game ever made, but it's by no means the first. As far back as the early 1980s, developers have been turning these movies into video games, with wildly mixed results. Over the years, across a variety of systems, we've seen arcade shooters, graphic adventures, platformers, strategy games, and even an ill-fated MMO. Most of these digital spin-offs, predictably, lean heavily into James Cameron's 1986 sequel, with its game-friendly xenomorph hordes, macho Marines and high-tech weaponry. Some, however, take a somewhat less predictable approach to the series – albeit with less than perfect execution. Alas, there are more bad *Alien* games than good ones, but a few classics can be found lurking in the air vents. Oh, and I've chosen to overlook the *Alien vs. Predator* games. Some of them are great, but I've decided to focus on those purely based on the *Alien* movies.

Alien
Year: 1982
Developer: Fox Video Games
Platform: Atari 2600

The first licensed *Alien* game doesn't quite do the source material justice. It's essentially a *Pac-Man* clone, where instead of gulping down pills, you destroy eggs; and instead of evading ghosts, you dodge xenomorphs. It's not a total copy, though: the unnamed protagonist, presumably a member of the *Nostromo* crew, can briefly deter the aliens by toasting them with a flamethrower.

Alien
Year: 1984
Developer: Concept Software
Platform: Commodore 64, ZX Spectrum, Amstrad CPC

This strategy game is much better at replicating the tension of the movie. You command the crew of the *Nostromo* as they hunt the alien using a menu-driven interface that looks like a blueprint of the ship. But you have to keep an eye on the crew's mental state, because if they become scared, stressed or hysterical, they'll refuse to follow your orders and probably get themselves killed.

Aliens: The Computer Game
Year: 1986
Developer: Activision/Mr. Micro Ltd
Platform: Apple II, Commodore 64, ZX Spectrum

This collection of interactive vignettes was the first of many video games based on James Cameron's action-packed sequel. It's a varied game for the time, mixing exploration, combat and basic puzzles. One minute you're landing a dropship on the surface of Acheron, the next you're creeping through Hadley's Hope with a pulse rifle mowing down pixelated xenomorphs.

Aliens: The Computer Game
Year: 1986

Developer: Software Studios/Mr. Micro Ltd
Platform: Amstrad CPC, Commodore 16/64, ZX Spectrum

Same name, different game. In this first-person take on *Aliens*, you control a squad of Colonial Marines searching for the queen's nest in an infested atmospheric processing plant. Despite its age, it's a surprisingly effective horror game, brilliantly capturing the confusion and chaos of those moments in the movie when our heroes are besieged by aliens on all sides.

Aliens: Alien 2
Year: 1987
Developer: Squaresoft
Platform: MSX

Today, Japanese developer Square Enix (formerly Squaresoft) is a popular purveyor of quality role-playing games. But one hot Tokyo summer in 1987 – long before it would go on to make its name with classic RPGs like *Final Fantasy*, *Secret of Mana*, *Xenogears* and *Chrono Trigger* – the fledgling studio developed and published a rare licensed game based on Cameron's blockbuster sequel.

Loosely following the events of the movie, you play as Ripley searching for Newt in the alien-infested colony of Hadley's Hope. As you descend into the stricken base you battle wall-crawling xenomorphs, slithering chestbursters and facehuggers launching themselves out of their eggs.

It's basic stuff – as most games were in the 1980s – but there's fun to be had in hopping between platforms and blasting xenos with Ripley's pulse rifle. Throughout the game you fight the alien queen, whose screen-filling sprite is suitably menacing, culminating in a final showdown in which you end her reign of terror for good. A skilled player can beat the game in twenty minutes.

Your reward for doing so is a heartwarming scene of Ripley

and Newt rushing into each other's arms, then an epilogue explaining that they both escaped Acheron along with Hicks, the last of the Colonial Marines. Just don't spoil the moment by thinking about what happens to them in *Alien 3*.

Aliens
Year: 1990
Developer: Konami
Platform: Arcade

This side-scrolling shooter, developed for arcades by Konami, is best known for its unusually bright, colourful take on what is typically a dark and subdued cinematic universe. Playing as either Ripley or Hicks, you use grenade launchers, flamethrowers and pulse rifles to blast through hordes of curiously fluorescent xenomorphs. A fun, if shallow, take on Cameron's sequel.

Alien 3
Year: 1992
Developer: Probe Entertainment
Platform: Super Nintendo, Sega Genesis

These moody side-scrolling shooters, released for Sega and Nintendo's rival 16-bit consoles, were based on David Fincher's infamously divisive sequel and had a lot in common – but were actually very different games. They were both set on Fiorina 'Fury' 161, the bleak prison planet Ripley's escape pod crash-landed on in the movie, and featured our shaven-headed hero rescuing prisoners and battling xenomorphs. But while the arcade-length Genesis version was all about fast-paced action and brain-boggling map memorisation, the SNES version was non-linear, atmospheric, exploratory and more reminiscent of games like *Super Metroid*. As for which version is best, well, that's a debate that will rage forever – but they're both absolutely worth playing.

Alien 3
Year: 1993
Developer: Bits Studios
Platform: Game Boy

Released exclusively for Nintendo's incredibly popular handheld, this Game Boy version of *Alien 3* was, once again, completely different from the others. This one featured a top-down perspective, focusing on exploration, survival, item gathering, and simple environmental puzzle solving. Unlike the movie's bittersweet ending, this more optimistic retelling of the story sees Ripley climbing back into her escape pod and leaving the planet.

Alien 3: The Gun
Year: 1993
Developer: Sega
Platform: Arcade

To truly experience this brilliant and intense on-rails shooter, you have to play it on the original arcade cabinet. Featuring a pair of wonderfully chunky lightguns based on *Aliens*' pulse rifles, *The Gun* saw you, a nameless Colonial Marine, battling your way through Fiorina 161 and mowing down hordes of xenomorphs and Weyland-Yutani commandos. Locations aside, it felt more like an *Aliens* game than an *Alien 3* one, but was pretty great all the same.

Aliens: A Comic Book Adventure
Year: 1995
Developer: Cryo Interactive
Platform: PC

Loosely based on Dark Horse's popular *Aliens* comics, this little-known curio is the first, and to date only, point-and-click adventure game set in the *Alien* universe. You play as a Colonial Marines commander tasked with investigating a distress call sent by a mining colony, which in this series can mean only one thing: xenomorphs. Sadly, boring grid-based combat, achingly slow pacing and poorly designed puzzles make this one hard to recommend.

Alien Trilogy
Year: 1996
Developer: Probe Entertainment
Platform: PlayStation, Sega Saturn, PC

The early-to-mid 1990s was the era of the '*Doom* clone', as developers tried to replicate the wild success of id Software's seminal first-person shooter. *Alien Trilogy* is *Doom* with xenomorphs, with levels *very* loosely based on the events of *Alien*, *Aliens* and *Alien 3*. The narrative is pretty flimsy and cuts a lot of corners, but that's not really the point here. The point is walking through dark, scary corridors and blowing away xenos, and in that regard it's a decent, if basic, shooter let down by some awkward console controls.

Aliens Online
Year: 1998
Developer: Mythic Entertainment/Kesmai
Platform: PC

Of all the games on the list, this has to be the most forgotten. Yes, there really was a massively multiplayer online game set in the *Alien* universe. Co-developed by MMO veterans Mythic, it sadly wasn't a *World of Warcraft*-style RPG, but an asymmetric team-based first-person shooter. Brilliantly, you could choose to play as either the Colonial Marines *or* the xenomorphs, and the latter was definitely more interesting. As an alien, you could scurry through ducts, climb into vents and get the jump on your opponents – which was essential, because all of your attacks only worked at close range. Don't worry about whether it's worth playing or not, though. In the year 2000, just two years after it launched, the *Aliens Online* servers were unceremoniously shut down.

Alien Resurrection
Year: 2000
Developer: Argonaut Games
Platform: PlayStation

Alien Resurrection, despite some excellent production design and a few standout moments, is widely considered to be one of the worst *Alien* movies. Yet this spin-off game, released exclusively for the PlayStation, is one of the best *Alien* games. When it launched, it was given a hard time by critics, including an infamous GameSpot review complaining about its 'terrifying' twin-stick control system – which would eventually become the standard control scheme for all first-person games on consoles. But time has been kinder to it, and over the past decade or so it's become something of a cult classic.

The game's story sticks to the movie relatively closely, taking place two centuries after the events of *Alien 3* and following the adventures of a cloned Ellen Ripley as she battles xenomorphs aboard the USM *Auriga*. You play as Ripley's clone for the majority of the game, but also get to control other characters from the film, including Winona Ryder's secret android Call, and two relatively minor mercenaries, Christie and Distephano.

While most *Alien* games up until this point had focused on action, *Resurrection* sprinkled some effective survival horror elements into the mix. There's plenty of shooting, but the game also takes some time to set the mood with flickering lights, xenos jumping out of the shadows, and a wonderfully gloomy atmosphere. This has proven to be a quietly influential game, inspiring an exciting new wave of PSX era-inspired horror devs. It's not quite *Alien: Isolation*, but it's the closest any other studio ever got.

Aliens: Thanatos Encounter
Year: 2001
Developer: Wicked Witch Software/Crawfish Interactive
Platform: Game Boy Color

This top-down shooter was developed especially for the Game Boy Color, and I don't blame you if you've never heard of it. The titular *Thanatos* is a spooky abandoned freighter infested with xenomorphs that you, choosing from one of five Colonial Marines, are tasked with eliminating. Cleverly, if you die, you can pick another grunt, replay the level and attempt to rescue the fallen ally. Otherwise, there isn't much that's special about this one: a forgettable action game that didn't do anything really interesting with the licence.

Aliens: Extermination
Year: 2006
Developer: Play Mechanix
Platform: Arcade

This lightgun shooter is about as basic as *Alien* games get. Set in Hadley's Hope after the events of *Aliens*, you play as a Colonial Marine sent to mop up any hostiles that somehow survived the movie's explosive finale. Don't think about it too much; it's just an excuse to blast hordes of xenomorphs and rampaging androids programmed by Weyland-Yutani to kill on sight for some reason. A deeply stupid arcade game that is probably more fun when drunk.

Aliens: Infestation
Year: 2011
Developer: WayForward/Gearbox Software
Platform: Nintendo DS

Now this is more like it. *Aliens: Infestation* is another great *Alien* game, taking inspiration from Nintendo's *Metroid* series. It features vivid comic-book-style art, crunchy side-scrolling combat and an interesting permadeath mechanic. If one of your Colonial Marines dies in battle, another in your party will take their place. You can replace dead characters with fifteen marines scattered around the game, but if your whole party is wiped out it's game over.

But for me, the real highlight of *Aliens: Infestation* is the song that plays over the end credits. It's a hilariously accurate Metallica pastiche, complete with comical James Hetfield-esque vocals, and features some truly wild lyrics about 'artificial persons' being impressed by the xenomorph's structural perfection, and the words 'concentrated acid for blood' sung in rapid succession. You have to hear it to believe it. Listen to the whole thing on YouTube right now. If you still own a DS, this one's a must-play.

Aliens: Colonial Marines
Year: 2013
Developer: Gearbox Software
Platform: PC, PlayStation 3, Xbox 360

Oh dear. Where to begin? *Aliens: Colonial Marines* had everything going for it. Legendary concept artist Syd Mead was hired to help design the levels. Gearbox had the full blessing of Fox to tell a new canon story in the *Alien* universe tying directly into James Cameron's sequel. Even some of the original *Aliens* cast, including Lance Henriksen and Michael Biehn, were involved.

But despite all this, the final product is half-baked, shallow, poorly designed, terribly written and riddled with bugs. The xenomorphs are a far cry from the perfect organism described by Ash, reduced to simple-minded cannon fodder. The level design is boring, repetitive and unimaginative. The Marines' dim-witted wise-cracking has none of the self-aware charm of the source material. It's just a really bad video game and comes across like a bad cover version of the movie it's based on. Avoid at all costs, basically.

Alien: Isolation
Year: 2014
Developer: Creative Assembly
Platform: PC, PlayStation 3/4, Xbox 360/One, Nintendo
Switch, iOS, Android

Things were looking bleak for *Alien* video games in the wake of *Colonial Marines*, but a year later, Creative Assembly emerged from the shadows and showed everyone how it was done. *Alien: Isolation* is the greatest *Alien* game ever made (I know, I'm a broken record), setting a new benchmark for the series by . . . well, just read the next chapter to find out why.

By the way, if you own a Switch OLED, I highly recommend getting hold of *Alien: Isolation* for it. Not only is the Switch edition the best-looking console port thanks to improved anti-aliasing, but the inky black shadows and atmospheric lighting look sublime on that display.

Aliens: Armageddon
Year: 2014
Developer: Play Mechanix/Raw Thrills
Platform: Arcade

Hey, it's another arcade game. But I gotta give this one props for its unhinged premise. Earth has been overrun with aliens and facehuggers, and your only hope to survive this xeno-apocalypse is to reach a rescue ship named the *Ark* (see what they did there?) and escape off-world. As far as on-rails lightgun shooters go this is fun enough, and seeing aliens running around Earth is pretty entertaining. A facehugger or alien queen somehow making it to Earth has been a looming threat in several *Alien* movies, so this is your chance to experience first-hand an absurd version of how that might play out.

Alien: Blackout
Year: 2019
Developer: Rival Games/Theory Interactive/D3 Go!
Platform: iOS, Android

Alien: Isolation fans waited five years for a sequel, and in 2019 we finally got one! Well, *kinda*. This mobile game reveals what happened to Amanda Ripley following the events of *Isolation*. She was rescued by the inhabitants of a Weyland-Yutani research outpost, Mendel Station, and placed in hypersleep. But when she awoke, she found the place terrorised by, yep, an alien.

The game is very different from *Isolation*: it sees you remotely controlling the station's doors and systems and guiding the crew of a docked ship, the USCSS *Haldin*, to safety. A cool enough idea, and by no means a terrible game, but perhaps not the best way to continue Amanda's story. A proper sequel would have been more appropriate, but hey, it's something.

Some angry backlash online to the revelation that *Alien: Blackout* was a mobile spin-off led to Fox briefly entering damage-control mode and clarifying that the project wasn't strictly a sequel. '[*Blackout*] is a standalone game that shares Amanda Ripley as a main character,' the studio tells *Game Informer*. 'But it's not related to, or a sequel of, *Isolation*.'

Aliens: Fireteam Elite
Year: 2021
Developer: Cold Iron Studios
Platform: PlayStation 4/5, Xbox One/X/S, PC, Nintendo Switch (2023)

I'll be honest: I've only ever played this co-op shooter solo. If you play on your own, you're assigned a pair of android marines, Alpha and Beta, to fight alongside you, which is a nice touch. Structurally, it couldn't be more basic. You move through a level, a door locks, and a massive group of xenos rushes you. You kill them all, the door unlocks, and you move to the next fight.

Story-wise, it's *Alien* by numbers. A squad of Colonial Marines is sent to investigate a refinery that's been invaded by xenomorphs. This leads to the discovery of a planet where Weyland-Yutani is conducting sinister experiments on humans, etc. You get the idea. The narrative in *Fireteam Elite*, if you can call it that, is really just an excuse to drag you to different maps.

However, as simple as it is, I find blasting through waves of aliens with my smartgun quite cathartic. The weapons feel good and some of the environments (particularly a city built by *Prometheus*'s enigmatic Engineers) are quite striking to look at. I don't know how I'd feel about it if I paid money for it but playing it for free via Xbox Game Pass was a fun way to kill a few hours.

Aliens: Dark Descent
Year: 2023
Developer: Tindalos Interactive
Platform: PlayStation 4/5, Xbox One/X/S, PC

Another game based on *Aliens*? After *Isolation*, I thought maybe developers would realise the potential in making games based on Ridley Scott's original movie. But here we are back in the familiar surroundings of Cameron Town. Colonial Marines. Swarms of xenomorphs. Cocky one-liners. You know the drill. I mean, I love *Aliens*, but *please*, watch any other *Alien* movie.

Dark Descent is, as tired as the premise is, pretty good. It's a real-time tactics game wherein you order your squad around, which instantly sets it apart from all the other *Aliens* games that have come before it.

I'd recap the story, but it's completely unremarkable. Space station. Xenomorphs. Marines. Again, the drill. You know it. There's an *XCOM*-inspired strategy layer where you can manage your squad, tend to their wounds, and unlock better gear and weapons for them, but the more time you spend here, the more the xenomorph infestation grips the next level.

Dark Descent is a decent *Alien* game, but I think it's time developers broaden their horizons. *Alien Resurrection*, *Prometheus* and *Alien: Covenant* – whatever you think of them – all bring something new to the mix. They're still fundamentally movies about a giant penis murdering people in sci-fi corridors, but each has its own perspective, aesthetic and flavour. That's why it's such a shame when a new *Alien* game is announced and, once again, it's steeped in the familiar atmosphere and visual design of the 1986 movie.

Beginnings

Making the ultimate Alien *video game.*

Somewhere out there, hidden in the depths of a movie studio archive I can only imagine looks like the warehouse from the end of *Raiders of the Lost Ark*, is a treasure many *Alien* fans would do unspeakable things to get even a brief glimpse of. A priceless assortment of production material from the creation of Ridley Scott's 1979 movie – including set blueprints, continuity Polaroids, props, scripts, storyboards, concept art, models and costume photography – was preserved by Fox and safely stowed away in its archives.

A lot of this material has, over the years, made its way into books, magazine articles and behind-the-scenes documentaries about the making of the first *Alien* movie. J. W. Rinzler's superb book *The Making of Alien* is not only an essential read for anyone interested in the creation of that film, but it also features some particularly rare nuggets plucked from this collection. However, much of the archive's contents remain unseen – at least by the general public.

In 2008, a group of hardcore *Alien* fans from Creative Assembly – a game development studio based in Horsham, England best known for making sports and epic military strategy games – was given the opportunity of a lifetime. Fox granted them access to this archive, which when digitised amounted to an astonishing six terabytes of photos, documents and art. (Well, that's one version of the story. I've heard six terabytes from one developer, and three from another. But you get the idea: there was a *lot* of amazing stuff in there.)

The team then began using this collection for pre-production on a new *Alien* game based on the original movie. They obsessed over its contents, deconstructing it to create a new world in the same style as the film world. As a lifelong fan of *Alien*, director Alistair Hope compared delving into this archive to the scene in *Pulp Fiction* where John Travolta opens the briefcase and is bathed in golden, otherworldly light from some mysterious treasure inside.

This unprecedented access was hugely inspirational for Creative Assembly's artists and designers. *Alien* superfans on the team who thought they knew the movie inside-out were humbled by this remarkable compendium, whose contents revealed a depth of detail and craft far beyond that which made it onto the screen. It inspired them to take the same approach as those production designers working in Shepperton Studios back in 1979: paying close attention to the fine details and the practicalities of this lived-in sci-fi universe.

But Creative Assembly weren't just *handed* an *Alien* game: they had to convince Fox they were the right people for the job. From the outset, the developers wanted to create a game in the spirit of *Alien*, not *Aliens*. Historically, as we saw in the previous chapter, most video games based on these movies were influenced by James Cameron's bombastic blockbuster sequel, not the slow-burning original. From a game design perspective, this makes sense. It's simpler to give a player a pulse rifle and throw dozens of aliens at them than pit them against a single hyper-intelligent xenomorph. But Creative Assembly weren't interested in *simple*.

Sega, parent company of Creative Assembly, had the rights to the *Alien* licence and had asked the studio to think about making a game set in that universe. After a slew of poorly received *Alien* games, Creative Assembly first wondered if this IP – as recognisable and popular as it was – wasn't something of a poisoned chalice. But then realising the potential for an *Alien* survival horror game, rather than the usual *Aliens*-inspired first-person shooter, Creative

Assembly decided this was an opportunity worth taking. Within a week, Alistair Hope had drawn up a five-page pitch in which he set out his vision for a tense, deliberately paced horror game, rooted in the hard sci-fi of Scott's movie, where the main antagonist couldn't be killed. You couldn't just shoot this thing; you had to outsmart it, outmanoeuvre it.

'From the moment we pitched the original concept to Fox, they were completely behind us,' Hope says in an interview with PC Gamer. 'I think because we were trying to stay true in spirit to the original, they felt like it was in safe hands. It was a collaboration, but I don't think we ever came across anything where anyone said no, you can't do that.'

It was a great idea, and Fox was on board, but Sega was resistant at first. Sega also had the rights to the licence for the Olympics and would have much preferred Creative Assembly to build something with that instead. This would be a much safer bet than a risky, tense horror game. Undeterred, however, a group of devs broke away from the main team and created a demo in five weeks designed to put across their vision for that currently formless *Alien* game. It was a mood piece, designed to give a sense of what it might be like to inhabit the dark, claustrophobic, retro-futuristic setting of the 1979 movie.

Interestingly, the demo was built using an engine Creative Assembly had previously used to create a console-focused action game named *Viking: Battle for Asgard*. Released in 2008, this hack-and-slash action–adventure was inspired by Norse mythology (long before Sony's *God of War* had success with a similar setting), and was an attempt by Creative Assembly to expand its horizons beyond its successful *Total War* strategy series. Reviews were mixed, but the technology powering the game gave the skunkworks team making the *Alien* demo – which was really only a handful of engineers and artists – a time-saving starting point for their intriguing new proof of concept.

Creative Assembly made the risky decision to create its own engine and toolset, rather than using an established engine like Unreal. This was partly because the developers wanted full control over the rendering and lighting systems so they could get as close to the look of the movie as possible. The *Viking* engine was therefore iterated on and modified, eventually becoming the in-house Cathode engine that ultimately powered *Alien: Isolation*.

Footage of this demo recently appeared in a documentary by Noclip, and it's a fascinating early look at what would eventually become *Alien: Isolation*. The player walks along a dark corridor as fluorescent strip lights flicker on around them, and a tranquil piece of classical music – Mozart's 'Eine kleine Nachtmusik', as heard in the film – drifts down the hall. A pair of drinking birds sip from a glass of water, the lights of chunky computers blink on and off, and the deep rumble of engines can be heard in the background.

Even at this early stage, in a hastily made and completely non-interactive demo used for illustration purposes, Creative Assembly absolutely nailed the atmosphere of *Alien*. We also catch several glimpses of the 1979 Weyland-Yutani winged sun logo – an indication of just how deeply rooted in the aesthetic of the original movie the team intended this game to be. The environments and lighting in the finished game are much more sophisticated, but it's amazing how much of the look and feel was already firmly in place.

The player moves to a brilliantly observed replica of the medbay set from the movie. The room is dark except for a spotlight shining on a facehugger that has attached itself to some poor soul's head. Then, from the shadows, more facehuggers appear, scuttling like spiders. The player flees the room, only to be confronted by the xenomorph itself. It drops from the ceiling – dark, slinky and terrifying – and lunges at the player with a bone-chilling shriek. The animation of the alien falling, almost *dripping*, out of the vent is wonderfully unsettling and uncanny, and a version of it actually made it into the finished game, when Ripley encounters the creature in Sevastopol's medical facility.

Mission accomplished. Everyone who saw this short but thrilling demo was immediately sold on the idea, including the executives at Sega, who wisely decided to make *Alien: Isolation* a reality. The nebulous, sketched idea of an *Alien* survival horror game was interesting, sure, but actually getting something in front of people – something they could *see* and *hear* – made a bigger, more immediate impact. If it wasn't for this demo, and the clear, confident vision of its creators, *Alien: Isolation* probably wouldn't have been greenlit.

Alistair Hope's next job was building a team to actually make this strange, ambitious game. At first, the team was just a handful of people stuck in the corner of the floor on which the *Total War* games were being developed. Then, as more people joined, the team was given its own floor. Around the time *Isolation* was being developed, a lot of British development studios were closing down, including Realtime Worlds, Black Rock and Bizarre Creations. It was a bleak time for game developers, but the *Isolation* team took comfort in the fact that they'd just been given an exciting new project with the enthusiastic backing of Sega and Fox.

Creative Assembly managed to attract a lot of talent to the project – which was, for a while, known as *Alien: Year Zero* – including developers from industry giants like Rockstar and Ubisoft. But, cleverly, the studio also hired outside of the games industry bubble. People from the world of film and TV were brought onboard, including lighting artists who had never worked on a video game before. Ridley Scott did something similar during the pre-production of *Alien*, famously hiring Swiss surrealist H. R. Giger and French comic-book artist Jean 'Mœbius' Giraud – neither of whom were part of the Hollywood system – to bring their unique aesthetic sensibilities to the movie.

Gary Napper, one of *Alien: Isolation*'s lead designers, left a job at EA Bright Light (a Guildford-based studio best known for making *Harry Potter* games) to join the project. He signed an NDA, got his hands on an early demo, and from the moment he saw the alien there was no question: he *had* to work on this game. Hiring continued gradually over time, and eventually there were around a hundred people working on bringing *Alien: Isolation* to life.

But there was one thing Sega still had concerns about: the perspective. Today, first-person horror games are both commonplace and incredibly popular. Games like *Dying Light, Devotion, SOMA,*

Phasmophobia and even recent entries in the *Resident Evil* series have let players see through the eyes of their protagonists. It's a more nerve-racking way to experience horror, so it's no surprise it's become the standard. But when *Alien: Isolation* was being pitched, this wasn't the case. Third-person horror was still the thing.

That first demo was positioned entirely from a first-person perspective and was all the more effective because of it. But to please Sega, and increase the chance of the game getting made, the studio decided, somewhat reluctantly, to shift to third person. Footage exists of this brief shift, and it's quite jarring to look at. The camera hangs over Amanda Ripley's right shoulder, similar to the likes of *Dead Space* and *Resident Evil 4*, and the distinctive intimacy and impact of *Isolation*'s eventual first-person perspective is conspicuously absent.

That's not to say it made for a bad experience, just a different one. In the footage, unearthed again by Noclip, being able to see Amanda's face as she hides from the xenomorph is quite striking. Her eyes widen with fear as she senses it closing in and you can see her breathing heavily as her heart rate quickens. The death animations are also more brutal. In first person, what exactly happens when the alien grabs hold of you is left to your imagination. But in third person, these violent ends are, for better or worse, much more explicit.

Thankfully, first-person prevailed. Though early first-person gameplay demos weren't quite working, after hacking the camera and repositioning it on Amanda's forehead, the view felt instantly better. Sega and Fox were both expecting a third-person survival horror game, which was the trend at the time, but Creative Assembly managed to convince both sets of execs that viewing the world, and the alien, through the hero's eyes made for a better game.

Even so, it still took Creative Assembly years to figure out exactly how all the different pieces of this unusual *Alien* game they'd dreamed up would fit together. As they tested while elements were still being worked on, there was some doubt in the studio about whether the game would work or not. That is, until the developers created what is referred to in the games industry as a *vertical slice* – a polished, refined, fully featured demo intended to give the player a clear idea of what the finished game will be like.

With animation, sound, lighting, special effects and other crucial features in place, *Alien: Isolation*'s magic began to emerge. People in the studio were playing the demo over and over again simply because it was so fun. The alien's AI was at a stage where the creature's behaviour in the demo level was unpredictable and surprising, and this in tandem with everything else made it obvious to Creative Assembly that they were onto something special.

A similar demo was eventually used for the media hands-on event that led to all those glowing previews – including PC Gamer's back in early 2014. This demo build was stripped down, with crafting, hacking and other elements removed to focus squarely on the alien AI and the stealth elements. But it spoke to the power of Creative Assembly's concept that, even reduced to its core, the game was still compelling, fun, and, more importantly, scary as all hell.

The idea of *Alien: Isolation* went against everything that typically defined a mainstream, big-budget video game based on a popular, world-famous IP. Creative Assembly put immense value on steady pacing, detailed world-building and deep systems-driven gameplay, resisting the urge to make something broad and approachable. This could have scared Sega away, but they believed in the team's vision enough to support it.

Resident Evil 4, released by Capcom in 2005 to widespread critical acclaim and record-breaking sales for the series, was something of a turning point for horror video games. Suddenly, everyone wanted to make their own action-packed over-the-shoulder horror shooter. Slower, more methodical games fell out of favour, especially in the AAA space. The developers of *Alien: Isolation* stuck to their guns, however, and were delighted when, as the game was being developed, a more considered style of horror made a resurgence thanks to the success of indie horror hit *Amnesia: The Dark Descent* and its many imitators.

Creative Assembly also took inspiration from games outside of the horror genre. The oppressive tone and stark brutality of

Playdead's monochrome puzzle–platformer *Limbo* was a big influence. So was Ion Storm's influential stealth game *Thief: Deadly Shadows*: specifically, the feeling it projects onto the player of being underpowered, surrounded by enemies and forced to lurk in the shadows to survive. The video-nasty violence of Monolith's *Condemned* series (also published by Sega) made an imprint on the developers too.

As for who the protagonist of this new canonical entry in the *Alien* series should be, Creative Assembly kept coming back to one person: Amanda Ripley. They thought about who would care that the *Nostromo* went missing. Weyland-Yutani, of course, but they needed someone with an emotional connection to the missing towing ship and its ragtag crew of space truckers.

Ellen's daughter was the obvious choice. Not only did she want answers about *why* the ship had vanished, but she wanted closure too. Was her mother dead? Or was she out there in deep space, lost and alone? Weyland-Yutani wouldn't *really* care about the fate of the *Nostromo*, at least not beyond the substantial financial hit suffered when it disappeared. But Amanda would be deeply invested in pursuing the truth, which would give the game a strong and resonant emotional underpinning. She was perfect.

Creative Assembly didn't think Fox would go for it, because she would be a major addition to the mythology and IP owners are generally very protective over such things. This is the daughter of *Ellen Ripley* we're talking about here, after all; arguably the most important character in the *Alien* series. Creative Assembly really wanted to tell this story, and the thought of the studio denying them the opportunity was a source of much stress among the team. Then, just like that, Fox gave them their blessing. They loved the idea, and besides a brief mention in the director's cut of *Aliens*, Amanda Ripley's life was a blank slate, giving the developers a lot of freedom to tell her story.

It was also important to Creative Assembly to have a female lead in the game. To them, this was fundamental to the *Alien* IP. Long before any story had been written, or the developers even knew they wanted Amanda to be the lead, early pre-alpha builds of *Alien: Isolation* featured a female crash test dummy with a pony-tail as the player character. It was just assumed the hero would be a woman, because that's part of the fabric of the *Alien* series.

That said, while promoting *Alien: Isolation*, Sigourney Weaver made it clear that the last survivor of the *Nostromo* being a woman wasn't some kind of bold feminist statement, but an attempt to surprise audiences by playing against their expectations. 'It was all male characters in the original script,' she tells the *Guardian*. 'Walter Hill and David Giler changed it, but only because they thought no one would ever expect the girl to be the hero.'

With Amanda Ripley established as the protagonist, writer Dan Abnett was hired to help flesh out a story. Abnett has been writing comics since the mid-1980s, working on the likes of *Transformers*, *Judge Dredd*, *Batman* and *Guardians of the Galaxy*. It was eventually decided that *Alien: Isolation* would be set fifteen years after the first movie. The *Nostromo*'s flight recorder has been recovered, having survived the destruction of the ship, and Amanda sets off on a mission to retrieve it – only to end up trapped aboard a dilapidated space station with a xenomorph, in much the same way her mother was.

There are a lot of parallels between the stories of the movie and the game, which was Creative Assembly's intention all along. The studio never wanted to make a straight adaptation of the film, but still wanted there to be a lot of connective tissue there. A mission set on LV-426, where another unfortunate starship crew is drawn to the egg-filled derelict, is an especially obvious example of this. The developers figured that if you're going to put an alien on a remote space station, you have to explain how it got there. Revisiting this iconic location was also an unmissable opportunity to let players experience one of the movie's most memorable, atmospheric scenes through their own eyes.

Through Fox, Creative Assembly also got a chance to meet a figure key to the making of *Alien*: editor Terry Rawlings. 'That was amazing,' says Alistair Hope. 'The man's a genius. He edited *Blade Runner* as well, so he can do no wrong. He was able to give us additional insight into the movie.' The slow, deliberate pacing of Rawlings' editing is an essential part of the film's magic, and Creative Assembly took this on board when figuring out the flow of their game's narrative. Knowing what to cut to keep things moving was one especially valuable piece of advice Rawlings gave, referring back to the infamous *Alien* deleted scene where we see Brett and Dallas being gruesomely mutated into eggs, which was cut because it distracted from the more pressing threat of the xenomorph.

With a story in place, a team established and a promising demo vindicating the designers' vision, *Alien: Isolation*'s development could begin in earnest. In 2013, Sega published Gearbox Software's ill-fated *Aliens: Colonial Marines*, the infamous FPS that was criticised for its technical shortcomings, lack of consistency with established *Alien* lore, one-dimensional AI, rote gunplay and uninspired level design.

'We looked at the negative reaction to *Colonial Marines* and noticed a common theme,' *Alien: Isolation* senior producer Jonathan Court tells VideoGamer. 'People wanted the game we were making. It was something people had wanted for a long time, and there was a frustration that no one was delivering it, which was very interesting for us to read.'

Fans were crying out for a smarter, scarier, *better Alien* game. A survival horror worthy of Ridley Scott's movie, not just another shallow, flashy shooting gallery. Little did they know, while the *Colonial Marines* backlash was raging online, a group of *Alien*-obsessed developers in a studio in Horsham were secretly working on the game of their dreams.

Building Better Worlds

Deconstructing one masterpiece to construct another.

Most sci-fi movies from the 1970s are beginning to show their age, but there are a few that hold up surprisingly well thanks to the quality and craft of their production design. *2001: A Space Odyssey*, *Solaris* and *Close Encounters of the Third Kind* are a few examples that I regularly revisit to marvel at how magnificent – and *convincing* – everything looks. But Ridley Scott's *Alien* arguably outclasses all of these giants of the genre. The director's preference for understated realism over flashy effects, and the squad of uniquely talented artists and craftspeople he formed to build his world, make this a movie that is startlingly immune to the passage of time. It'll look great forever.

This is thanks to the broad range of wildly different, seemingly incompatible artists Scott hired to bring his vision to life. Macabre Swiss surrealist H. R. Giger is rightly famed for his biomechanical alien and derelict ship designs, but he was just one part of a larger team of seriously talented creatives contributing to the hard-edged, lo-fi sci-fi of *Alien*. Scott wanted anything relating to the creature, including the derelict, to feel unnerving and otherworldly, which aptly describes both Giger's work and the man himself. He more than fulfilled the brief, creating some truly haunting and horrifying visuals that have been permanently inscribed into the minds of moviegoers all over the world.

Scott also recruited legendary French comic artist Jean 'Mœbius' Giraud, of *Heavy Metal* fame, and costume designer John Mollo – both of whom contributed to, among other things, the film's iconic, idiosyncratic pressure suit designs. All these artists had very different styles, disciplines and visual sensibilities, which makes *Alien* one of the most textured, believable and sophisticated science-fiction movies ever made. Scott, who studied art before making films, has always had a keen visual eye, and bringing these creative giants on board only heightened that aspect of his craft.

But the unsung hero of *Alien* is undoubtedly Ron Cobb. He was renowned for his attention to detail and to the actual functionality of the things he designed. When he designed, say, an airlock door, he didn't just make it look good: he drew detailed schematics describing how it would open and close. This is why the *Nostromo* is so convincing. Everything serves a purpose, even if you only see it for half a second as the camera sweeps past it.

In an interview in Paul Scanlon's *Book of Alien*, Cobb says: 'I resent films that are so shallow they rely entirely on their visual effects. I've always felt that a lot of effort should be made to render each environment as convincingly as possible, but always in the background.' And that's what *Alien* and *Alien: Isolation* do so well. These are credible sci-fi worlds that don't rely on far-fetched tech and fancy special effects to convince you that you're in the future.

You *believe* you are because it seems real. The more grounded a setting is, even if it's fantasy or science fiction, the easier it is to relate to it. That's why something like *Prometheus*, with its holographic computer interfaces, isn't as convincing as *Alien*, despite advances in effects technology.

Reflecting his practical approach to set and prop design, Cobb had a very distinctive visual style. Look at his sketches for *Alien* – whether it's a patch on the arm of a flight suit, a futuristic cat carrier or a bulkhead door – and you'll see many of them have the same precise, considered aesthetic, carefully drawn on graph paper with felt-tip pen and pencil. These images feel more like real-world architectural or product design schematics than concept art for a

Hollywood sci-fi movie. I've always loved studying Cobb's work on *Alien*, and so did the *Alien: Isolation* development team – which is evident in how well the game's environments mirror the sets he designed for the movie.

When it came to creating concept art for Sevastopol, Creative Assembly's artists had a genius idea. They decided to do it in the style of Cobb, putting themselves in his shoes, imagining this new setting in the same headspace he would have been in when dreaming up the interiors for the *Nostromo* in the 1970s. Some of these concepts have since been released by Sega, and it's impressive how closely the game's art team managed to capture the look and feel of Cobb's designs. It's a mental experiment that paid off, because if any location from Sevastopol appeared in *Alien*, it would slot in perfectly.

Creative Assembly also took a very 1970s approach to the game's colour palette. Although the majority of the game is metallic and industrial, whenever there are flecks of colour, the tones are always period-accurate. There are a lot of browns and mustards and garish patterns, which you don't typically see in hard science-fiction worlds – especially modern ones. Rugs, bed sheets and other home comforts, scattered around the station to make life in deep space less oppressive for Sevastopol's citizens, all look like they could have been ripped straight out of the pages of a seventies homeware catalogue.

The artists also made liberal use of another of Cobb's most important contributions to *Alien*: the Semiotic Standard For All Commercial Trans-Stellar & Heavy Element Transport Craft, or the Semiotic Standard for short. This is a set of bold, minimalist icons – meticulously sketched out on graph paper by Cobb – that represent a variety of different locations and functions aboard the *Nostromo*. Radiation Hazard, Exhaust, Pressure Suit Locker, Artificial Gravity Absent, Medical, Computer Terminal and Organic Storage are just a few of the symbols that make up the Semiotic Standard, drawn in bold lines and colours, intended to be easily read and recognised by the people working on the ship.

In the movie these icons are visible in places where they would really serve a practical purpose on a ship like the *Nostromo*, and Creative Assembly took the same approach when introducing them into Sevastopol. Lead UI artist Jon McKellan also designed some new ones exclusively for the game, which as a fan of Cobb's originals was something of a career highlight for him. The Semiotic Standard has become an iconic and instantly recognisable part of the *Alien* aesthetic, as much as the *Nostromo* or the xenomorph has, so it was only right that Creative Assembly should so enthusiastically factor it into the design of its world. In fact, I'm writing these very words on a custom mechanical keyboard with a keycap set inspired by the Semiotic Standard.

The locations in *Alien: Isolation* are new, and feel new, but every design element – from the architecture all the way down to individual props – is extracted from the movie's visual language. Creative Assembly totally immersed themselves in the world of the film, even playing it on screens in the studio on a loop. This detail was mentioned by several developers during the first wave of press for the game, and many assumed it was an exaggeration. But according to several developers I've spoken to, this was the reality of working on the game. Anyone whose desk happened to be near one of the TVs repeatedly screening the movie would see it in their peripheral vision for eight to ten hours a day, for over four years. Some people on the team even refused to watch other movies in the series during development, ensuring no visual or thematic elements from the sequels subconsciously slipped into their work on the project.

Creative Assembly's 1979 role-playing extended to the game's vast collection of objects – from decorative props to the many weapons and gadgets Ripley uses. The movie's production designers would cobble sci-fi props together using everyday objects. Computers, machinery, tools, and even the *Nostromo* itself were created using pieces of military model kits, scrap from disused aircraft, and other assorted junk sourced from various places. In that spirit, *Alien: Isolation*'s art team took the same approach when it came to littering Sevastopol with the detritus of everyday life. If a propmaker in 1979 couldn't make something with objects available at the time, the developers couldn't either.

During pre-production, *Isolation* art director Jude Bond was lucky enough to see some of the original screen-used props from the movie up close, and he was struck by how cheaply cobbled together they were. 'You're essentially being sold a lie on the screen,' he tells *Edge*, 'which reaffirmed everything we'd seen from the production shots Fox gave us. You could actually see where they'd coloured things in with felt-tip marker pens. Ripley's flamethrower was made of wood! This totally fed into how we designed our props. The idea of these objects being ad hoc and strapped together from other bits and pieces.'

Clutter is a crucial part of what makes the *Nostromo* such a tangible space. I've never been a fan of super clean and tidy sci-fi settings, because humans love *stuff*. Where is everything? The *Nostromo*, however, is a wonderful mess. Every surface is littered with junk, trinkets, discarded cigarette packs, crushed beer cans, and other remnants of the people who live and work there. *Alien: Isolation* takes the same approach to making Sevastopol feel like a place where people exist, and locations like the bullpen in the Colonial Marshal Bureau, the bridge and lounge aboard the *Torrens*, and the many living spaces and offices tucked away in the station are scattered with assorted bits and pieces.

Sevastopol is riddled with technology of all kinds, but none of these designs reference anything built after 1979. There are no touchpads, holograms or tablets. Instead, inspiration was drawn from old radios, portable TVs and reel-to-reel tape recorders – clunky, *tangible* tech with buttons, sliders and dials that would have been the height of technology in the late seventies. This is also reflected in both the game's UI and the many interactive computers that litter Sevastopol.

Jon McKellan went to great lengths to make this aspect of the game's aesthetic as convincing and authentic as possible, particularly the VHS distortion that gives the world's computer systems a tangibly analogue feel. He would record UI elements onto old, beaten-up video tapes, play them back, and create distortion by deliberately magnetising the screen and cables. Then he'd record the output directly off a CRT screen, resulting in beautiful, degraded tape effects that no software would be able to simulate nearly as well. Creative Assembly tried using video effects software to create these effects in a more convenient, streamlined way, but it never looked quite real enough. Some of these effects just can't be replicated accurately by a machine.

The developers also had to reverse-engineer UI elements from the film and make them interactive in the game. *Alien* is full of computer screens displaying all manner of futuristic looking (well, at least for 1979) graphics, wireframes, graphs and 3D imagery. Jon McKellan assumed this would make it relatively easy to create interactive mini-games, user interfaces and hacking challenges in the same style. Then he dug into the design on a more practical, mechanical level, and became aware of a fairly significant limitation.

Excluding the bridge consoles and MU-TH-UR, the supercomputer Dallas and Ripley interact with via a chunky keyboard, nothing else on the *Nostromo* is actually interactive. Everything is a readout or a gauge – a means of displaying information rather than inputting or controlling it. This meant Creative Assembly had to dream up their own ways a person might interact with these arcane-looking lo-fi computer displays. They designed original interactive interfaces but built around the visual language of the movie in terms of style, colours, borders and so on. This is one of several examples of the developers of *Alien: Isolation* having to take something designed to be purely visual and figure out a way for the player to actually do something with it.

An important part of constructing Sevastopol was *deconstructing* the *Nostromo*. Studying the movie, Creative Assembly identified and isolated five distinct locational themes: habitation, science, medical, engineering and technical. Habitation covered the crew of the *Nostromo*'s living spaces, including the communal dining area and the hypersleep chamber. Although nowhere on the cramped, claustrophobic *Nostromo* is *really* comfortable, these are the parts of the ship where its human inhabitants would feel the most at ease in deep space. Science and medical are the parts of the ship where science officer Ash would often be found, analysing the deceased facehugger and silently hatching his plan to return the xenomorph to his Weyland-Yutani masters.

Engineering and technical represent the ship's internal organs, where beleaguered engineers Brett and Parker – yearning for a bonus that will never come – spend their days preventing the *Nostromo* from falling apart. These are the most oppressive areas of the ship, particularly the labyrinthine, warren-like tunnels in the lower decks and a dark, silent hangar cluttered with the silhouettes of mining equipment and heavy machinery. All of these different parts of the ship, although visually consistent, have a look and feel of their own, which Creative Assembly then used to build Sevastopol.

The artists dissected *Alien*'s incredible, convincingly lived-in sets down to the last bolt and generated an in-house style guide. Whenever a new environment was being worked on, this guide was the bible for maintaining a consistent visual language throughout the whole station – and one that, crucially, constantly made the player feel like they'd stepped into the movie. Every corner of Sevastopol references the movie in some way, from the overall design to the smallest seemingly insignificant detail. You probably didn't notice a lot of these visual callbacks, but on a subconscious level, even when it isn't immediately apparent, you always feel like you've stepped inside *Alien*.

When you visit the San Cristobal Medical Facility, the visual language of the entire location is extracted from the *Nostromo*'s medical bay. The beds in the wards echo the retractable bed Kane lies on in the movie. You can find the same fold-out drawers containing medical instruments. Rows of microscopes in a laboratory are the same as the one Ash uses to study the facehugger. Creative Assembly created plenty of its own props, details and visual flourishes too, but every one can be traced back to that original medical bay set.

The same applies to Sevastopol's living spaces. Whenever you see restaurants, dining areas, offices or other spaces designed for human habitation, the DNA of the *Nostromo*'s iconic lounge set is evident. You'll even find several lounge/kitchen areas that are almost identically laid out. This could simply be an easy callback to the movie, but in my head-canon these living spaces are manufactured by the same company and supplied as a modular plugin for space stations and starships. This is exactly the kind of money-saving technique that would be popular in *Alien*'s hyper-capitalist dystopia.

Descending into the guts of Sevastopol, connections to the *Nostromo*'s engineering decks are viscerally obvious. These are the scariest parts of the station, with dim lighting, low ceilings, cramped corridors and ominous-looking futuristic machines looming in the darkness. When *Isolation*'s xenomorph claims its first victim, it happens in a cavern-like chamber with chains hanging from the ceiling, swaying gently in the breeze of the station's air-conditioning system, dripping with water. This is a direct reference to the area of the *Nostromo* where Brett meets a similarly gruesome end.

Creative Assembly's meticulous attention to detail even stretches as far as the individual lights that illuminate the world. 'We're very aware of the period when *Alien* was made,' Jude Bond tells *Edge* magazine. 'So we're conscious of what lights we should be using and what the colour temperature of those lights should be. There are no LED lights in our game at all. We appropriated a lot of the production methodology of the original film.'

Creative Assembly also tossed a new element of intriguing world-building into the mix in the form of the Seegson corporation. In the *Alien* series, we're used to hearing about the wealthy, successful Weyland-Yutani corporation and its monopoly over space. But while the Company *does* have a presence on Sevastopol, it's Seegson whose presence is more strongly felt. They're responsible for day-to-day operations on Sevastopol, but it's clear from the state of the place – and clues buried in terminals and audio logs – that this is a company struggling to make a name for itself in the galaxy.

It's a refreshingly unique perspective on the setting. We know Weyland-Yutani control basically everything, but what about the little guys? The gulf between the two corporations is most evident in the designs of its synthetics. Company androids are indistinguishable from humans, but Seegson's Working Joes are rubbery, robotic and could never be mistaken for a real person. Sevastopol is in the process of being decommissioned during the events of *Alien: Isolation*, but there's the distinct sense that it probably didn't look much better when it was still operational. Seegson is a mid-tier corporation in a universe ruled by an all-conquering one, and this adds massively to the downbeat, melancholy atmosphere of this dreary backwater dump.

Creative Assembly didn't want the station to feel like it was built yesterday. It had to feel like a place that had existed for years, accumulating decades of grime and decay. Seegson's branding was important too, because its logo, advertisements and other visual ephemera are seen throughout the station. The artists imagined they were a design agency and Seegson was a client. They wanted this to feel like a company that could really exist. Would its logo look convincing at the top of a letterhead or on the arm of a uniform? This is another example of the developers placing themselves inside the setting they were creating, rather than just observing it passively from afar.

But making Sevastopol feel like a real place was only half the battle. It was important for it to be a fun play space as well as a convincing world. When constructing *Alien: Isolation*'s levels, Creative Assembly's designers had to think like a player. Multiple paths through the levels were essential, especially with a dynamic AI-driven predator stomping around. As you play the game, you notice that there's always some kind of escape route nearby if the beast gets too close for comfort. It just wouldn't be fun if you were constantly backed into a corner with no way to flee. It's a good thing this station has such a wide-ranging and conveniently human-sized ventilation system.

Creative Assembly also dedicated a lot of pre-production resources to the game's costumes. The rumpled, scrappy, grease-stained outfits of the *Nostromo* crew – and all those little personalised touches like Lambert's cowboy boots, Brett's Hawaiian shirt, Parker's headband and Ripley's unzipped flight suit – have become an iconic aspect of the movie's production design.

For the game, the artists took the same approach as they did when constructing the new environments, closely studying and back-engineering the source material. 'The subtle nuances of the costume design fascinated us,' says Jude Bond. 'They seemed to be an extension of the crew's character. They're wearing uniforms, but they're dishevelled and informal, each with their own personal touches. The costumes were partly responsible for seeding our obsession with the deconstruction of the original film.'

Early concepts for Amanda Ripley's clothing, created by artist Calum Alexander Watt, were heavily inspired by the exotic, colourful art of Mœbius. 'Jean Giraud was a long-time hero of mine,' says Watt. 'These early explorations were an opportunity for me to directly reference his work for the original film.'

In the end, a more conventional outfit was chosen, more in line with Ellen Ripley's utilitarian costume in the movie. But these stylish sketches – including one of Amanda Ripley in a shiny red jumpsuit with padded pauldrons and kneepads, looking like some kind of futuristic sci-fi quarterback – are a fascinating glimpse at what could have been had the team leaned more into the Mœbius look.

A curious detail on Amanda Ripley's final costume is the key hanging around her neck, which looks like it fits something small like a lockbox or a filing cabinet. It's never mentioned in the game, and when I asked director Alistair Hope about it during an interview for *PC Gamer* magazine, he was reluctant to answer. After a pause he said: 'I don't think we need to explain everything.'

Calum Alexander Watt also produced concept art of dozens of Sevastopol residents, their costumes incorporating visual elements from those of John Mollo: patches, pins, epaulettes, trucker caps, canvas sneakers, flight jackets, jumpsuits, quilted trims and cargo trousers with big pockets. All creased and stained, true to the grimy 'space trucker' aesthetic established by the film.

Concept artists, including Edouard Caplain, looked at what people wore in the late 1970s to ensure every costume on Sevastopol, no matter how minor the character is, feels period appropriate. 'We browsed through a ton of 1970s photos that we scavenged online and we used bits of their fashion to build characters,' says Caplain in *The Art of Alien: Isolation*. 'I think the end result shows the variety of style there was back then very well.'

The really remarkable thing about *Alien* is that, despite being made in the late 1970s, it doesn't look old. Okay, so maybe a few minor details like Ripley's hair and Dallas's beard give the game away a little. But for the most part this is a truly timeless film. On the other hand, look at *Alien 3*, *Alien Resurrection* or *Prometheus*. I appreciate the quality of the production design in all of these films, but they look very much like products of their times.

By piggy-backing on *Alien*'s rich aesthetic, *Alien: Isolation* becomes timeless itself. Sevastopol will look and feel every bit as immersive, lived-in and believable ten, twenty, maybe even thirty years from now. It's one of the most accomplished settings in the history of video games, and there's no finer digital haunted house in which to be repeatedly half scared to death.

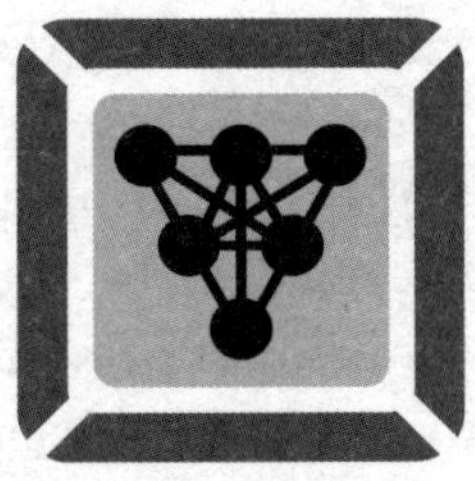

Structural Perfection

Building the ultimate killing machine.

When considering how *Alien: Isolation*'s titular otherworldly predator might behave, an important rule had to be established: the player can't be scared all the time. The best horror, in any medium, is the kind that shows some restraint, carefully picking the right moment to scare us rather than subjecting us to an all-out terror assault. In video games this is doubly important, because an enemy that is too relentless will make the player just give up and go play something else. No one wants to feel like they can't win.

This is why Creative Assembly put a lot of effort into making *Alien: Isolation*'s particular brand of AI-driven horror as varied and textured as possible. A number of devilishly clever techniques were used to ensure the player is in a constant state of nerve-gnawing tension. But, crucially, the player never loses hope that they *just might* be able to evade or outfox the creature.

Chief among these is the fact that the xenomorph is quietly tethered to the player. This is why it always seems to be in the right place at the right time. Or is that the *wrong* place? The AI doesn't know where you're going or what you're going to do next. But by simply making sure the alien gets in your way, it creates interesting – and, more importantly, terrifying – situations for the player to deal with. However, how actively it hunts, and how aggressively it behaves, can vary wildly depending on how you've been playing the game.

Everything you do in *Alien: Isolation*, and everything the alien does, is monitored and reacted to by the all-seeing AI director. This hidden presence is your own personal Ridley Scott, making sure what's happening to you at any given moment is as exciting, tense, thrilling and scary as possible – but in a measured, calculated way. This is achieved using a system referred to internally by Creative Assembly as the 'menace gauge'. When the alien is near you, in your line of sight, visible on your motion tracker, or otherwise in a position that gets your heart racing, the menace gauge gradually increases.

Then, when it reaches a critical level, the director will tell the alien to cool it for a while, move to another part of the level, or climb into a vent. Not only does this make *Alien: Isolation* a better horror game, dynamically creating a varied ebb and flow of gameplay, but it gives you time to actually *play* the game. There are hundreds of objectives – powering up generators, hacking doors, and so on – and the AI director telling the alien to back off gives you a chance to complete them. If it never left you alone, you'd never make any progress.

But the director is only one part of the equation. It's important to note that it'll never cheat and tell the alien exactly where you are – but it *will* point it in the right direction. This is when the creature's own senses take over, responding to any noises you make or any glimpse of you if you stray into its field of view. The beast's AI is composed of over a hundred nodes, all dictating different behaviours, levels of aggression, reactions to what's happening around it and more. The sheer amount of reactivity contained within the xenomorph's simulated brain is what makes it seem *smart*, and why you get a sense that it's a thinking, feeling being you're battling against, not just an animatronic puppet.

One of the most chilling things about playing *Alien: Isolation* for a prolonged period of time is the uncanny feeling that the beast is learning how you play and reacting to it. This is true.

Well, kind of. When you first meet the alien, it only has access to a small portion of the nodes in its brain. But as you perform certain actions – like, say, repeatedly hiding in lockers to escape from it – new nodes are unlocked, and the alien will begin to exhibit new behaviours. The node that makes it search in lockers more frequently will be unlocked as a response to you, creating the illusion that it's getting wise to your tactics. It's genius, and it really works, because you'll *swear* this thing is second-guessing you.

But don't think playing conservatively will save you. If you've progressed through the game without unlocking certain nodes, the game will trigger them anyway, increasing the alien's intelligence and spread of behaviours whether you've played a certain way or not. This is also part of why the creature is harder to deal with later in the game. This gradual unlocking of behaviour nodes creates a sense of escalating threat and makes dealing with the beast in later levels notably trickier than when you first cross its path.

For visualisations of how *Alien: Isolation*'s remarkable AI works, be sure to check out the fantastic YouTube channel AI and Games: particularly the video titled 'Revisiting the AI of *Alien: Isolation*'. Dr Tommy Thompson, an AI researcher, lecturer and games industry consultant, is the foremost expert on how *Alien: Isolation*'s creature thinks and has made some fascinating discoveries about the inner workings of its brain. You could almost write an entire book about what's going on inside this thing's head.

In an interview with *Edge* magazine, conducted while the game was still in active development, *Alien: Isolation* art director Jude Bond described the alien as a 'living thing'. 'We review the game every day in a darkened room,' he says. 'And every day someone shrieks and leaps out of their chair, because you never know what's going to happen. Yes, it's a piece of AI, and yes it has parameters we can tune, but its network of behaviours is so insanely complicated that the thing is almost sentient.' The developers would often be so surprised by something unexpected the alien did in a playtest that they'd have to dig through the game's code to find out exactly what it just did and, import-antly, *how*.

'Over the course of the game's development, the thing I really didn't expect was the fact that, as a team, we'd still be getting caught out by the xenomorph,' Alistair Hope recalled in an inter-view with Kotaku. 'Even towards the end of the production cycle we'd still die and jump and yell and be surprised by it. In fact, even now when I play it, my heart is still thumping away.'

Design lead Gary Napper, speaking to *Edge*, recalled a moment when the team was crowded around someone playing the game. 'He was hiding behind this bit of cover, and you could see the alien walk off to the right,' he says. 'The exit was straight ahead and he just had to get to the door, but the alien turned around and started heading back towards him. We were all shouting "Go!" and as he dashed for the exit everyone started cheering. It was incredible that you could have an experience like this three years into development.'

While prototyping the alien, a small group of developers put together a proof-of-concept demo, which in its earliest form had, surprisingly, a player-controlled xenomorph in place of the complex decision-making tree that would eventually dictate its behaviour. Someone would actually control the alien, hunting another person playing as Amanda. This was set up to give the developers a sense of how this beast, as an intelligent, thinking being, would hunt its prey. The decisions made by the player-guided alien in these experimental games of hide-and-seek would then be used to figure out how the AI would behave.

The developers also took part in an amusing thought exercise when imagining how the alien could behave and how players could interact with it. In an oft-repeated story, told to numerous media outlets during the promotion of the game, director Alistair Hope said they imagined a tiger had just been set loose in the studio. 'We found it was fascinating to talk about how we'd sur-vive,' he said in an interview with MCV. 'We'd get behind a desk and look for an escape, trying to peek around and see where the tiger was. Okay, we need to get to the fire escape at the other end of the office now. How do we do it? Some people would throw things to distract it or crawl from desk to desk.'

At some point during development, while tweaking and balancing the creature's AI, it would loudly announce in an emotionless computerised voice what it was doing and what it was going to do next. *'I'M LOOKING FOR YOU NOW.' 'I'VE LOST TRACK OF YOU.'* This was a useful tool for determining exactly how its behaviour tree was responding to the environment and the player's actions, but had the unintended side effect of being absurdly hilarious. I wish they'd left this in as an unlockable bonus mode.

Creative Assembly also invested heavily in the animation of the creature. It has seven layers of animation running simultaneously, representing different parts of the body. A mix of motion-captured and procedural animation, and a sophisticated system of blending these together, is what gives the xenomorph such an uncanny and convincing range of movement. It's an intimidating, weighty presence, and you can almost feel the ground shudder as it stomps past you when it's in patrol mode. Then, if it senses something, it slows down, leans its head forward, and *prowls*, searching for the source.

In *Alien*, six-foot-ten (or seven-foot-two according to some sources) Nigerian artist Bolaji Badejo was hired to strap on H. R. Giger's KY Jelly-smeared rubber suit and portray the xenomorph. He was drinking in a pub in London's West End when a member of Ridley Scott's casting team, who was actively seeking a tall, slender person to play the alien at the time, spotted him. Peter Mayhew, who famously played Chewbacca in the *Star Wars* movies, was briefly considered for the role, but ultimately lost out to Badejo. Despite a complete lack of acting experience, his incredibly long legs were of particular interest to Ridley Scott, which he felt gave the creature a suitably alien quality.

However, in *Alien: Isolation*, the xenomorph is significantly taller than Badejo, standing at almost ten feet tall. This was partly to create a sharp contrast between the game's small, claustrophobic environments and a creature that felt truly massive. 'We wanted to create an alien that was physically huge,' says Alistair

Hope in an interview in the official *Alien: Isolation* art book. 'We wanted it to look *down* on the player. This is a form of the alien we felt hadn't been experienced in games based in the franchise before.'

Alien: Isolation's xenomorph is notably slower than the athletic, wall-crawling creatures we've encountered in other *Alien* games, but according to animator Simon Ridge, speaking to *Edge*, that was both intentional *and* true to the source material. 'Ask someone to describe how a xenomorph behaves and they tend to describe the creatures from the later movies. But if you analyse the first film, it doesn't move very much at all. It's very slow. But we also wanted it to be agile and deadly, which was a difficult challenge for the animation team. In some early tests it felt too bulky and weighty, like an ice hockey player. But we managed to find a nice balance of power and agility.'

For Gary Napper, a key realisation happened when seeing players encountering the alien and not immediately wanting to attack it. 'That was a big moment for us,' he tells *Edge*. 'It was saying: this isn't like other *Alien* games.' Until *Alien: Isolation*, the usual reaction to seeing a xenomorph in a video game was pulling the trigger of your pulse rifle and giving it hell. But in this game weapons wouldn't save you. You'd have to *outsmart* this thing. Internally, Creative Assembly would talk about their desire to 're-alien the alien'. They wanted to create a creature that felt like *the* alien, not another cannon-fodder space bug. 'We wanted a huge creature that looked down on the player and didn't run around below their waist like an angry dog,' Alistair Hope tells PlayStation Blog, accurately describing, whether intentionally or not, the enemies in *Aliens: Colonial Marines*. 'And we wanted an alien that recaptured a sense of mystery and the unknown.'

No antagonist in any other video game comes even remotely close to *Alien: Isolation*'s xenomorph. This is the apex predator of an entire medium, and no matter how many times I play and replay the game, it still manages to find new and exciting ways to make my heart leap out of my chest. No horror game before or since has taken such a systemic approach to scaring the player, which is a major part of why this game is a modern classic. Of course, the developers had amazing source material to work with. The concept of the alien, and H. R. Giger's iconic designs, already tapped into our most primordial fears. Creative Assembly just took this to another, freakier level by giving it a *brain*.

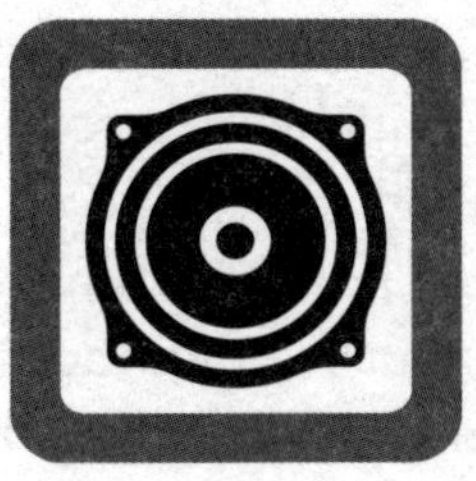

Sounds of Sevastopol

Silence, synthesizers and psychoacoustics.

Jerry Goldsmith's darkly beautiful *Alien* score is a vital part of the movie's distinctive, haunting sonic atmosphere. But things could have been very different. In 1976, Japanese composer and electronic music pioneer Isao Tomita released his own unique take on Gustav Holst's *Planets* suite. Ridley Scott listened to this offbeat masterpiece – a dramatic and bewitching collision of orchestral music and synthesized sounds – and fell in love with what he heard. He wanted Tomita to compose the music for *Alien*, but Fox president Alan Ladd Jr insisted that someone more traditional took the job.

Goldsmith, of course, nailed it. Romantic and stirring, yet with a sinister undercurrent running through it, the music he composed for *Alien* is magnificent. Creative Assembly were well aware of this when they started work on *Alien: Isolation* and wanted to recreate the feel of Goldsmith's score in their own soundtrack. Musicians Joe Henson and Alexis Smith, collectively known as The Flight, were hired for the job. Previously, the duo had written and performed a selection of multiplayer music for *Assassin's Creed IV: Black Flag*, a song for *LittleBigPlanet 3* and soundtracks for a couple of indie games. But scoring *Alien: Isolation* was a much bigger job than any of those projects.

'They wanted it to sound like the 1970s,' says Smith in an

interview with Den of Geek. 'And it had to be scary. They're some pretty specific barriers, but they trusted us.' The Flight faced an interesting challenge, though: *Alien*'s score only amounts to around twenty minutes of original Jerry Goldsmith music. It's a movie with a famously sparse, minimalist soundtrack, which meant creating a *lot* of new music especially for the game – but, crucially, music that felt like it could have been composed by Goldsmith back in the late seventies.

The duo picked out a few cues from the score that they thought captured the essence of the movie, leading to Creative Assembly securing the rights to ten minutes of Goldsmith's music for use in the game. These recognisable motifs – including the flutes that are elemental to *Alien*'s ethereal, otherworldly atmosphere – gave the composers enough familiar component parts to build with.

Henson's brother Christian, a fellow composer, also contributed to *Alien: Isolation*'s score. He handled the more orchestral, cinematic music in the game's few linear cutscenes while The Flight focused on the in-game music. While the music in the opening chapters is pure Jerry Goldsmith, helping to reinforce that the game is part of the same universe as the 1979 movie, the composers were able to get a little more experimental later in the game.

They discovered that when they combined vintage synthesizers from the period with Goldsmith's entirely orchestral score, these instruments didn't feel out of place. An example of can be heard as Ripley first encounters the murderous Working Joe androids, when electronic elements and manipulated guitar samples creep into the score. 'We were determined to avoid any kind of pastiche when we were composing the music,' the composers say in an interview with The Sound Architect. 'So we quickly moved into new and hopefully fitting territory.'

Alien: Isolation's score is also dynamic, reacting to what the player is doing. The Flight created layers of music and sounds that the game would then intelligently thread together to match whichever level of tension, fear or drama the player was currently experiencing. 'Apart from in the scripted scenes, you rarely hear a piece of music the same twice,' Henson tells Den of Geek.

'Sometimes it's seamless and brilliant, and other times we would notice. But we like hearing how the game pieces the music together.'

Sadly, *Alien: Isolation*'s score has never been officially released due to some unknown legal issues. But you can still listen to it online, ripped from the game by fans. Hearing it in isolation, it's easier to appreciate how perfectly The Flight managed to capture the spirit of the movie. In the heat of the game, whether you're fearfully creeping past a Working Joe or being lunged at by an angry xenomorph, it can be hard to pick out the nuances of the music.

The *Alien: Isolation* soundtrack was reportedly used as a placeholder during the editing of Ridley Scott's sequel, *Alien: Covenant* – and there are some similarities between it and Jed Kurzel's final score. I've also heard that the game itself actually inspired parts of *Covenant*. A poster showing Katherine Waterston's character, Daniels, pinned against a wall, hiding from an alien lurking around a corner, is very similar to a piece of key art Creative Assembly created for *Alien: Isolation*, even down to its green tint.

Accompanying the score is some of the best audio design I've ever encountered in a video game. The *Nostromo*'s claustrophobic soundscape – chirping computers, distant echoes, whirring machinery, and the constant drone of its immense fusion engines – adds to *Alien*'s pervading sense of unease. *Isolation* recreates this aspect of the movie perfectly.

Creative Assembly were given access to archive materials used in the film, which were then used as layers to build the game's atmosphere. Director Alistair Hope dug into Fox's archives and found some dust-covered quarter-inch tape cartridges, lying forgotten in a dark corner, unheard for thirty-five years. *Alien: Isolation*'s sound team digitised them and were amazed to discover that they were the actual analogue tapes on which the film's sound team had recorded their sound effects. It was a gold mine, and the perfect reference point.

'They were sitting at the bottom of an old cardboard box in the Fox archives,' Alistair Hope tells the *Guardian*. 'They didn't know what they were, but we asked for them anyway, and it was the original sound effects archives. Lots of weird noises, moaning sounds. You could even hear the British sound engineers from the seventies calling out take numbers prior to recording.'

But the audio on these 8-tracks was too fuzzy and degraded, so the audio team had to recreate some of them with modern technology. 'In some cases we used the isolated stems for reference material to replicate the recordings,' sound designer Sam Cooper tells The Sound Architect. 'Some of the archive material was very old and grainy, which was what we wanted sometimes. But in other situations it was preferable to recreate it at a higher fidelity.'

If you've watched *Alien* as many times as I have, the sounds of the *Nostromo*'s computers and the other ambient sounds that characterise the ship will be burned into your brain. Playing the game and hearing those same sounds really makes you feel a part of that world. The sound designers also got to have fun with it, manipulating these recognisable effects to create new sounds for Sevastopol. 'We were able to take the original recordings and put a modern spin on them,' says sound designer Byron Bullock. 'Double tracking, sub harmonics, morphing, time-stretching, adding strange impulse responses. All kinds of things to create interesting new variations of these iconic sounds.'

The sound team recorded a *lot* of new audio for *Alien: Isolation*, including, according to Bullock in an interview with Kotaku, 'explosions, metal impacts, large industrial machinery, animals, humans, fruit and vegetables, old analogue computers, old toys, and electromagnetic information captured with special microphones.' Adding to the game's authenticity, some of these Foley recordings were made and edited at Shepperton Studios (now merged with Pinewood Studios), where Ridley Scott filmed *Alien* decades previously, as well as *Blade Runner*, *G.I. Jane*, *Gladiator*, *Robin Hood* and *Prometheus*.

But *Alien: Isolation* didn't just have to sound like the movie; it had to make players *feel* something. During pre-production, the sound team did research into psychoacoustics and the human body's innate conditioned response to certain sounds and frequencies. They created an evolving, dynamic soundscape that would rise and fall depending on whichever situation Ripley might find herself in. Creative Assembly also used sound to keep players on edge, mixing ambiguous, abstract sounds into the station's ambience.

The audio mix in *Alien: Isolation* reacts intelligently to the player *and* the alien. If the creature is nearby, the music and sound will intensify accordingly. If you're hiding somewhere, the mix may be reduced and leave you in near silence, adding to your feeling of hopelessness and isolation. 'We've not been afraid to use quiet and silence in the game,' says Bullock. 'It's these quiet moments that help to heighten your senses and increase the tension.'

This is something *Silent Hill 2*, another horror masterpiece, also does brilliantly. In that game you'll often enter a room and be plunged into a sudden, stark silence, with only the echoing sound of your footsteps to break it. 'The job of a sound designer is not just to create sounds,' says *Silent Hill 2* composer and sound designer Akira Yamaoka in a documentary about the making of the game. 'We also have to know how to use silence. I actually think that selecting moments of silence is another way of producing sound.'

'We tried to use silence as a weapon,' says lead audio designer Mark Angus in an interview with Sound of Life. 'So we'd put the player into environments that were very minimal and very quiet so they could hear themselves moving and breathing – as well as the movement of the alien. We wanted the player to think that every little sound they heard could be the creature lurking, and those became some of the scariest moments in the game.'

Alien's soundscape is also characterised by the distinctly analogue, mechanical sound of the *Nostromo*'s computers and machinery. When MU-TH-UR picks up the distress beacon on LV-426 and wakes the ship up, we hear a cacophony of chittering, whirring and clunking as its systems kick into gear. To recreate this feel, Creative Assembly not only recreated sounds based on those priceless archive tapes, but created their own by recording and sampling floppy disk drives, tape machines and other old hardware.

According to Sam Cooper, *Alien: Isolation*'s audio team made heavy use of Sennheiser MKH 8040s – professional cardioid microphones that cost upwards of £2,000. 'They have an extended frequency range,' says Sam Cooper. 'This allows for heavy pitch shifting when recorded at a high sample rate, which is very useful when you're recording sounds intended for a huge space vessel.' The team also used a home-made coil pickup microphone, borrowed from a friend of Byron Bullock, which 'picks up all kinds of strange sounds'. The distorted, glitchy analogue sound that accompanies the Sega logo at the beginning of *Alien: Isolation* was achieved using this unusual hardware.

When it came to implementing audio in the game, the sound team's lives were made easier by Creative Assembly's powerful in-house Cage scripting tool. This gave the designers easy access to advanced scripting ('one of the most powerful development tools I've ever used,' says Bullock) and allowed them to populate the world with sounds in a quick, easy and visual way. Cage also let developers from different fields – VFX, lighting, AI, game design and so on – work on levels simultaneously, which allowed for rapid, efficient iteration.

Horror benefits from being tightly scripted, and the genre masters always figure out just the right moment to trigger something and make the viewer or player jump. But in a dynamic, reactive game like *Alien: Isolation*, that's much more difficult. Creative Assembly had to develop tools, including Cage, to give the feel of a scripted horror experience, but orchestrated by systems, not people.

If you're running away from the alien, having just alerted it, the music and sound mix will be at full intensity. But if you manage to escape into a locker, the sonic ambience will slowly lower in intensity, and some elements may be removed from the mix altogether. If you're in a locker, and haven't alerted the alien yet, but suddenly catch a glimpse of it through the grill, the audio engine will know to play a sudden sting of music to make your heart leap. It's a jump scare that feels authored and linear – and is every bit as impactful and effective as one – but that was in fact created on the fly by the game itself.

'It's all about the little details,' says Mark Angus. 'All the little ticks and whirs, the little movement sounds, the background pipes and the humming of the engines of the spacecraft. We built a world that reacted how you imagine it would, with reflections and reverb, obstruction and occlusion. This makes you feel like you're in a real place, increasing your immersion.'

It can't be understated how vital *Alien: Isolation*'s music and sound is to the experience. It's a game I always make sure I play with quality headphones or a good speaker setup, because it does such an incredible job of drawing you into the world. But it's also a useful tool, accurate enough to let you track the alien's movements entirely by ear. When I play the game, I find myself using audio to keep tabs on the creature more than the motion tracker.

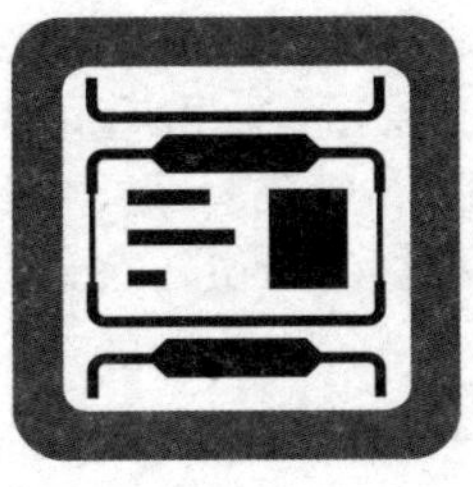

Crew Log

The lost souls of Sevastopol.

Alien: Isolation is, as the title suggests, a pretty lonely game. Ripley spends most of her time fending for herself, although she does occasionally bump into other people as she explores the station. Not counting the dozens of unidentified, panicky survivors you see running around the place, there are almost thirty named characters in the game. Some play major roles in the story, while others appear mostly, or entirely, in audio logs and terminal messages. Here's everyone worth knowing on Sevastopol.

MAIN CHARACTERS

Amanda Ripley

When Amanda was just ten years old, her mother disappeared. Ellen Ripley was serving as a warrant officer aboard the USCSS *Nostromo* – a towing ship transporting 20 million tonnes of mineral ore from the planet Thedus to Earth – but she never made it home. The ship vanished, along with all seven of her crew, somewhere in deep space. *We* know what happened to them, of course, but for Amanda it's a mystery that has haunted her ever since.

In the years following her mother's disappearance, Ripley joined Weyland-Yutani as an engineer. She worked on starships and space stations in the region of space where the *Nostromo* went missing, which is where she meets a Company android named Samuels. He tells her the *Nostromo*'s flight recorder has been recovered in the Zeta Reticuli system, and that it's being held on a space station named Sevastopol – an encounter that leads to the events of *Alien: Isolation*. For Amanda, despite a justified mistrust of her shady, immoral employers, this is her chance to finally get some closure.

In Keith R. A. DeCandido's official *Alien: Isolation* novelisation, whose inconsistencies with the game have led some fans to consider it non-canon, we learn more about Amanda's backstory. She was conceived during a layover between long-haul space trips, leading to her mother and father, Alex, being reprimanded by Weyland-Yutani for contravening corporate policy. After her mother disappeared she was raised by her stepfather, a man named Paul Carter (Ellen Ripley's second husband), with whom she had a fraught and troubled relationship. She ran away from home several times before developing a passion for engineering and eventually turning this into a career.

Amanda's likeness is based on Welsh actor Kezia Burrows, who also provided motion capture for the game's cutscenes, as well as assorted grunts, shrieks, heavy breathing and strains of effort. Burrows is often wrongly credited as being the voice of the character too; she is in fact voiced by American TV, film and theatre actor Andrea Deck. Burrows was originally going to voice Ripley along with doing her motion capture, and had even finished recording her lines. But Deck was brought in at a later date to re-record them, according to Burrows in an interview with the Perfect Organism *Alien* podcast (hey, cool name), in a more 'authentic' American accent.

In a restored scene in the Special Edition cut of *Aliens*, Weyland-Yutani exec Carter Burke reveals to a distraught Ellen that Amanda died of cancer aged sixty-six. This might seem like a bleak end for the character, but can you really trust anything the slimy, corrupt Carter Burke says? Weyland-Yutani wanted Ellen to lose all hope of reuniting with her family and travel back to LV-426, and an organisation like this always gets what it wants – regardless of the morality at play. I don't think we've seen the last of this character.

Christopher Samuels

In the *Alien* series, androids fall into two distinct categories: the nice, friendly, helpful ones who will help you through thick and thin, and the ones that want to either A) perform bizarre experiments on you or B) murder you. When we first meet Samuels, who introduces himself as an employee of Weyland-Yutani, we can be forgiven for thinking that he might be the next Ash: a synthetic who, if ordered, will destroy any pesky, fleshy human whose interests contradict those of the Company. Luckily, Samuels is less Ash and more Bishop.

It would have been easy to mimic *Alien* and have him turn on Ripley, but Creative Assembly wisely decided to take the less predictable route. Samuels is one of the good guys, and some of his efforts to help Ripley escape Sevastopol (and to help a badly injured Taylor) are nothing short of heroic. But don't be fooled: he can handle himself in a fight. Confronted by a Working Joe, Samuels dispatches it with ruthless efficiency. A reminder that beneath that charming exterior he has capabilities beyond any mere human.

Samuels is voiced by veteran video game actor Anthony Howell, who also played Cyril in *Final Fantasy XVI*, Margit in *Elden Ring*, Elias in *Diablo IV*, and an advanced AI named SAM in *Observation*, a horror game created by former *Alien: Isolation* developers. On this project, he was reunited with Kezia Burrows, who played *Observation*'s astronaut protagonist, Dr Emma Fisher.

Marshal Waits

Sevastopol is basically a self-contained city, and every city needs a police force. Marshal Waits (named Jethro in the *Alien: Isolation* novelisation) is head of the station's embedded Colonial Marshal Bureau, and has a remarkable knack for taking a bad situation and making it worse. In the events leading up to the Sevastopol incident, and frequently during it, he makes a number of rash, bone-headed decisions that risk the lives of everyone on the station. Waits is voiced by, and his appearance is based on, the actor William Hope. You may recognise Hope as the actor who portrayed Lt Scott Gorman in *Aliens*, one of the Colonial Marines who travels to Acheron with Ellen Ripley.

Ricardo

Deputy Ricardo is Waits's shadow, but more honest and well-meaning than his scheming superior. He goes out of his way to help Ripley on several occasions and generally seems like too nice a person to be trapped on a space station with a killer alien. Like all the characters in *Alien: Isolation*, however, he never really gets a chance to say much, leaving his true personality, his past, and what brought him to Sevastopol something of a mystery.

Ricardo's likeness and motion capture were provided by Syrus Lowe, an actor who has appeared in TV shows including *Sherlock* and *Avenue 5*. His dialogue was performed by Richie Campbell, whom you may have seen in an episode of popular British–French detective drama *Death in Paradise*.

SUPPORTING CHARACTERS

Diane Verlaine

Verlaine is the owner and captain of the USCSS *Torrens*, the commercial transport vessel that brings Taylor, Samuels and Ripley to Sevastopol. She's professional, proud of her ship and clearly reliable, otherwise Weyland-Yutani would never have trusted her with such an important job. If you're a fan of the *Hitman* games, you may recognise Verlaine's voice – albeit in a different accent than you're used to. She's played by Jane Perry, who is perhaps best known for playing Diana Burnwood in IO's assassination sandbox.

Nina Taylor

Taylor is a young Weyland-Yutani executive, which should immediately make you suspicious of her. But she's actually a rare example of a Company suit who isn't deeply morally corrupt. This is likely due to the fact that she's new and inexperienced, finding deep-space travel stressful and struggling to deal with the dangers thrown at her on Sevastopol. Taylor is played by Emerald O'Hanrahan, who also stars in long-running BBC radio series *The Archers*.

Henry Marlow

Marlow owns and runs the *Anesidora*, the deep-space salvage ship that unwittingly brings the alien aboard Sevastopol. His wife, Catherine Foster, dies after being impregnated by a facehugger, and after her death he makes it his personal mission to kill the xenomorph. However, with his judgement clouded by grief, he resorts to increasingly extreme methods to stop it.

The *Alien* series is full of references to the writing of Joseph Conrad, and it's likely this character is named after Christopher Marlow, a recurring character in his books. Marlow is played by Sean Gilder, a British actor with roles in a few Hollywood movies, including Martin Scorsese's *Gangs of New York*.

Axel Fielding

Shortly after arriving on Sevastopol, Ripley has a tense run-in with this sarcastic Scottish survivor. He fills her in on what's been going on, teaches her some survival tactics, and gives her a flashlight. He's twitchy and paranoid at first, rudely holding a gun to Ripley's head, but he eventually warms to her. His name is a reference to Axel Stone and Blaze Fielding, characters from Sega's *Streets of Rage* series, and he's portrayed by Scottish actor George Anton. Think of any classic British TV show – *Taggart*, *Casualty*, *A Touch of Frost*, *The Bill* – and Anton will have appeared in at least one episode.

B. Ransome

Ransome is a Seegson executive who never actually appears in the game, but is featured in numerous audio logs and terminal messages. He's the archetypal corrupt corporate scumbag, more concerned with profits than the safety and happiness of his employees. He's played by Argentine-born British actor Ben Cura, who recently appeared in *Bridgerton* spin-off *Queen Charlotte*. Side note: Cura is the ex-husband of Andrea Deck, the voice of Ripley.

Dr Kuhlman

Kuhlman is one of San Cristobal's resident doctors. His colleagues suspect that he's become addicted to his own medication and is secretly helping himself to the hospital's supplies. He meets Ripley briefly early in the game, and while he seems helpful, there's something strangely off about him. His character model is based on *Alien: Isolation* lead programmer Clive Gratton, but there's some debate about who plays him as no actor is credited.

MINOR CHARACTERS

Mike Tanaka

Although only a minor character, Tanaka actually has a more fleshed-out backstory and personality than some of the main cast. Working on Sevastopol as a systems archivist, he kept a diary as the xenomorph began rampaging around the station. Entries from this journal were posted, in character, on the Twitter account @MikeTanaka2095 – an official profile created by Creative Assembly. He also posted sketches of his co-workers, the station and the alien, which were in fact drawn by *Alien: Isolation* concept artist Calum Alexander Watt.

Dr K. Lingard

Sevastopol's chief medical officer was at ground zero when the xenomorph was unleashed on Sevastopol. She tended to Catherine Foster when she was brought aboard the station, not realising the grave existential threat posed by the facehugger attached to her. Lingard is a selfless and good-natured person who always does what's right for her patients – even if it means dealing in Sevastopol's black market to acquire life-saving medicine.

Jake Sinclair

Through this character we get a sense of what life is like on the station for the gangs of aggressive survivors Ripley encounters. Once a security officer, Sinclair now takes a more lawless approach to surviving the Sevastopol incident. But in a revealing audio log he expresses regret for the blood he's spilled and laments the loss of his wife and children. Sinclair disobeyed quarantine procedures and let Foster on the station, inadvertently kickstarting the events of the game. The face on his ID tag is that of Gary Napper, *Isolation*'s lead designer.

W. 'Chief' Porter

Sevastopol's chief engineer, who is becoming increasingly concerned about the stability of the station's systems, and the fact that several members of his engineering team have gone missing. His name and ID tag photo are a reference to *Alien: Isolation* writer Will Porter. In audio logs, he's played by actor Mac McDonald, who has appeared in numerous sci-fi films and TV shows, including *Aliens*, *Red Dwarf*, *The Fifth Element* and *The Empire Strikes Back*.

Julia Jones

A reporter for the *Colonial Times* who has been living on Sevastopol for two months. Critical of how Seegson are running the station, she often writes exposé articles that are critical of the corporation and its executives. She also reported on a revolt against the Colonial Marshals before the incident.

William Connor

The USCSS *Torrens*' navigator and comms officer. Absolutely nothing of note is revealed about this character in *Alien: Isolation*, and even his fate at the end of the game is left mysterious. It's a shame Verlaine's right-hand man is essentially a glorified extra.

Francis

A survivor who, along with a small band of followers, ends up cornered in the depths of Seegson Synthetics by the alien. Mahoney and Peterson are also part of this group. Not much is revealed about these characters.

Zachary Watson

A resident of Sevastopol with a drinking problem. After finding him drunk and disorderly, the Colonial Marshals lock him in an evidence room to sleep it off. This would, sadly, be his final resting place, but the maintenance jack he has gripped in his hands will prove to be very useful for Ripley.

Bartholomew Hughes

Hughes is Seegson's communications manager, encountered by Ripley as she explores an android-infested Seegson Communications. He has a wife, Marie, and a daughter, Claire. Despite the obvious danger, Hughes ventures into the comms hub to re-establish contact with the outside world.

Catherine Foster

Foster was part of the *Anesidora* landing party that investigated the beacon on LV-426, falling victim to a facehugger while investigating an egg in the derelict. She was the wife of the ship's captain, Henry Marlow.

Heyst

A member of the *Anesidora* crew, Heyst can often be heard cracking childish jokes and teasing his colleagues. Although he initially went along with Marlow's plan to illegally hack the *Nostromo* black box and dig for valuable data, he now regrets it and wants to distance himself from his former captain.

Meeks

Another *Anesidora* crew member. Meeks finds it difficult to cope with the chaos unfolding on Sevastopol – which, as part of the ground team who investigated the beacon on LV-426, was partly his fault – and resorts to alcohol to help him get through it. However, mirroring Ripley's protests in the movie, Meeks fights with Marlow over bringing Catherine Foster aboard the *Anesidora* without going through proper quarantine procedures. If they had listened to him, this would have been a very different story.

Lewis

An engineering technician working on the *Anesidora*, who stays aboard the ship while the rest of the crew investigates LV-426.

Smythe

Seegson's beleaguered head of synthetic development who has repeatedly struggled to sell the company's technically unimpressive and increasingly out-of-date Working Joe androids to potential clients.

G. Spedding

A Seegson employee serving as an android liaison executive. He works closely with Smythe pitching Working Joes to clients and is in a relationship with Suzanne Archer, a Seegson Synthetics receptionist.

D. Turner

A Colonial Marshal who, when the creature begins running rampage around the station, is sent in with a small strike team to kill it.

The Story So Far

A tale of two Ripleys.

In the year 2120, a commercial towing vessel, the USCSS *Nostromo*, heads for the planet Thedus. Located fifty-nine light years from Earth in the Epsilon Reticuli system, this world is loaded with valuable minerals and home to a number of large, lucrative mining outposts. Two years later, dragging an expensive payload of 20 million tons of refined mineral ore behind it, the *Nostromo* begins the long journey home. But the crew is pulled out of hyper-sleep early, and its voyage to Earth is interrupted, when the ship picks up a strange signal coming from an uncharted moon in the uninhabited Zeta Reticuli system.

Despite protests from the crew, who are eager to return home, Weyland-Yutani policy states that they must investigate. Ash, the newly installed science officer, insists they send someone to take a look. A small landing party explores the surface of this barren, wind-blasted and primordial planetoid, which is designated LV-426. While exploring, they find a crashed spacecraft of unknown origin and venture inside. Executive officer Kane has an encounter with a strange parasitic creature and returns to the *Nostromo*, giving 'birth' to a vicious alien creature that grows to an immense size in a matter of hours. Warrant officer Ellen Ripley warned against bringing Kane back aboard without a quarantine procedure, but she was overruled by her crewmates.

Science officer Ash, secretly a Weyland-Yutani android, turns on the crew. He's instructed by his paymasters, via the ship's MU-TH-UR computer system, to protect the creature at all costs and return it to Earth for study. The Company's warfare division wants to find a way to weaponize it, despite the incredible existential threat it poses to the entire planet – and maybe even the entire *universe*. Why let that get in the way of a little profit, huh? The crew manages to subdue Ash, stopping his rampage, but the creature proves more formidable. It kills the entire crew, bar one: the resourceful Ripley.

Ripley activates the *Nostromo*'s self-destruct system, kills the alien by jettisoning it into space, and escapes in a shuttle with the ship's cat, Jones. In fifty-seven years, Ripley and her fellow feline survivor will be awakened from hypersleep and rescued, setting the events of James Cameron's *Aliens* in motion. Corporate Company representatives will grill her about what happened, scoff at her story, and hold her accountable for the destruction of the ship.

But until then, the *Nostromo* and her crew are considered missing and Weyland-Yutani takes a staggering financial hit. That's a lot of ore to just misplace somewhere in the depths of space, and the bean counters are not happy. But the Company *knew* what was on LV-426, having secretly installed Ash as a sleeper agent aboard the *Nostromo* to ensure they investigated the source of the 'distress signal' – which was actually a warning. Weyland-Yutani never expected the crew to survive, coldly declaring them expendable, but they didn't account for the loss of an expensive ship and 20 million tons of ore.

The apparent disappearance of the *Nostromo* was huge news, and speculation about what might have happened to it spread all over the galaxy. The Company tried to sweep the story under the rug, and even speaking about it became taboo among executive employees. Eventually, people lost interest, and the ship was officially registered as having been lost without a trace.

Ripley has a daughter, Amanda, who is understandably devastated by the unexplained disappearance of her mother. Developing a passion for engineering in her teens, she finds work with the Company as a technician and requests a work placement near the sector where the *Nostromo* disappeared. She thinks that if she gets a job in the same region of space, a new clue could emerge and she might find, at long last, some kind of closure.

Amanda is very much cut from the same cloth as her mother. She's tough, talented, practical and utterly single-minded. She also inherited some of her mother's distrust of authority. Part of what makes Ellen Ripley such an interesting and enduring character is that she was an ordinary person thrust into an extraordinary situation, forced to fight for her survival, and the same can be said for her offspring. This quality runs in the family.

Amanda never loses hope that her mother might be found, and her faith is rewarded when, fifteen years after the events of *Alien*, she receives a visit from a Weyland-Yutani employee named Samuels and her story truly begins. She's only twenty-six years old at this point and loaded with emotional baggage brought on by the loss of her mother, but that's not going to stop her.

Mission Guide

Alien: Isolation, *level by level.*

Now to the real meat of *Perfect Organism*. I've always been a fan of companion books designed to be read alongside TV shows and movies. In the 1990s and early 2000s, Fox published a series of episode guides for each season of *The X-Files*. After finishing an episode, I used to love (and, in fact, still do) reaching for the relevant book, flicking to its entry, and learning more about what I just watched. A similar companion book was published to accompany the superb British horror anthology series *Inside No. 9*. As I write this, I'm rewatching *The Sopranos* with Alan Sepinwall and Matt Zoller Seitz's superb companion, *The Sopranos Sessions*, in hand. I've also owned a DVD box set of the original *Twilight Zone* for years that comes with a book featuring impressively detailed recaps of each episode and loads of brilliant backstory. But no one, as far as I know, has written anything like this for a video game yet – which is a big part of what inspired me to write the book you're holding now.

It's also an expression of the fact that, whenever I finish a novel, movie, TV series, video game or whatever, I immediately go online and absorb as much related ephemera as I can, no matter how trivial. I scour IMDb, Wikipedia, TV Tropes and ancient, forgotten GeoCities fan sites preserved in the depths of the Wayback Machine for random nuggets of trivia, references

I might have missed, old reviews from the time, goofs or anything else even vaguely interesting. If you're the kind of person for whom a piece of media doesn't end when the credits roll – and this moment is, in fact, the beginning of a whole new voyage of discovery – you'll get an extra kick out of *Perfect Organism*.

When I play a game, I spend a lot of time just *looking* at stuff. From the moment I got my first console (a Sega Master System with *Alex Kidd in Miracle World* built-in), I've been fascinated by environment art, audio design and other aspects of game development that contribute to atmosphere, world-building and creating a sense of place. Doubly so in *Alien: Isolation*, a game based on a film whose production design I've been fascinated with for most of my life. I play games to *be* somewhere, and Sevastopol is among the most convincing, immersive, lovingly crafted virtual worlds I've ever spent time in. In fact, I could tell from the moment I saw the title screen, where Sevastopol floats in a starry void – a lonely speck dwarfed by an ominous, swirling gas giant – that the people who made this thing were as hopelessly besotted with the 1979 movie as I was. That they *got* it. And that was incredibly exciting.

The following chapters, then, are the result of this urge to study, analyse and pore over every shadowy corner of Creative Assembly's modern masterpiece and the classic sci-fi movie that inspired it. As a games journalist, I would often write about games in this way, but I was always restrained by a pesky word count. Here, however, with an entire book at my disposal, I'm now free to go *much* deeper; an opportunity I will take full advantage of. This is a game that is absolutely heaving with detail and craft, and every part of Sevastopol – down to the most unassuming office or storage room – has something worth studying in it. That's not something you can say about many other games.

So what can you expect from this mission guide? Well, a bit of everything. Observations about level design, art and audio. Easter eggs, trivia and movie callbacks. Connections to other *Alien* media. Things I love. Things I don't. I may love *Alien: Isolation* enough to write an entire book about it, but that doesn't mean I don't think there are some things Creative Assembly could have done better. I'm going to take you through the whole game, level by level, and hopefully by the end you'll have a deeper understanding of and appreciation for this remarkable game. Think of it as a director's commentary (remember those?), but by an *Alien: Isolation* superfan who has spent far too many hours obsessing over every inch of this stricken backwater space station and trying to get inside the heads of both its hero and her nightmarish adversary.

If you're playing the game for the first time, don't worry: I'll be avoiding spoilers. I won't directly reference anything in a chapter that hasn't appeared in the game up until that point. This means you can read the book as you play without fear of any big surprises being ruined. I might *hint* at certain plot points, but only in a way people already familiar with the game will understand. If you're replaying the game (welcome back, we missed you), having *Perfect Organism* on hand to read after completing each level will be a fun and rewarding way to revisit Sevastopol. I've written the book with dipping in and out in mind, but if you want to read it all in one sitting, that works too. It's your call. There's no right or wrong way to use this mission guide.

Alien: Isolation is so faithful to the source material, and captures its look and feel so perfectly, that these two pieces of media – separated by decades and existing in very different mediums – comfortably occupy the same space in my head. I don't think of *Isolation* merely as a video game based on a movie: to me, it's an extension, a *continuation*, of what Ridley Scott and his talented crew achieved in Shepperton Studios all those years ago. I'll talk about this, and much more, as we progress through the game step by step – from Amanda Ripley's explosive arrival on Sevastopol to its thrilling climax.

MISSION 1

Closing the Book
Like daughter, like mother.

A figure in a welding mask hunches over some unidentifiable piece of futuristic machinery. Sparks fly from a plasma torch, but their work is interrupted by a voice: 'Ripley?' They raise their mask, revealing a woman's face with dark, intense eyes and a forehead moist with sweat. This is our introduction to Amanda Ripley, daughter of Ellen Ripley, an engineer working in a remote corner of space. The man – or, more accurately, *artificial person* – is Samuels, a representative of the powerful, space-conquering Weyland-Yutani corporation. 'I'm Samuels,' he says. 'I work for the Company.'

This is a loaded word in the *Alien* series. Weyland-Yutani's reach extends so far, and the organisation is so entrenched in the everyday industry, politics and economics of space, that the need to refer to it by name has long since passed. Ripley pointedly pulls her mask back down and reignites her torch. This makes her attitude towards the corporation clear. Her mother was on their payroll when she went missing, and she understandably holds a grudge.

In the comic *Aliens: Resistance*, written by Brian Wood and published by Dark Horse Comics, we learn that Ripley's attempts to get a straight answer from Weyland-Yutani about what happened to the *Nostromo* and her missing crew have been frustratingly fruitless. 'They string me along, give me just enough bureaucratic red tape to wade through to keep me hoping,' she tells a Company-appointed therapist she suspects has been hired to encourage her to move on and stop asking questions. 'They want me on a leash.'

Then Samuels mentions something that makes her drop her guard. A commercial salvage ship, the *Anesidora*, has located the *Nostromo*'s flight recorder: a potential clue to the whereabouts of her mother. It's being held on Sevastopol, a backwater space station, and Samuels wants her to go there with him. As he details the mission, Ripley makes him a cup of coffee – a nice callback to

Aliens, where her mother did the same for Carter Burke and Lt Gorman as they tried to convince her to travel back to LV-426 with them.

'I've been cleared to offer you a place on the *Torrens* if you want to come along,' says Samuels, referring to a ship that we'll be visiting soon. 'Maybe there'll be some closure for you.' The camera lingers on Ripley's face as she processes everything she's just learned. It's clear she doesn't want to play ball with the Company, and doesn't trust Samuels, but can she really give up an opportunity to find out what happened to her mother?

The next thing we see is Ripley emerging from a transparent, sarcophagus-like hypersleep pod aboard the *Torrens*. This octagonal, padded room is quiet except for the distant rumble of the engines and the chirps of nearby computers. This location will be instantly recognisable to anyone who's seen *Alien*, as it's a near-perfect replica of the hypersleep chamber from the 1979 movie. This iconic set was designed by Benjamín Fernández, a Spanish art director, who used hidden hydraulic rams to make the flower-like pods open slowly.

Ripley inserts an ID card into a terminal, presumably to alert the crew of the *Torrens* that she's awake. Explore the room and you'll find a few interesting objects, including a book with a medieval coat of arms on the cover titled *War in Totality* – a reference to developer Creative Assembly's popular *Total War* series of military strategy games. There are several photos stuck to the walls too, including a picture of the White Cliffs of Dover. Details like these make the *Torrens*, and later Sevastopol, feel real and lived-in.

The hypersleep chamber also marks the first of many appearances of *Alien*'s famous drinking bird. This novelty toy, whose head bobs up and down as it appears to sip from a glass of water, was one of many strange knick-knacks decorating the *Nostromo* – which *Alien* writer Dan O'Bannon explained as being 'from various gift shops around the universe, wherever they stopped off. I figured that wherever you go there will always be gift shops.' Sevastopol and the *Torrens* are similarly littered with toys and other assorted junk collected from around the galaxy. Life in deep space is hard, so it's no surprise that people want to liven up the places where they live and work.

Ripley leaves the hypersleep chamber and it's immediately obvious from the layout of the ship that the *Torrens* has a lot in common with the *Nostromo*. Both vessels are Lockmart CM-88B Bison towing ships, but the *Torrens* has been refitted as a transport vessel, used for moving people around rather than large cargo like the refinery in *Alien*. This is reflected in its appearance, which is more comfortable and less industrial than its 1979 counterpart. It's not quite the *Enterprise-D*, but for a spacecraft in the *Alien* universe it's positively luxurious. Warm colours and soft lighting set this vessel apart from its submarine-like cinematic counterpart. As Ripley moves through a corridor, fluorescent lights flicker on and make it feel like the ship is waking up alongside her.

Move the camera down towards Ripley's feet and you'll notice that she's in her underwear. Ridley Scott originally wanted the crew to be completely naked in their hypersleep pods, but the studio was dead set against it. Scott actually shot the scene twice – once with the cast wearing underwear and once without – just in case they had a change of heart. 'I wanted to have a total sense of reality and rawness to this whole film,' he said in a director's commentary recorded for *Alien*'s original DVD release. 'Because the realer and truer you get, the scarier it gets later. But I lost that argument for obvious reasons.'

In a nod, perhaps, to influential first-person shooter *Half-Life*, Ripley locates a locker with her name on it and retrieves her clothes. You can take a shower, too, whether you already have your clothes on or not. A crew roster on a screen reveals who she's travelling to Sevastopol with, including Christopher Samuels (the synthetic human we already met in the intro), another Company employee named Nina Taylor and the *Torrens*' skeleton crew: Diane Verlaine, the ship's owner and captain, and William Connor, her second officer.

Nearby, a random assortment of papers is stuck to a wall – including one bearing the name Weylan-Yutani, without the D.

This is what the Company was named in the original movie, before it was retconned to Weyland-Yutani in *Aliens*. According to production designer Ron Cobb, who came up with the name, he originally wanted to call the company Leyland-Toyota, suggesting an alliance between the British and the Japanese in this vision of the future. But this wasn't allowed for copyright reasons, 'so changing the letters gave me 'Weylan', and 'Yutani' was a Japanese neighbour of mine.'

This otherwise unremarkable scrap of bureaucratic paperwork also has the lesser used 1979 version of the corporation's logo printed on it, which Cobb based on the winged sun: a solar symbol associated with divinity, royalty and power that was used by the Egyptians, Persians and Mesopotamians in ancient times. *Alien: Isolation* is impressively zealous when it comes to honouring the original movie and using it as the primary source material, but all other references to Weyland-Yutani in the game, including later appearances of the logo, are based on the series' current official post-*Aliens* canon. This random piece of environmental decoration, possibly left over from an earlier iteration of the game, makes me wonder if this wasn't always the case.

Exiting the locker room, you can now decide who to speak to first: Samuels in the medbay or Taylor in the communal kitchen/lounge area. The dialogue changes slightly depending on who you bump into first, but not in any significant way. You can also head straight for the bridge if you're feeling anti-social, but you'll miss out on some interesting world-building.

In the medbay, Ripley asks if Samuels woke up early. 'Well, I don't really need as much sleep as the rest of you,' he says, pointedly reminding us that he's not made from the same flesh and blood as the rest of the crew. He notes, as if we hadn't guessed already, that the *Torrens* is a 'very similar model' to the *Nostromo*. Ripley says she's worked engineering jobs on ships like this before. We get the sense that space travel is nothing special for her, which is a nice echo of the original film, where it was treated with a similar lack of reverence. This is not the final frontier: just a place where people go to do a job.

The medbay is a brilliant recreation of the infirmary set from the movie. It even has a functional CT scanner – based on a design by Ron Cobb – which folds away into a concealed, glass-covered chamber when a button is pushed. The room's ambient background noise, including a rhythmic, pulsing sound that sweeps in hypnotic waves, is also lifted directly from the film. Fans of Ridley Scott's other masterpiece, *Blade Runner*, may recognise this sound. It was reused as part of the futuristic ambience of Deckard's apartment.

In the lounge, Taylor is struggling with the hangover-like after effects of hypersleep. 'I don't do long-haul very often,' she says. 'Most legal execs don't travel further than the coffee machine.' Ripley reassures her that you get used to it, another clue that our hero is accustomed to travelling in deep space.

Taylor is, as her previous dialogue suggested, part of Weyland-Yutani's legal team. She's been tasked with overseeing the handover of the *Nostromo* flight recorder and compiling a final accident report detailing exactly what happened to the missing ship. In a revealing line of dialogue she notes that this will look great to her superiors – before realising how insensitive that sounds. Ripley is unfazed. 'It's okay. We'll both get what we want, right?'

The lounge will be instantly familiar to anyone who's seen *Alien*, being a near-identical replica of the room where Kane famously 'gave birth' to the xenomorph that terrorised the crew of the *Nostromo*. In the kitchen there are replicas of the futuristic-looking coffee dispensers that appeared in the movie. *Alien*'s set designers used a pair of real-world Braun Aromaster KF20 coffee machines as the basis for these, as well as a Krups 223 coffee grinder – which also appeared, more famously, in *Back to the Future Part II* as Mr Fusion, the 'home energy reactor' retrofitted to Doc Brown's time machine.

Overflowing ashtrays, discarded beer cans and other junk give the *Torrens* a similarly untidy, lived-in feel as the *Nostromo*'s shared spaces; although Verlaine's ship isn't quite as grimy. On a nearby terminal, Ripley reads a message sent to Taylor outlining the *Nostromo* incident and listing the missing crew. The author, a Weyland-Yutani employee named Saul, writes about this tragedy in the cold, matter-of-fact way only a true Company man could.

Ripley moves to the bridge and meets Verlaine face-to-face for the first time. The captain is wearing a clean, neat uniform, reflecting the pride she takes in her ship. Under the jacket we catch a glimpse of a pink paisley shirt, which recalls Brett's Hawaiian shirt. Sartorial details like this reinforce the idea that *Alien: Isolation* is presenting us with a seventies vision of the future.

While Ridley Scott was overseeing the construction of the *Nostromo* bridge set, he asked the carpenters to lower the ceiling to add to the crew's feeling of isolation and claustrophobia. Even though the *Torrens'* bridge is much brighter, this dropped ceiling still gives the place an oppressive feel. It's a subtly brilliant piece of off-the-cuff set design from Scott, and one that informs many of the new areas Creative Assembly went on to design for Sevastopol.

You can also catch a tantalising glimpse of the *Torrens'* humming, womb-like MU-TH-UR supercomputer chamber here through a window – but, alas, it's sealed off. You can only access this iconic location for yourself, albeit on another starship, in the game's *Nostromo* DLC missions. Then, when you're done exploring, it's just a matter of picking up a briefing file and triggering a dramatic cutscene that sets *Alien: Isolation*'s story fully in motion.

Bringing an image of Sevastopol up on a flickering CRT screen reveals that the station is seriously damaged – including, in a stroke of bad luck for Ripley and co., the dry-dock bay. This means Verlaine is unable to dock the *Torrens* and attempts to contact the station for help, only to receive a garbled radio message from someone named Waits, a Colonial Marshal. Through the static we can make out the words 'serious situation', but not much else.

Ripley, Samuels and Taylor are left with no choice but to strap on the *Torrens'* yellow pressure suits and spacewalk over to Sevastopol via a precariously long cable. Then, suddenly, disaster strikes. An explosion sends a hulking chunk of metal debris hurtling towards the cable, snapping it and sending the three characters spinning off in different directions. Ripley manages to grab hold of the station before she's swept away into the darkness of space, narrowly escaping into an airlock, unaware of the nightmare that awaits her.

MISSION 2

Welcome to Sevastopol
Into the abyss.

Ripley shakes off the impact and we take control of her once again. The screen is framed by the helmet of her pressure suit, condensation beading on the reinforced glass. We hear the frantic rhythm of her breathing, adrenaline still pumping through her veins, and the hiss of the oxygen tanks. She moves into an airlock and dumps the suit in a locker. The yellow *Torrens* suit stands out among Sevastopol's, which are white and muted – similar in style to the one her mother wore when she ejected the alien from the *Narcissus* shuttle.

In a dimly lit storage area, a monotone beeping sound alerts us to our first save point on the station. *Alien: Isolation*, somewhat controversially, forces you to rely entirely on manual saves. There are almost no checkpoints and no autosaves. Over the course of the game, this beeping becomes a source of comfort, because you know that once you jam your keycard into the slot you'll never have to repeat the preceding section again.

A loud rumbling sound echoes through the dark, claustrophobic hallways. The lights flicker, the screen shakes and dust falls from the ceiling. 'Sevastopol stability compromised,' says a disembodied, presumably computer-generated voice emanating from some unseen source. The station's stabilisers have been damaged, compromising its orbit around KG-348 – the gas giant you saw from the bridge of the *Torrens*. This will come into play later.

A jet of flame explodes violently from a broken gas main. Ripley bypasses it by slipping into a vent, whose oddly sinister, iris-like covering opens with a distinctive metallic scraping sound – which is lifted directly from *Alien*. The film's BAFTA-winning sound design team, led by Derrick Leather, Jim Shields and Bill Rowe, was instrumental in bringing a uniquely absorbing sonic atmosphere to the *Nostromo*, and atmosphere which *Alien: Isolation* replicates brilliantly. There's something quietly unnerving about the way the vents grind open, like a mechanical eye opening in the dark and peering at you.

Ripley emerges from the vent and finds the first of many Sevastolink terminals glowing in the gloom. The green-and-black monochrome monitor and keyboard-driven interface are loosely inspired by IBM PCs from the seventies and eighties. Ripley finds a post by chief engineer W. Porter (named after *Alien: Isolation* writer Will Porter) revealing that Sevastopol is in the process of being decommissioned, along with a message warning the employees hired to dismantle it not to treat it as a 'lucky dip', implying there have been problems with scavenging and looting on the near-abandoned station.

The way forward is blocked by a collapsed floor, over which a pair of boards have been precariously placed. Ripley steels herself and steps onto the makeshift bridge, but it immediately gives way. She tumbles into a void of sparking wires, smoking electronics and twisted cables, finding herself on a baggage carousel deep in the guts of the station's spaceflight terminal. The whole area has been plunged into darkness by the many power cuts plaguing Sevastopol, forcing Ripley to light the way by igniting a conveniently placed flare.

She climbs a ladder and finds herself in a small storage room where music is playing quietly from a stereo. The design of these stereos – which can be found all over Sevastopol – seems to be based on the real-world SKR 700, a cassette recorder produced in East Germany that was popular in the Soviet Union in the early-to mid-eighties. Its manufacturer in the game is Generic Electric, an obvious parody of American electronics conglomerate, General Electric.

What you hear on this radio, and every radio in the game for that matter, is different every time you play. It's entirely randomised, pulling from a selection of thirty-five songs and fuzzy, distorted audio clips. The highlight is an eerily tape-warped version of Mozart's 'Eine kleine Nachtmusik', which Dallas listens to in *Alien* while enjoying a quiet moment away from the crew in the *Narcissus*. There are also bluegrass guitar instrumentals, a haunting music-box rendition of 'Silent Night', and songs by a band called Dead Sea Navigators, whose bassist Nik Williams worked on *Alien: Isolation* as a programmer.

There are some curious voice recordings too. In one, a man attacks the Seegson corporation and calls for a social revolution. In another, someone reads feverishly from *The Book of Delight* – a twelfth-century collection of short stories by Joseph Zabara. Whether this text has any thematic connection to the game, or was simply chosen because it sounds cool, is a mystery. A passage from Mary Shelley's *Frankenstein* can also be heard, which has some relevance (albeit coincidentally) when you consider David's activities in *Alien: Covenant*. There's also a recording of a passage from Franz Kafka's *The Metamorphosis*.

But back to Sevastopol. Ripley finds herself in a darkened lobby with a model of the station perched on a pedestal in the centre of the room. She activates a generator, restores power, and the model is suddenly illuminated. The design of Sevastopol's exterior is heavily based on the colossal ore refinery the *Nostromo* was towing through deep space in *Alien* – only with three towers rather than four. Even though there's no up or down in space, the large platform at the base was deliberately placed there to give a sense of a 'ground' level, helping players mentally navigate the station as they move through it.

On a terminal near the generator, Ripley reads a note saying no one goes to the spaceflight terminal anymore 'after what happened', which is one of many small pieces of ominous foreshadowing littering this section. Even though we know an alien is loose – the game is called *Alien: Isolation*, after all, and we've all seen the movie – these still ratchet up the tension on a first playthrough, simply because they make you wonder exactly *when* it's going to show up.

Greed, corporate overreach and the soulless commodification of space are some of the *Alien* series' most prominent themes, and *Isolation* contributes to this by covering the corridors of Sevastopol in garish, corny advertisements. They're all hand-drawn in a vintage seventies style, which gives them a curious charm. One features a satisfied-looking man reclining in a chair, raising a glass of whisky. 'On your way back to Thedus?' the copy reads, referencing the mining planet that was the *Nostromo*'s last port of call before its fatal encounter on LV-426. 'Toast your return with Davenport Rye.'

Another features a woman with a terrifying rictus grin, showing off her perfectly maintained teeth. 'Smile with confidence!' it reads above the logo of the San Cristobal Medical Facility, which Ripley visits later. Seeing these chirpy, aspirational, often comical adverts clinging to the walls of such a dilapidated, miserable and forgotten place creates an interesting visual contrast. Sevastopol is what happens when capitalism goes unchecked, which these faded, peeling remnants of its not-so-distant past only serve to highlight.

Ripley makes her way through a departure lounge, ducking under exposed wires and navigating past heaps of abandoned suitcases, and finds herself in one of the game's most visually striking, evocative areas: the spaceflight terminal. Looking up through a large atrium window we see KG-348 and the endless turmoil of the storms roiling on its surface, set against the cold void of space. In Sevastopol's prime this was a vibrant, lively hub – then the space traffic dried up and left it in the sorry state we see it in now. Artist Bradley Wright, who designed this location, thought of it as a huge, monstrous flower.

Dotted around the terminal are public communication devices called VIDCOMs, whose design is somewhat reminiscent of the video-phone Deckard uses to call Rachael in *Blade Runner*. *Alien* and *Blade Runner* are often thought of as inhabiting the same universe, and there are more overt references to Ridley Scott's existential cyberpunk masterpiece to come.

There are a few businesses here too: Xing Xang, a boarded-up noodle bar that was apparently once 'the best on the station'; a place called CRED-OP Amusements, containing a row of dusty arcade machines and an air hockey table; and a predatory short-term loan company that offered no doubt massively high interest advances on Sevastopol employees' wages – with the full backing of Seegson. This area does a lot of legwork in terms of world-building, painting a vivid picture of what a dreary, soul-sucking place Sevastopol is.

As Ripley moves through the terminal, the immense silhouette of the *Torrens* suddenly begins to rumble slowly past the atrium window. A spotlight spills through the glass, but Verlaine doesn't notice Ripley. She watches helplessly as metal shutters groan to life, drop down and cover the glass. When he designed these, Bradley Wright imagined them being used to protect the fragile exterior of the terminal from space debris or other drifting junk.

After activating another generator, bright light pours out of the entrance to Xing Xang, revealing the shadow of a fast-moving figure inside. First time players will wonder if this is finally the moment where they come face-to-fangs with the alien, but not quite. Inside, an audio log from journalist Julia Jones talks about unrest in the terminal, resulting in a riot and a gun being fired at the Colonial Marshals. Ripley crawls through a vent and makes her way through a half-destroyed lounge with a collapsed air vent. We see a cleaning robot with friendly glowing eyes and the name Harold printed on its side in a retro typeface. This is almost certainly a reference to the cheery-faced Henry brand of vacuum cleaners, which are something of a design icon in the UK.

On a departures board we see a variety of destinations once served by Sevastopol's spaceport, now permanently cancelled. These include Barnard's Star, Ross 154, Procyon, Groombridge 34, Alpha Ceti, Capella, Delta Pavonis, Canopus and Arcturus, which are all real stars or star systems. When you're in the baggage reclaim area, crank up the volume and listen carefully – ideally with headphones. You'll hear a cat's meows coming from a distant vent. Then, as you move through the area, its mewing will be suddenly cut short and you'll hear an eerie hissing sound. I'll let you fill in the blanks here, but I don't think this unseen feline will be as lucky as the *Nostromo*'s cat, Jones.

Ripley's journey is halted when she finds many of the doors in the next area of the station blocked by pneumatic barriers. This sends her on a detour to a Colonial Marshals customs office, where she finds the bloodied corpse of a man named Zachary Watson who, despite being locked in a safe and secure evidence room by Marshal Waits for being drunk and disorderly, has somehow (well, *we* know how) ended up dead. Ripley winces as she prises a heavy-duty maintenance jack from his stiff, cold hands – a tool that will let her unseal those aforementioned pneumatically braced doors. She can also use it as a makeshift bludgeon, which will come in very handy later on.

But when you solve one problem in *Alien: Isolation*, another isn't far behind. Ripley is about to move deeper into the station when she feels the cold steel of a gun barrel pressed against her head. A wired, paranoid survivor, Axel Fielding, tells her there's 'a killer' on the station. She manages to talk him down, offering him a place on the *Torrens* if he helps her contact Verlaine. Axel, played by Scottish actor George Anton, wears a jacket bearing the logo of manufacturing company Watatsumi, suggesting he may have been an employee.

All the noises and disturbances we've seen and heard so far – the clattering in the restaurant back in the spaceflight terminal, a table being knocked over near where we found the maintenance jack – have all been Axel, who has been secretly following Ripley. This is confirmed if you use a freecam to break out of the game's boundaries, from where you'll see Axel's character model lurking, even though we don't see him until now when he holds us up.

Stay away from other survivors, he says. 'They don't like strangers.' This is the game telling us that gun-toting humans on the station will shoot on sight. Axel leads Ripley to a small room he's been living in. There's an acoustic guitar propped up against a wall, a sorry-looking mattress, rice bowls with dirty chopsticks, and scattered playing cards. A real bachelor pad.

Axel gives Ripley a headset with a design almost identical to the modified Racal Amplivox RA-150 Minilite worn by the crew of the *Nostromo* in *Alien* and the Colonial Marines in *Aliens*. Because of its futuristic appearance, this headset appeared in countless other sci-fi movies in the seventies, eighties and nineties, including *Star Wars*, *Superman*, *Moonraker* and *Demolition Man*.

Axel and Ripley sneak past gangs of nervous, twitchy survivors. He's taking Ripley to the Lorenz SysTech Spire, one of Sevastopol's three towers, where she can contact the *Torrens* for help. But then our Scottish friend meets a sudden, gruesome demise. A strange, viscous liquid drips on Axel's shoulder. Then, the alien, making its first unforgettable appearance in the game, grabs him, brutally impales him through the chest with its tail, and drags him shrieking into an air vent. Ripley flees in terror, escaping onto a local transit system. If you make too much noise while waiting for the train, or loiter when its doors noisily open, the alien can show up and kill you long before it's formally introduced in a later mission. Climb on board and she's safe – for now. Alas, things are about to get a lot worse.

MISSION 3

Encounters
You're not alone.

With Axel almost certainly dead, Ripley is on her own again. Her destination is Seegson Communications, where she hopes she'll be able to contact the *Torrens*. Exploring the transit station, Ripley downloads a map of the area from a brightly glowing terminal. These are obviously telegraphed all over Sevastopol – however, there are a few tucked away in the depths of the station that are easy to miss, making navigating this labyrinth much more difficult.

Continuing on, Ripley finds herself at an airport-style security checkpoint. We'll pass through here later, but for now she heads towards the Lorenz SysTech lobby. Lorenz SysTech is one of the *Alien* universe's many powerful mega-corporations, albeit a much smaller one than the all-conquering Weyland-Yutani. This deep-space construction company actually built Sevastopol, funded by the GeoFund Investor banking corporation. Work on the station started in 2095 and finished in 2105, two years behind schedule.

Depending on which version of *Alien: Isolation* you're playing, this door may take a while to open. The next area is quite large, and the game uses the hissing and beeping of the automatic doors – creating the illusion of a creaky, worn-out mechanism whirring to life – to mask the game engine loading in the next chunk of map. When the doors finally slide open, Ripley finds herself in one of Sevastopol's most visually memorable environments.

We're in a cavernous lobby dominated by an immense starship engine hanging from the ceiling. This area has been described by Creative Assembly as a showcase for the tech companies based in the SysTech spire. Other pieces of spacefaring machinery litter the place, although there's a sense that this centre of industry's glory days, if it ever had any, have long since faded.

A young woman's voice echoes in the distance. 'What the hell is wrong with this thing?' she curses. 'Work, damn you!' Ripley approaches cautiously and the woman blindly fires a revolver at her. She stops unloading and sprints upstairs, shouting for some unseen friends, giving us a moment to investigate whatever it was that was frustrating her so much when we arrived.

Ripley approaches a locked door and finds a security access tuner hastily abandoned on the floor. The design of this chunky, lo-fi hacking device is somewhat reminiscent of early handheld televisions, particularly the 'Watchman' range of pocket TVs manufactured by Sony in Japan in the early 1980s. 'She was trying to hack the elevator's security,' Ripley says to herself, helpfully informing the player as to the purpose of this piece of sci-fi gadgetry. Alas, its circuits are fried, but we're playing as an engin-eer, remember? 'Easy fix,' says Ripley, who speaks to herself a lot in the game, as we receive a fresh objective: locate a new data cell to revive the dead tuner.

Search the nearby reception desk and you'll find one of the fifty ID tags scattered around Sevastopol. The characters these tags belong to are all named after people who worked on the game. This one, for example, bears the name A. Hutchinson: a reference to senior brand manager Amy Hutchinson, a member of the *Alien: Isolation* marketing team. Each tag also comes with an ASCII portrait of the person in question. The quality of the reward earned for finding them all, which is no mean feat, depends entirely on how much you value the PlayStation trophy or Xbox/Steam achievement you receive for doing so.

There's an audio log here too, recorded on an old seventies-style reel-to-reel tape player. In it, a Seegson Communications manager named Bartholomew Hughes records a message for his wife, Marie, urging her to leave work and pick up their daughter, Claire – and their cat – then head home. He clearly sensed something bad was happening on Sevastopol. We'll meet this guy later.

Anyway, now it's time to find that data cell, which is located in an area beneath where Ripley currently is. Problem is, the trigger-happy woman from earlier has returned with a group of similarly on-edge friends in tow. This is a light stealth challenge to kick things off, and there are a number of ways to sneak by unseen. You can attempt to attack the group head-on, but your chances of survival are slim. The game wants you to think your way out of this predicament – or, alternatively, you can just make a mad dash for the objective marker on your map. The survivors won't follow you down into the lower levels, for reasons that will become clear shortly. 'No way,' the would-be hacker says, her voice filled with fear. 'I am NOT going down there.'

As we descend a staircase we catch a rare glimpse of Sevastopol's exterior through a tall window. The gas giant KG-348 looms above the station, creating an ominous sense of scale. Shattered chunks of debris float past the glass, wreckage from the explosion that rudely interrupted our EVA walk earlier. Eventually, Ripley's descent leads her to tech support HQ. Sometimes, but not always, you can catch an early, brief glimpse of the xenomorph here. It'll disappear through a doorway, then you'll hear a

distant hiss as it noisily clambers into a vent and leaves the area –
for now.

In this area you'll see a vending machine that dispenses hot
food. The reheated calorie-dense delights on offer include pizza,
french fries, chicken nuggets and horse burgers. Delicious. But,
more excitingly, inside the tech support office Ripley finds her
first gun: a .357 revolver from firearms manufacturer Spearhead
Armoury. The design of this weapon seems to be based on the
Mateba Model 6 Unica, an Italian revolver – albeit with a more
squared-off silhouette, presumably to give it a sci-fi edge. The
Unica was released in 1997, which is one of the only examples in
Alien: Isolation of a prop not being rooted in the design of a real-
world counterpart from the 1970s. Even so, the hefty, utilitarian
design of this gun feels right at home in this world.

It's just a shame it's useless. Well, nearly. The xenomorph will
shrug bullets off like mosquito bites, so don't bother wasting your
ammunition. You *can* kill human enemies and, with five to six
well-placed headshots, Working Joe androids with it – but the
noise will aggressively alert the xenomorph to your position, so
it's something of a double-edged sword. If the alien moves near a
propane tank and you think fast on your feet, an accurate shot
from the revolver will cause the tank to explode and scare your
pursuer away for a while.

Ripley moves deeper into the tech support floor, finding herself
in a workshop littered with gutted computers and assorted scrap,
some of which she can pick up and use later to craft gadgets,
including smoke bombs – the easily-missed blueprints for which
are located on a desk in this area. In a circular room whose walls
are lined with flashing, chirping computer terminals, Ripley gasps
at the sight of a bloodied corpse slumped in a chair. Whoever this
guy was, it looks like someone blasted him several times with a
shotgun. This is a stark reminder that the alien isn't the only violent creature lurking on Sevastopol.

Then, a stroke of luck. Entering the room where the data cell is
located, Ripley stumbles upon something much more valuable:
the *Nostromo*'s recovered flight recorder. The design of the black

box is clearly based on the self-destruct device from the movie – in particular, the piston-like tubes that rise up as Ripley goes through the achingly slow, tense process of blowing up the *Nostromo*. This is a neat way of making this new prop, created especially for the game, feel like a visually authentic part of the ship we saw in the film.

She grabs it excitedly, tapping at a small keyboard, trying to activate it, but is dismayed to discover that the data is corrupted. It seems the closure our hero has been desperately seeking will have to wait. Adding insult to injury, her presence in this room triggers a security lockdown. Alarms begin to scream, which when you first play the game instils an almost unbearable fear that the xenomorph will be lured towards the source of the racket.

Luckily, Ripley is left alone long enough to solve a simple environmental puzzle, which involves moving power-activated archive shelves in a specific order to reveal the data cell that will let us, finally, activate the access tuner. She plugs it into the hacking tool and watches it fizz to life, meaning it's time to return to the code-locked door that resisted the efforts of the revolver-toting woman who tried to kill us earlier. But before that, a nearby audio log gives us a clue as to what could have happened to the busted *Nostromo* flight recorder.

W. Porter, Sevastopol's chief engineer, reveals that he, under orders from Marshal Waits, broke corporate confidentiality agreements and tried to access the black box data. But besides the Weyland-Yutani logo, there was nothing on it. 'Someone aboard the *Nostromo* could have asked its MU-TH-UR core to wipe it clean,' he says. Could it have been Ash? This tracks with his single-minded mission to secure and protect the xenomorph specimen at all costs. Whoever the culprit was, Ripley is left devastatingly empty-handed.

Now it's time to get out of here, but first Ripley has to find a way to disable the security lockdown she accidentally triggered. In an ominously dark, shadowy room filled with softly glowing computers, she locates the terminal that will free her. The keyboard here is also based on the *Nostromo*'s self-destruct device, whose peculiar controls were designed by *Alien* production artist Simon Deering. 'Ridley Scott asked me to make some nice buttons,' he said in a 2009 interview. 'Complicated but interesting, because they won't be on screen for more than a second or two.' If you pause the film you'll see a number of strange phrases on the self-destruct controls, including SHAKTI EXCESS, PADME, LINGHA and YONI – which are all references to *The Secret Doctrine*, a pseudo-scientific esoteric book written in 1888 by Helena Blavatsky that Deering happened to be reading during the production of *Alien*.

The security terminal keyboard in *Alien: Isolation* is heavily based on Deering's design – as are several other computers throughout the game. But the texture is sadly too low-resolution to make out any of the odd phrases that make this such a compelling piece of production design. When Ripley lifts the lockdown, we finally get our first good look at the alien. It drops from a vent above her, then slowly rises to its feet. But a second before we see its face, Ripley shrieks and quickly ducks behind a desk. She holds her breath, racked with a pure, visceral terror as the creature's tail drops in front of her and slithers between her legs. She hears the beast moving away and peeks cautiously over the desk. It creeps into the next room, giving her a brief window to escape. If you're playing on PlayStation, PC or Xbox you'll earn a Trophy/Achievement here titled, appropriately enough, 'The Perfect Organism'.

Your goal now is getting back to the room with the hanging engines without being brutally killed by the alien, which involves a lot of quiet, careful sneaking. The survivors from earlier, including the woman you liberated the access tuner from, aren't quite so light-footed, however. Get back to where you started and you'll see the creature rampaging into the group, tearing them limb from limb. You don't have to worry about these guys anymore at least, but it's cold comfort in light of the fact a xenomorph is now on the loose.

Ripley manages to evade the alien and make it to the locked door the woman was trying to get through. She uses the newly repaired access tuner to bypass the lock. The shape-matching hacking minigame isn't much of a mental challenge in and of itself, but with an alien breathing down your neck it suddenly feels ten times more difficult. The door finally slides open, revealing an elevator that will take Ripley to Seegson Communications. If she can contact Verlaine on the *Torrens*, maybe she can find a way out of this nightmare.

MISSION 4

Seegson Communications
A rude awakening.

The elevator judders to a halt and Ripley exits, finding herself in the depths of Seegson Communications: a network hub that handles all internal and external communication on Sevastopol. By now you'll have seen and heard the name Seegson multiple times, leading you to believe they're the owners of the station. But while they do have a presence in every corner of it, they're actually more of a service provider. When Lorenz SysTech built Sevastopol they intended to sell it to a large corporation, but with no offers forthcoming it became an independent free port – which Seegson stepped in to handle infrastructure for.

Seegson, originally known as Sieg and Son, is a corporation created exclusively for *Alien: Isolation*. *Colonial Times* reporter Julia Jones describes it as 'a company we all forgot' and a 'second-tier' corporation, giving a sense of how little impact this group has made in the *Alien* universe – especially compared to Weyland-Yutani. Poor products, over-expansion and a number of other bad business decisions ensured Seegson never lived up to their full potential, which Ripley finds evidence of all around the station – and, when she approaches the reception desk in Seegson Communications, staring her in the face.

The desk is manned by an eerie, blank-faced mannequin with dot-like glowing eyes. This is Ripley's first encounter with a Working Joe, the low-tech android workforce that keeps Sevastopol operating – even when the majority of its human inhabitants have fled or been killed. These unconvincing artificial people seem unbothered by the emergency currently engulfing the station, and go about their duties as normal. Created by Seegson, the Working Joes are generations behind Weyland-Yutani's lifelike androids. They're built to be cost effective and easily replaced, with basic functionality and no personality. A cheap Nokia to Weyland-Yutani's sleek iPhone.

Creative Assembly based the mannequin-like appearance of the Working Joes on resuscitation dummies from the 1970s. In early concept renders they have rubbery-looking hairpieces on their heads, but in the final game, to help players differentiate between the Joes and the human survivors, the artists decided they should all be bald. Ripley asks the Joe at the reception desk for help accessing Seegson Communications, but the android simply asks her to take a seat and wait. The cold, slightly distorted voice of these mechanical beings is quietly chilling. They're polite and well-spoken, but in a frightening, uncanny way. None of them attack Ripley in the first part of the chapter, but they're still unnerving. Their beady, staring eyes are totally devoid of humanity.

'No wonder Seegson is losing the tech race,' Ripley says to herself as the android wanders away, ignoring her. As she searches for a way in, we hear a chirpy recorded voice reading out an advertisement. 'Here at Seegson, we remember that the ultimate goal is clear communication,' it says. 'That's why all our communications are serviced by local APOLLO AI.' This is the first time Ripley hears the name APOLLO, and it won't be the last.

Ripley continues deeper into Seegson Communications, hopelessly trying to get the attention of the Working Joes, who regard her with total indifference. 'APOLLO has the situation in hand,' one says, brushing her concerns off. It's clear something has gone wrong with these machines.

Interestingly, early in development, Creative Assembly toyed with the idea of making Ripley an android. Before the developers were certain Fox would let them use Ellen Ripley's daughter as a protagonist, they considered making her a synthetic, which would be revealed to the player late in the game.

Ripley finds a small workshop at the end of a long hall, in which she discovers one of the most important gadgets in the game: the motion tracker. But this, along with the *Aliens*-era Weyland-Yutani logo featured in the game, is another thing in *Alien: Isolation* inspired by James Cameron's follow-up rather than the 1979 original. In the first movie, the crew of the *Nostromo* use a boxy-looking motion tracker (built by Ron Cobb out of a Panasonic Ranger-505 portable TV with, strangely enough, an ice cube tray attached to it), which features a bare-bones UI comprised of simple dots on a glowing square grid.

This looks good on the screen, but implemented in a game as-is, it just wouldn't relay enough information to the player. This is why Creative Assembly decided, wisely, to use a tracker with a UI based on the much more readable, practical one used by the Colonial Marines in *Aliens*. The moment Ripley picks up the tracker, a blip immediately registers on its radar-like display as a Working Joe creeps up behind her to ask her what she's doing. This is a clever, and fairly devilish, way of instructing the player how the tool works.

On a nearby terminal Ripley finds another audio log from Bartholomew Hughes, telling his wife that he's heading to Seegson Communications to try and re-establish communications with the outside world. She continues on, using a vent to bypass another jobsworth Working Joe who won't let her into the deeper facility. Then, through a crack in the vent, she sees Hughes in the flesh. He's shouting at a Working Joe about re-establishing comms, but the Joe attacks him, saying he's 'being hysterical'. Hughes unloads a revolver into the android, but it has no effect besides making it recoil briefly – a clue to the player that it'll take more than a bullet to stop these things. Ripley watches in horror as the Working Joe wrestles Hughes and slams his head repeatedly against a wall, coldly murdering him. Androids going rogue in an *Alien* story is no surprise, but the sudden, unceremonial brutality of this scene is a shock to the system. When the Joe is finished with Hughes, it quips 'good day' and strolls away.

Up until this point the Working Joes have been a benign presence, but now they'll attack Ripley if she crosses their path. They're slow and easily outmanoeuvred, but if they grab hold of you they can deal a huge amount of damage – killing you outright if your health is low. There are several ways to kill them, including shocking them with a stun prod and finishing them off with a swing of your jack. But there's always the risk of this kind of violent noise-making alerting other Joes or, worse still, the xenomorph.

Ripley dodges a few Working Joes – who are, for now, easy to avoid – and takes a nearby elevator to her next destination: the Seegson Communications hub. When she arrives, an audio transmission from Verlaine crackles over a speaker. 'What the hell just happened?' she says. 'Did any of our EVA team make it onboard?' But the message is falling on deaf ears, with only the uninterested Working Joes there to receive it. Verlaine says that 'the explosion' (the same one that almost killed Ripley earlier) has damaged the *Torrens* and she's had to leave Sevastopol space for repairs. 'Systems will be down while we repair, I can't say for how long.' Damn.

Ripley accesses a terminal and finds the garbled message the *Torrens* received as she approached the station, now clear as day. It's Marshal Waits trying – and evidently failing – to send a long-range emergency signal outside of Sevastopol space. Something appears to be blocking the transmission. Ripley tries to send an external communication herself, to the *Torrens*, only to hear an automated voice say that it's been denied by order of APOLLO. The voice adds that local communications are still active on select channels, and Ripley wonders if there's anyone else on Sevastopol she can contact. But, to do so, she'll need to move deeper into Seegson Communications and locate another terminal.

The communications hub is another memorable location and seems to have been heavily inspired by an oft-published, but unused, piece of Ron Cobb concept art for the bridge of the *Nostromo*. Through a large atrium window we can see the screen-filling mass of KG-348, ancient, silent and oblivious to the chaos unfolding on the station. We also see an array of enormous satellite dishes, which is actually a digital matte painting (of the kind beloved by Hollywood, especially around the time *Alien* was made) rather than a 3D space.

This is one of the first real stealth challenges in *Alien: Isolation*, with enough Working Joes roaming around that you really need to think before you move. Luckily, the area is full of stuff to hide behind, including rows of comms terminals with handy little alcoves beneath them to squeeze into, as well as a hidden vent system that helps you stay out of sight and bypass a few of the androids. With a little patience, you can make it through this area without being seen, eventually moving out of the hub and into internal communications.

Inside, Ripley hears another overlooked transmission – this time from Samuels. He's calling for help, saying it's urgent, but as usual the Working Joes ignore his pleas and robotically go about their daily routine. There are more places to hide in this part of the level, and plenty of shadows to slip into, but the tension is ramped up massively by the fact that there are blind corners and tight corridors everywhere. This oppressive closeness encourages, or more accurately *forces*, you to use your new motion tracker to keep your eye on the Joes wandering around as you edge slowly towards the internal comms terminal.

Ripley finally locates it and activates it, which involves completing a series of simple shape-matching puzzles. The stylish, almost abstract visuals for these mini-games were extracted from the visual language of the *Nostromo*'s many computer displays – an idea lead UI artist Jon McKellan would develop and build upon in his own game, 2019's *Observation*, which is considered by many to be something of a spiritual successor to *Alien: Isolation*.

A cutscene is triggered and a face appears on the terminal's screen through a glitchy syrup of deliciously analogue, authentic-looking VHS distortion – which, as explained earlier in the book, was done with actual degraded tape rather than a digital simulation. It's Samuels, who is relieved Ripley is still alive. Ripley explains the situation, including the murderous androids and the lethal creature on the loose. He tells her he's in the

Medical transit station with Taylor, who has been badly injured. He's going to send a car for Ripley, which means going back to where we started – a task made difficult by the fact that interacting with the internal comms terminal has triggered an area-wide security alert.

Alien: Isolation will often do this: making the player retread a known location, but with some twist to mix things up. In this instance, a loud, distressing alarm begins to shriek, alerting nearby Working Joes that someone unauthorised has been meddling with the internal comms. So not only are the Joes more alert for your return journey, but the ceaseless screaming of the alarm makes using your ears to help you determine their movements almost impossible. On a more psychological level, this repetitive, unpleasant sound – accompanied by red flashing lights – makes an already stressful situation almost unbearably so. Regardless, Ripley has to get back to the station, relying on her motion tracker more than ever.

In one of the narrow corridors here, you might notice a vent in the ceiling dripping and hear a soft hissing emanating from within. This is not a coolant leak, but the viscous drool of the xenomorph. Walk under the vent and you'll be suddenly, violently killed by the waiting creature: an easy-to-miss trap that still catches me out even after finishing the game multiple times.

Before you leave, make sure you find the terminal with the words USCSS *NOSTROMO* glowing tantalisingly on the screen. This is the first of ten audio logs recorded by the original cast of *Alien*. In this one, Tom Skerritt reprises his role as Captain Dallas and complains about Weyland-Yutani replacing his usual science officer at the last minute – a reference, of course, to Ash. This is the easiest *Nostromo* log to find, sitting basically out in the open. The others are hidden in the station's depths or require certain kit to access.

Ripley makes it safely back to the transit terminal, finding the car sent by Samuels waiting for her. So far, the alien has largely kept itself to itself, but from this point on it becomes more of a clear and present existential threat. We're only four missions into

Alien: Isolation, with a long way to go, but we're about to set foot in one of the scariest locations in the entire game.

MISSION 5

The Quarantine
Above all, do no harm.

Ripley steps off the transit car and finds Samuels looking after Taylor, whose uniform is ominously stained with blood. 'She needs treatment,' says Samuels. 'Medical is nearby, but I didn't want to leave her.' Which means, naturally, it's up to us to visit Sevastopol's hospital – the San Cristobal Medical Facility – in order to locate a life-saving trauma kit. San Cristobal is one of the many islands that make up the Galapagos archipelago. It's also Spanish for Saint Christopher, the patron saint of travellers, nightmares and plagues. I'll let you decide which of these this deep-space medical facility was named after.

As Ripley makes her way towards Medical, an automated voice announces that APOLLO has initiated a station-wide transit shutdown. Guess we aren't leaving this spire any time soon. The main entrance is locked by a device we don't currently have the required tool to bypass, forcing a detour. Entering a sterile-looking waiting room, a row of metal shutters suddenly clunks to life, slowly pulling back to reveal another impressive view of KG-348. Then we hear a voice: 'You. Hey, you. Need some help?' This unknown survivor sounds friendly enough and activates a locked elevator, inviting Ripley upstairs.

Medical is in a state of lockdown, by order of the Colonial Marshals, and Ripley is forced to crawl through the ventilation system to proceed. She emerges in a place a sign identifies as a 'welcome area', although it's far from welcoming. San Cristobal is in a sorry state, with evidence of recent unrest, heaps of trash and flickering lights. Behind a glass-walled office, Ripley finally meets the source of the voice that beckoned her here: the enigmatic Dr Kuhlman.

If you've watched any behind-the-scenes material for *Alien: Isolation*, this face may be vaguely familiar to you. Kuhlman's appearance is modelled after Clive Gratton, the game's lead programmer, who has done several interviews about the development of *Alien: Isolation* over the years. Most of the people you meet on Sevastopol are in fact based on Creative Assembly staff members and their friends and family. This is actually quite common in the games industry. The patrons in *Batman: Arkham Knight*'s diner intro sequence, to give a random example, are all people who worked on the game too.

Kuhlman says there are no medical supplies up here, but that Ripley will be able to find some in the lower hospital. The doctor suggests we visit Morley's office, which is located in the nearby psychiatric ward, to find a passcode that'll let us take an elevator down. He refuses to join Ripley, saying he's 'in no fit state', though he seems healthy enough. It'll become clear very soon why Kuhlman prefers to stay tucked safely away behind that thick wall of glass.

In the psychiatric ward, Ripley hears a distant thump and clatter – one of many examples of *Alien: Isolation*'s sound designers trying their best to freak unnerved players out. Kuhlman's voice crackles over the radio and informs us that this part of San Cristobal was home to 'unstable patients' who had trouble adapting to life in deep space. 'Far from the rhythms of Earth, sunrise, sunset,' he says, 'the mind has a tendency to wander.'

Spend some time exploring here before heading to Morley's office and you'll find some interesting world-building. In a padded room, a serene female voice describes comforting terrestrial images of leafy forests and the smell of a home-cooked breakfast – which contrasts sharply with the gruesome corpse at Ripley's feet. In an interview with AvP Galaxy, writer Will Porter reveals that, in writing this part of the game, he wanted to avoid the tired cliches of a 'gore-dripped madhouse' (something a lot of games are guilty of) and use the *Alien* universe's inherent realism to highlight some interesting concepts.

'The human mind isn't built for the vastness of space, or even prolonged removal from the natural rhythms of Earth,' he says. 'Mix this in with a touch of what we'd now recognise as the 1970s' misapprehensions in mental health treatment, through signage and language, and all of a sudden you've got a space to explore that feels subtly different to where most games have gone before.' He admits that a lot of players might not pick this up when they're frantically trying to escape from a killer alien, but even subconsciously it's a powerful framing device to complement the 'cold dread' of the gameplay.

In a communal day room, an audio log suggests Kuhlman has been dipping into the hospital's supply of drugs for himself. 'I tried to use the dispensary today and found I was locked out!' he gripes, blaming two fellow doctors, Morley and Lingard, and threatening to file a complaint. We'll find out more about Lingard, Sevastopol's chief medical officer, later.

It's possible Kuhlman's addiction was inspired by, or perhaps a *very* subtle reference to, the *Alien* movies. In *Aliens*, while Ripley is being grilled by those obnoxious Weyland-Yutani suits, dossiers of the *Nostromo* crew can be seen in the background. These are unreadable in the movie, but available to view on the *Alien Anthology* Blu-ray set. They reveal that Kane, John Hurt's character in *Alien*, was expelled from medical school for becoming addicted to the medication he was prescribing – which sounds a lot like Kuhlman. However, these dossiers also say that Dallas worked for *Blade Runner*'s Tyrell Corporation, so quite how canon they are is somewhat questionable.

Ripley uses the access tuner to hack her way into Morley's locked office. On his computer we find a note from a concerned staff member about dwindling supplies of mood stimulants, which Kuhlman is 'handing out like candy' after multiple visits to the dispensary. More evidence of his addiction. The elevator passcode we're looking for is on the terminal too, but things are never simple in *Alien: Isolation*. We need Morley's physical key-card too, which Kuhlman says he keeps on his person at all times. But where *is* he?

First, however, a more pressing matter: the station's now familiar automated voice pipes up again to warn Ripley that a quarantine breach has been detected in Medical. Red lights begin to flash in the hallway outside. As we head back to the psych ward, a jet of steam suddenly blasts from a vent in the ceiling, then a black, clawed hand reaches menacingly through it.

Creative Assembly cleverly placed a hospital gurney here, which most players instinctively duck under to hide from the beast. It drops from the vent and begins stomping around the ward, which is bad news for us because we need to pass through this area to locate Morley's keycard. As you navigate this part of the level, the xenomorph is constantly on the move, walking in and out of rooms, slipping in and out of vents, and investigating any noises you might foolishly make. It's *very* active, which makes the moment where you have to carefully enter a code into a keypad to progress distressingly tense.

On my first playthrough of *Alien: Isolation*, my eyes did most of the work. I spent the vast majority of the game carefully poking my head around corners, desperately trying to keep the xenomorph in my line of sight. I felt like if I could see it, I'd instinctively know the best way to slip past or distract it. This is a perfectly valid way to play the game, because there is a lean button, after all. But now, a hardened *Alien: Isolation* veteran, I realise that *seeing* is only half the battle. Your ears are just as valuable for outsmarting the alien.

The sound design is exceptional throughout. The oppressive, claustrophobic corridors of Sevastopol are alive with sound: creaking bulkheads, chirping computers, steam-spewing vents, Working Joe androids muttering sinisterly to themselves. You even hear the rubbery squeak of Amanda Ripley's canvas sneakers on the floor if you quickly shift position. A lot of attention has been paid to how the game sounds, which also feeds into the gameplay.

At a certain point, you can play *Alien: Isolation* almost entirely by ear. Now when I play it, I try my damnedest not to see the xenomorph. For one, the slightest glimpse of the thing is enough to make my Apple Watch send me an elevated heart rate warning – even after playing through the game many times and knowing it inside out. It's just so damn unpredictable. But secondly, and more importantly, I don't really need to. Thanks to that peerless sound design, I can almost always tell where the alien is and what it's doing by just carefully listening to it – especially when I play with headphones.

The most terrifying sound in *Isolation* is the menacing hiss that heralds the alien's arrival in the level, slithering out of a ceiling vent. This is your cue to stop dead in your tracks. Then it's a matter of listening out for those heavy footsteps. The xenomorph may be the perfect organism, but it's not light on its feet. I love this sound because it really gets across how massive and heavy this beast is – but also because it's a vital positioning tool. You can accurately track where the alien is relative to you, especially with a pair of good headphones.

When the alien gets bored of trying to find you it'll skulk away into one of those ceiling vents, and this AI routine has a very specific sound attached to it: a clumsy, metallic thump as the beast drags its immense frame back into the cooling ducts. This means that, for a while at least, you're relatively safe. If you do something daft like sprinting or firing a gun it'll appear in a flash and murder you. Stay quiet, though, and it won't bother you until it re-emerges.

In a locker room, Ripley finds a staff rota scribbled on a whiteboard. I've always loved how, despite *Alien*'s vision of a distant spacefaring future, old-fashioned physical media is still a thing. In the movie, and all over Sevastopol, we see document-stuffed binders, scattered paperwork, and sticky notes stuck to computer consoles. On the whiteboard Ripley notices a list of patients, which rooms they're in, and their attending doctors – including, crucially, Morley and his keycard. Time to investigate rooms A-29, C-21 and A-26.

Our next destination is a rotunda ward with several rooms attached to it like petals on a flower. If you just want to get in and out, Morley's gruesomely mutilated body can be found in room

A-29. Search his corpse to find the keycard. But if you can't help but explore a location thoroughly before moving on, visiting the other rooms on the ward will earn you some bonus goodies in the shape of a decent haul of crafting materials and a less useful ID tag. Look out of the windows in these rooms and you'll see the San Cristobal lobby down below – a location we'll visit soon, although it will look very different.

Now that we have the keycard and passcode, it's time to return to Kuhlman. It's obvious now that he knew the alien was in the psychiatric ward, but sent us down there anyway. 'Now that's unfair,' he says when an understandably angry Ripley challenges him. 'I *thought* it might be there. There's a difference.' Not cool, man. When we tell him the passcode, he suddenly perks up. Conveniently enough, where we're going also happens to be where the drug dispensary is. He moves to the next room, primes the elevator and tells Ripley that he's just going to go back and collect his things and then he'll join her.

But Dr Kuhlman won't be joining us. In one of the most striking, terrifying moments in the game, the doctor approaches an automatic door and turns his head to look at Ripley, failing to notice the towering xenomorph suddenly emerging from inky black shadows behind him. The creature's slow, considered, almost graceful movement here is absolutely chilling. In a flash, it grabs the screaming Kuhlman and pulls him into the darkness. There aren't many scripted moments like this in *Alien: Isolation* – most of the time the AI-powered xenomorph is dynamic and reactive to the player – but it's always hugely impactful whenever Creative Assembly decides to use one.

Ripley makes a hasty exit, heading to the elevator that we've been trying to access for the last forty-five minutes. When you break it down, the tasks you have to complete in *Alien: Isolation* are always pretty simple. In this chapter, all we've done is locate a passcode and a keycard. Yet, thanks to the unpredictable nature of the alien, the environmental storytelling, and the narrative through-line of Kuhlman's secret addiction, it feels much more engaging and interesting. Complicated objectives would just distract from the tension and horror, which is the true fast-beating heart of the *Alien: Isolation* experience.

MISSION 6

The Outbreak
Where it all started.

Now to secure that trauma kit. Ripley finds a door jammed by the next addition to her arsenal: the stun baton. This is the only non-lethal weapon in *Alien: Isolation*, and it's completely silent too, meaning it won't attract enemies when you use it. The design of the baton is lifted directly from the improvised cattle prod Brett and Parker hastily construct in *Alien*. It's a little far-fetched that someone on Sevastopol would jury-rig an identical device, but I'll let Creative Assembly off as it's a nice callback to the movie. Look closely at the baton and you'll see the brand Generic Electric printed on the handle – the same company that manufactures Sevastopol's many music-spewing stereos.

Generic Electric is just one of several new corporate entities *Alien: Isolation* adds to the hyper-capitalist *Alien* universe. Others whose logos you'll see printed on tech, weapons, machinery, shipping containers and packaging include Arious, Karnak, Gustafsson Enterprise Ltd, Koorlander cigarettes (named after one of the game's producers, Paul Koorlander), Henjin-Garcia Armament Co., Lunnar-Welsun Industries, Mühler & Milland and Samani.

Samani, incidentally, is the manufacturer of Ripley's distinctive two-faced digital watch, the Samani E-125, which you can see being advertised on billboards around Sevastopol. The design of this retro-futuristic timepiece is based on the one Sigourney Weaver wore as Ellen Ripley aboard the *Nostromo* in *Alien* – which was, in fact, a pair of Casio F-100 digital watches cleverly combined by the movie's art department. To *Alien* fans' delight, Casio recently released a new version of the F-100, the A100, which retains the late seventies vibe of the original, but with a few tasteful modern tweaks.

Ripley yanks the stun baton out of the door and it slides open, revealing a computer terminal and a message from Lingard. 'I've got a body up here that's part of a Marshals investigation,' it reads. 'Female, late thirties, chest wound.' The significance of this will become clear soon, but you don't need to be Poirot to figure out what a 'chest wound' means in this particular sci-fi setting. Adding to the sense of foreboding, Ripley finds herself in the hospital morgue. Frozen, eerily staring corpses, shoved into half-open body bags, are carelessly strewn around as if they've been tossed here in a hurry. Some haven't even been put in bags. It's clear the medical staff were not prepared for this level of bloody chaos. After solving a simple environmental puzzle involving locating and plugging in a coolant canister, Ripley continues deeper into the medical facility.

Dropping from a vent, she lands in a locker room that Creative Assembly decided, for whatever reason, should be one of the most impressive showcases of their Cathode engine's real-time lighting. A portable CRT television is propped up on a bunk, cycling through channels and casting a dramatic, colour-shifting glow over the otherwise forgettable room. In the next area, Ripley hears a spine-chilling, uncanny hiss in the distance – a clue that the alien is nearby – as a fluorescent light flickers to life, illuminating a gruesomely mutilated corpse lying in a pool of blood. The atmosphere has darkened significantly in this part of San Cristobal, and now we have to make our way through these narrow, twisting corridors with the xenomorph eagerly hunting us.

In a break room we're treated to another channel-switching CRT screen casting a flickering glow over the room – presumably the work of the same lighting or level artist. On the wall is a psychedelic concert poster featuring a mellow-looking bearded man with an afro and the words DOC SAMMI printed above him in a trippy font. Below it says: FIRE! FROM THE GODS. Someone on Sevastopol seems to be a fan of this guy's music. The design of this particular piece of world decoration is a lot more reminiscent of the 1960s than the late 1970s, which makes it feel a little out of place here.

The previous area we explored was plunged almost entirely into darkness, but here some of the corridors are blazingly bright, lit up by the harsh, eye-searing glow of fluorescent strip lights. Horror is hard to do in a brightly lit environment, but *Alien: Isolation* loses none of its tension when the shadows have been banished by a stark light source. If the alien grabs you in here, you'll get a very clear look at the creature in all its horrifying bio-mechanical glory – which may well happen, as there are a lot of long, uninterrupted hallways here with no place to hide if you suddenly see the xeno at the end of one of them.

Our next stop is the security office. If you take the right-hand path, you may (if you're particularly eagle-eyed) notice a couple of conspicuous traffic cones placed next to a dodgy-looking gas main. This is a very subtle warning which, inevitably, most players will miss. Move forward and there will be a sudden, shocking, and extremely loud explosion, releasing a deadly jet of impassable flames. This ear-shattering noise will alert the beast too, so it's wise to make a sharp exit. Alternatively, if you take the left-hand path you can avoid triggering this fiery hazard altogether. Just don't accidentally double-back on yourself down the other hallway; it will still trigger.

In the security office, Ripley finds a computer terminal with a message addressed from Marshal Waits to Dr Morley. 'I want you out of San Cristobal NOW,' it reads. 'You know what we've set up in there.' Ripley doesn't know what Waits is talking about here, but she will soon. There's also an audio message for Lingard from a Seegson chief executive named Ransome, who talks cryptically about wanting in on an 'interesting find'. But the most revealing message is found on a computer in the head of medical's office down the hall. It's a medical report filed on 13 November 2137 by a distressed-looking Lingard, who speaks through waves of grimy VHS fuzz.

If you were wondering why this chapter was called 'The Outbreak', well, you're about to find out. 'I want to state for the record that I have been placed under duress with regards to the compromised patient zero,' she says with a mix of anger and fear. 'Ransome, Seegson's head of operations, he . . . made certain threats towards my career and certification. But God help me, that woman needed help. I don't know what type of parasite she had encountered, but it had planted something inside her.' So now we know where the xenomorph currently terrorising Sevastopol came from. A woman had a close encounter with a facehugger, was taken to San Cristobal and promptly 'gave birth' – which is almost note-for-note what happened aboard the *Nostromo*.

Back in the security room, Ripley accesses a locker where we find – as well as a keycard that will let us progress in the level – an origami unicorn, which is of course a reference to Ridley Scott's other sci-fi classic, *Blade Runner*. There's also a carved statue of a panther, jaguar, or some other large feline predator, although what this may be alluding to, if anything, is lost on me. If you triggered the explosion, you can use the terminal here to turn off the gas.

Ripley slots the keycard into a nearby door and finds herself in another wing of San Cristobal, which is in a serious state of disarray. The few lights still functioning flicker on and off, furniture has been violently tossed, and bodies lie bloodied in dark corners. The trauma kit we need to save Taylor's life is nearby, however, in the operating theatre. In here we see the corpse of Catherine Foster, a character we'll learn more about later, lying on an operating table with a familiar gaping wound in her chest. This grisly, blood-splattered scene is the source of all the horror on Sevastopol – the same kind of harrowing 'birth' Kane suffered aboard the *Nostromo*. Ripley grabs the trauma kit from a nearby table and begins the long trek back to the transit station.

In an audio log, Waits instructs his staff to tape off San Cristobal in the wake of the outbreak, frustrated that Ransome – there's that name again – has been using his status as a top Seegson exec to stick his nose in. Yes, even when faced with the existential threat of an unstoppable extraterrestrial killer, people are still quibbling over bureaucracy, which is very *Alien*.

The only way out of this part of the medical facility is through reception, but the door is locked. Samuels suggests activating an evacuation procedure, which Ripley can trigger in a nearby power plant. She has to power up a generator to proceed; a convoluted process, each step of which makes an incredible amount of noise: a symphony of grinding, groaning and screeching metal that you really don't want to hear when the alien is prowling nearby.

Powering the generator up also awakens a Working Joe snoozing in a nearby charging pod, who for years I would carefully do my best to avoid. But in my most recent playthrough, I realised that his eyes are white, meaning he's operating normally and won't try to kill Ripley if he spots her. It's always worth taking a look at a Joe's eyes before you waste your time trying to stealth your way around it. There aren't many non-violent ones, but there are a few who have somehow managed to avoid whatever afflicted the others.

Naturally, once the evacuation has been triggered, a loud siren starts wailing and security lights flash on and off disorientingly. There are some jets of steam too, just to keep your stress levels high. It's the same thing that happened back in Seegson Communications, and it will happen again. The route back to the transit station is straightforward, at least in terms of layout, but the flashing lights, the presence of the alien, and a few human survivors lingering around make this a particularly nerve-racking stretch of gameplay. You can at least manipulate the alien, perhaps by crafting and tossing a noisemaker, to encourage it to attack any hapless humans in your way. An effective, economical tactic for sure, but one that always makes me feel a *little* icky each time I use it.

Ripley reaches the exit, bolts through the door and emerges into a large lobby – the same one, in fact, that we could look down at from the wards upstairs in the previous chapter. We have a brief moment to register stacks of strange barrels littering the area before the alien makes a dramatic entrance. Ripley shrieks as it drops from above and lands in front of her. She falls backwards in a panic and the creature slowly stands upright, readying itself to attack, but is interrupted by a circle of dazzling spotlights

clunking on. Red lights on the barrels flick on one by one, revealing the grimly explosive truth: someone set a trap for the alien,
but Ripley has been caught in it too.

The barrels detonate in a blaze of fiery destruction, Ripley is
knocked unconscious and the screen fades to black. When she
wakes up, the lobby has become a raging inferno and is rapidly
filling up with deadly, lung-clogging smoke. Hang around here
for too long and you'll choke to death and unceremoniously die.
But exploration-minded players do get a few minutes to visit a
nearby dental surgery and listen to an audio log from journalist
Julia Jones, in which she quizzes Lingard, unsuccessfully, about a
rumoured incident in the hospital, suggesting bad news travels
fast on the station.

But back to more pressing matters, like not dying horribly in
a fire. Back where Ripley encountered the alien is a ladder that
she can climb to safety, which involves some frantic button-
tapping. Near the top she briefly loses her grip and we see the
blaze roaring below, but she manages to yank herself up and out
of the lobby safely. We crawl through a vent, descend a ladder,
and find an elevator leading to our next destination: Seegson
Synthetics.

MISSION 7

Seegson Synthetics
Desperate times, desperate measures.

The elevator grinds to a halt. A fault has been detected and it's no
longer operational, forcing Ripley to take a detour through a
dark, smoke-filled vent system. The explosion that almost killed
her has caused fires to break out around this part of the station.
She finds another elevator, but it's missing a part: a compression
cylinder. Which means, yes, it's time to delve into yet another
dangerous part of the station to locate it. Almost immediately,
Ripley is confronted by a group of paranoid survivors yelling at

each other to calm down. They're armed and twitchy, having just survived a fight.

Human interaction in *Alien: Isolation* is one of its weakest links, falling into two categories: people who want to kill you and people who don't. The latter sit around lamenting their situation, if they say anything at all, and usually end up being killed by the alien. The former run around shooting at you and frequently suffer the same fate. I obviously love *Alien: Isolation* – I mean, I'm writing an entire book about it after all – but this is one aspect of the game I find disappointing. I just wish I could *talk* to these people. Maybe you could convince people to put down their guns or trade items. If you spared a few bullets, perhaps someone would unlock or reveal an alternate path. Richer interaction like this would make the setting feel so much more alive. A lot of the NPCs in the game are utterly lifeless, rarely reacting to you or anything you've done, feeling more like set dressing than actual people a lot of the time. A *Mass Effect*-style conversation system with dialogue choices would also show us a lot more of Amanda's personality. She's something of a closed book in this game, rarely revealing much about herself or what makes her tick.

A nearby scattering of bodies reveals a violent skirmish broke out here shortly before we arrived. This group of survivors, led by a man named Francis, were attacked by looters but managed to defend themselves. You can sneak through this area with a little patience, but luring the alien in with a noisemaker to kill Francis and co. makes getting through here easier. Dealing with one alien is more convenient than keeping tabs on multiple shooty humans.

The survivors you encounter on Sevastopol are perhaps a little too aggressive. I get that a situation like this would make people paranoid and territorial, but these supposedly normal citizens are a little too eager to shoot anyone they see without asking questions first. Sometimes, very rarely, they'll raise their gun and warn you to stay back. But for the most part they issue a death sentence the instant they see you, forcing you to resort to violence yourself.

But as flawed as this is from a narrative perspective, messing with these enemies is hugely entertaining. The xenomorph is your enemy, but it doesn't discriminate. The fact that it hungrily lunges at anything with a pulse can be used to your advantage, and I end up feeling, weirdly, like it's my friend. When I toss a noisemaker and watch it eviscerate my enemies, it's like a loyal attack dog. I almost feel proud of it. That'll do, xeno. That'll do.

Ripley slips into another vent and overhears a group of survivors above her, voices drifting through a grate, discussing the explosion that she narrowly avoided dying in back in San Cristobal. 'What do you think caused it?' one says. 'Gotta be Waits,' his buddy replies. 'I heard he's trying to kill that creature by setting traps. Remote charges. Can you believe that?' So now we know who put all those explosive barrels in the lobby. We also hear another interesting piece of intel: that Waits has set up 'a safe haven' in the Galleria.

But for now we have to venture deeper into Seegson Synthetics and find that compression cylinder. On a terminal, Ripley finds a note from Smythe, Seegson's head of synthetic development. He explains that Seegson is years behind Weyland-Yutani's most basic model android, and that they desperately need investment to have any hope of beating, or even *equalling*, their corporate rival.

In response, Ransome (Seegson's head of operations) says there's no money to spare, and that Smythe was hired because he's 'the cheapest, not the best'. After boasting about how much his suit costs and how fancy his executive suite is, Ransome says: 'Find a way to bring these costs down, huh?' Even in a universe filled with soulless corporate suits, Ransome is especially evil.

Ripley continues searching for the elevator part and finds herself on the other side of the room where we first encountered those armed survivors at the beginning of the chapter. If you didn't deal with them earlier, or call in the alien to do so, you'll hear one of them shout, 'There's something up in the vent!' Then the creature will drop down and do its thing. It kills the group and drags Francis into the vent. The terrified voice of a man named Mahoney (a friend or ally of Francis) crackles over a radio, having just witnessed all this chaos from another part of Seegson Synthetics through a security camera feed.

None of this has anything to do with Ripley, however, who continues deeper into the facility. There's a nice sense in this level of other people having a bad time on Sevastopol. *Alien: Isolation* is good at not making the player feel like the centre of the universe. There are hundreds, maybe thousands, of people on this vast station, all enduring their own traumas, dramas and horrors. And in the game's DLC, which we'll take a look at later in the book, we actually get to see the events of the game unfold through other people's eyes.

On another terminal we find an audio message from Seegson's android liaison executive, G. Spedding, addressed to Smythe. 'Have you been practising the script for the VIPs visiting today?' he says. 'We *need* to impress. Noise from upstairs says they're the last potential bidders for Sevastopol's Working Joe roll-out. If they go for Weyland-Yutani cast-offs instead, our jobs are on the line.' This is a nice insight into the corporate machinations at Seegson, and how desperate its employees have become in the face of the company's failures.

Finally, Ripley finds the elevator part she's been looking for. It's in Component Storage, a large warehouse that provides some spatial relief from the claustrophobic corridors we've been skulking through for the last hour or so. But to get it, we're going to need the help of a Working Joe. In a charging pod, a Joe stands motionless, head slumped forward, lit by an eerie red glow. Naturally, your first instinct is to question whether willingly bringing one of these things online is a good idea – but Ripley has no choice. However, to juice this guy up she needs to upgrade her security access tuner. A level two upgrade in a nearby office – which lets us hack higher security computers – does the trick.

Before we make our way back to Component Storage, we find a terminal that reveals how Smythe's presentation to the VIPs went. 'You totally fucked up the android presentation,' says Spedding. 'They're not interested.' It seems Seegson failed to raise interest in its androids, and Smythe was fired as a result. Anyway, not our problem. Ripley has an android to power up. She hits the button to activate the Working Joe and whispers, 'Now, play nice . . .' cleverly mirroring the player's nervousness at having to mess with one of these freaky killer machines. Luckily, its eyes are white. She asks it where the compression cylinder is and it dutifully reveals its location: row one, stack B.

Ripley follows the Joe into the warehouse where the part is being stored, before the android stupidly walks into an exposed electrical outlet and fries itself. It's no surprise the VIPs didn't want to invest in these things. If you feel bad about this idiot zapping himself, there's a nearby switch you can press to cut the electrical supply off. But you have to be quick about it.

Ripley raises and lowers a series of automated shelves – one of several simple environmental puzzles in *Alien: Isolation* – to get past the electricity and snag the compression cylinder. Then it's time to retrace our steps and go back to where we started. It's interesting how many objectives in this game involve going somewhere, picking something up or activating something, then backtracking. But you don't really notice it in the heat of the moment because there are so many existential threats to constantly worry about.

The area where Francis and his crew were hanging out is now eerily silent. All that's left are several bloodied and battered bodies: a macabre mix of the people the alien killed earlier and looters with gunshot wounds. This is a good time to (quietly) scour the area for missed scrap, items or ammo – as well as an ID tag on the floor in the corridor leading back to the broken elevator. Once we've gutted the place of anything useful, we slam the compression cylinder into the elevator and watch it groan and spark back to life. Our next and final stop in this relatively short chapter is the Synthetic Fluid Plant.

Ripley enters a large refrigerated factory with a loud, clunking assembly line looming above her head. Racks of the white fluid androids in the *Alien* universe use for 'blood' roll overhead, one by one, seemingly forever. Concept artist Bradley Wright helped design this space, using photographs of hanging carcasses in a butcher's freezer as a visual reference point.

This is where Seegson manufactures its Working Joes, and it seems production is still very much in full swing. This scripted moment is easy to miss, but watch the balcony in the distance closely. You'll see the alien suddenly appear, grab someone and leap off into the depths of the factory with them in its claws. Gunshots ring out as the victim's allies panic and try to shoot the creature, and they'll turn their weapons on you too if you get too close. These survivors are likely the group led by Mahoney, the guy whose voice we heard over the radio earlier. This part of Seegson Synthetics is one of the smallest, but also one of the *busiest*, places in the game. There are humans everywhere.

Ripley sneaks past them, finds an elevator that leads to the SciMed tower, and that's it. There's no dramatic end to this level; just pressing an elevator button and a slow fade to black. After the previous chapter's dramatic ending, maybe it's nice that this one finishes like this. *Alien: Isolation* is a pretty intense, full-on game, and any moment of respite should be enjoyed while it lasts. We're approaching the halfway point now, and there's a lot more drama in store for Amanda Ripley and everyone else stuck on Sevastopol.

MISSION 8

Haven
The eye of the storm.

Ripley steps off the elevator into familiar surroundings. We're back near where we first encountered the ill-fated Dr Kuhlman. But we're done, thankfully, with San Cristobal for now. Ripley returns to the transit station and startles Marshal Waits, who points a gun at her. We've heard this guy's voice plenty, but this is the first time Ripley meets him in the flesh. Satisfied she's not a threat, he lets her tend to Taylor, who is now lying unconscious. Ripley asks Waits what the creature is and where it came from. 'I dunno,' he says, a weariness in his voice. 'Something brought here by Marlow, the captain of the *Anesidora*.' This catches Samuels' attention, who reminds us that this is the very same ship that discovered the *Nostromo*'s flight recorder.

There's nothing that can be done for Taylor here. We need to get her to the Marshal Bureau, where Waits says there's a basic life-support unit. But guess what? The transit system is down. Isn't it always. Because Ripley is seemingly the only person who does any work around here, Waits asks her to go to Transit Control and fix it. 'Samuels says you're an engineer,' he says. 'Go and make yourself useful, seeing as *you* screwed up the trap.' It seems Waits is still a little bitter about that explosive mishap we had back at Medical.

We also meet a new character here, deputy Ricardo. He's Waits's right-hand man and, unbeknownst to Ripley, was indirectly involved in an incident that almost killed her earlier in the game. We'll learn more about this in the DLC mission 'The Trigger', in which we actually play as Ricardo.

Ripley takes a nearby elevator to Transit Control – a big room filled with computers, with a large display on the far wall that should be showing the current status of the station's transit cars, but is currently dark. We also hear a sound coming from a nearby utility room, which sounds an awful lot like someone, or something, banging on the door. This is a common scare in horror games, and I can't help but think of the moment in *Silent Hill* when you hear banging coming from a locker, only for a cat to burst out.

She tries to reactivate the system, but everything has been powered down. Then someone, an armed and hostile human survivor, enters the room. 'Hello?' he shouts into the darkness. 'I know someone's down here.' Turning to the banging sound, he adds: 'Calm down in there, you android fuck!' It seems the noise is coming from a Working Joe he somehow managed to trap in the room. If you restore power the door will slide open, freeing the Joe, who will then kill the human for you. Or you can deal with him yourself first. Whatever the case, once the area is clear you can reactivate the transit system.

The elevator we took down to Transit Control is busted, so we need to find another way back to the station. Ripley, aware that Taylor needs urgent care, tells Waits and the others to go ahead and take the train without her. Our next stop is the utility room that imprisoned the Working Joe. Inside we find a dead body, presumably killed by the frustrated android. But we've seen so many corpses by this point that they're now little more than macabre set dressing. In a small adjoining room, Ripley finds her next gadget.

You may have noticed a few vents around Sevastopol blocked by bulky metal panels. Well, this is how you access them. The first of many is waiting outside, and Ripley uses her engineering skills to neatly slice her way through the obstacle. In the intro, we saw Ripley wearing a welding mask, but with no such luxury here she has to rely on a small built-in eye guard on the gas torch itself. She crawls through the newly opened vent and finds an audio log recorded by Jake Sinclair, Seegon's head of security. 'I found an area in Habitation where we can seal ourselves in and wait for rescue,' he says. 'I've got guys welding vents and shutting off elevators. The plan is to make it watertight.'

This is a nice way of explaining why Ripley encounters so many obstacles as she moves around the station. Obviously, this is primarily for gameplay reasons. The player needs things to *do*. But rather than just hand-wave it, I like that this audio log was written to give Sevastopol's myriad blocked, locked and broken doors some in-universe context. Sinclair adds, gravely, that there's no room left for more people in their newly founded Habitation sanctuary. 'If we're going to get through this alive,' he says, 'there's no room for pity.'

Ripley makes her way back to the SciMed transit station and, as expected, Waits, Taylor, Samuels and Ricardo have made a sharp exit. Complicating matters, a train arrives carrying a group of shotgun-toting survivors. We have to avoid them while we wait for the train to come, then we can escape and journey to our next destination: the Solomons Habitation Tower.

If you're an *Alien* fan, you'll remember Ripley saying, 'This is commercial towing vehicle *Nostromo* out of the Solomons,' which one might assume is a reference to Earth's Solomon Islands. In fact, this is a collection of mineral-rich moons on the very edge of explored space in the *Alien* universe. This part of the galaxy is home to numerous mining colonies, which is why the *Nostromo* found itself there, towing that immense refinery back to Earth. Sevastopol's Solomons Habitation Tower is, presumably, named after this region.

The train arrives and Ripley's surroundings suddenly change dramatically. This is the part of Sevastopol where people actually live, which is reflected in the lighting, decoration and architecture. There are open spaces, high ceilings, bright lights, and even *plants*. After hours of industrial environments, it's a nice change to see a smidge of greenery. Of course, comfort is all relative on a deep-space station. The Habitation Tower is still pretty cold and oppressive, but slightly less so than the places we've visited so far.

As you play this level, you might notice that it's eerily quiet. Usually, exploring Sevastopol is punctuated by the unnerving sound of the alien crashing around, hissing and rumbling through vents. But in this level, at least based on my own experiences, the creature never turns up. You can sprint around madly and you won't draw its attention, which is a relief after many hours of slow, meticulous creeping. The explosion in Medical must have scared it away.

Ripley leaves the transit station and makes her way into a wide, curving corridor that you can imagine bustling with shoppers, workers and Colonial Marshals before everything went to shit – like a high street in space. But now it's covered in anti-Marshals graffiti and littered with junk, and the metal shutters on all the stores have been pulled down to deter looters. Around the corner Ripley finds the entrance to the Marshal Bureau, which has FUCK THE MARSHALS spray-painted on the door in big red letters.

Ridley Scott aficionados will know that the director is partial to a backlit fan. Well, there's a nice homage to this visual flourish here: a spotlight shining through a slowly turning fan, casting an atmospheric shadow over the floor. Whether or not this was an homage to the filmmaker, I don't know, but it's one of many examples of *Alien: Isolation* mirroring not just the design and aesthetic sensibilities of *Alien*, but how the movie was lit too.

In *Alien*, the crew of the *Nostromo* wear pin badges on their uniforms designating their rank aboard the ship. These were designed by the film's costume designer, John Mollo, who had an affinity for military uniforms and insignia. Before working in movies, he wrote and illustrated several well-regarded books about the history and design of military uniforms. He then went on to become an advisor for historical films such as *Charge of the Light Brigade*, *Nicholas and Alexandra* and Stanley Kubrick's *Barry Lyndon*, before being invited by George Lucas to design costumes for the *Star Wars* saga.

Characters in *Alien: Isolation*, including Ripley, wear similar badges. But the reason I'm mentioning this here is because of the big Colonial Marshals emblem hanging over the entrance to their HQ. It looks like a pretty standard sheriff-style badge at first glance, but peer a little closer and you'll notice that the pattern inside the circle is the same as John Mollo's executive officer badge, as worn by Kane in *Alien*. This is a neat example of Creative Assembly drawing from the visual language of the movie to build their world.

Ripley enters the Marshal Bureau and we're treated to that rarest of encounters: a group of humans who don't want to immediately pump Ripley full of lead. Some survivors are holed up in the lobby, pacing, fretting and waiting for help that they probably know deep down will never arrive. A woman thanks Ripley for getting the transit system running again as she makes her way into the main office, where Marshal Waits is holed up. He tells her that Taylor's condition has been stabilised and that she'll be walking again soon.

The walls here are lined with wanted posters, with portraits in the same ASCII style as the game's collectible ID cards. It's obvious that the criminals on parade here are, in fact, the game's developers. You can always tell, in games, when devs have put themselves on wanted posters in police stations because they look less like street-hardened criminals and more like mild-mannered programmers with neat haircuts. There are a lot of empty beer cans lying around too, suggesting Sevastopol's cops are having as hard a time keeping calm as the people under their protection.

There's a save point here, and interestingly, it always says 'hostiles nearby' even though this is one of the safest places in the game. You can fire your gun, run around and knock stuff over and the alien simply will not show up. This could just be a bug, or perhaps (and I'm reaching here) a subtle reference to something that will happen later involving Marshal Waits.

Waits tells Ripley that a guy named Marlow is in a holding cell, and that he's the person who recovered the *Nostromo*'s flight recorder. He also reveals that Marlow's ship, the aforementioned *Anesidora*, is in orbit around the gas giant and Marlow won't give up the command codes to bring it in to dock. 'Maybe you can get more out of the unhelpful bastard,' he says. 'Go talk to him.' Looks like Waits wants us to do more work for him.

Ripley locates the holding cell and finds Henry Marlow, captain and owner of the salvage vessel *Anesidora*. This character, despite playing a pivotal role in the story, only appears very briefly in *Alien: Isolation*. However, unused script files uncovered by modders reveal he was originally going to play a much larger role. Rather than just finding him waiting patiently in the cell, Ripley would have to hunt him down and bring him in. As part of this cut level he would have accompanied Ripley, similar to how Axel briefly joined her earlier in the game. Alas, in the final game he doesn't get much to do at all.

Ripley introduces herself and tells Marlow that she's with the Company, which feels a little out of character for someone who clearly has no love for Weyland-Yutani. 'Here for your empty box already?' he spits. 'You guys are keen, I'll give you that.' Ripley explains that she's here for personal reasons, that she's searching for her mother. He softens a little at this, explaining that while they did find the black box, they never found any trace of the ship. Then it's story time. Marlow wants to cut a deal and get out, and Ripley wants to know everything about the discovery of the flight recorder.

MISSION 9

Beacon
Warning signs.

We're now experiencing the events of *Alien: Isolation* through someone else's eyes. Taking control of Henry Marlow, mission nine opens aboard his ship, the *Anesidora*. However, before we get into the meat of this level we have to talk a bit about this salvage vessel. Firstly, that loaded name, which is an epithet of several goddesses and mythological figures – including, who is almost certainly the reference here, Pandora. In Greek mythology, Pandora infamously opened a jar (no, not a box) and unleashed all the evils of humanity. Oops. You should keep this story in mind as we work our way through this mission.

If you own Sega's excellent official art book, *The Art of Alien: Isolation*, you might be confused as to why many, many pages are dedicated to the *Anesidora*, even though we only catch a few glimpses of it in the finished game. This is because the ship was originally going to play a much larger role. The more time you spend digging through concept material and unused audio and script files, the more you realise just how much this game's story changed during development. A detailed exterior based on microscopic parasites and deep-sea crustaceans, and even some interiors, were designed for *Anesidora*. It's an amazing-looking, curiously bug-like ship, and it's a shame it's never been properly seen anywhere outside of the art book. A detailed 3D model of the *Anesidora is* in this level; it's just completely obscured by fog.

Back to the mission, and the only good look we get at the inside of the *Anesidora* is a pretty unremarkable loading dock. Marlow, his wife Catherine Foster, and crew members Heyst and Meeks are suited up and ready to explore the surface of a moon that *Alien* fans will instantly recognise. After some banter that gives you a sense that the crew of the *Anesidora* have been in deep space together for quite some time, a large metal door opens revealing the wind-blasted, blue-tinted and barren surface of LV-426 – the moon where the crew of the *Nostromo* had their fateful encounter with a xenomorph egg, and where a squad of Colonial Marines would endure their own horror.

Some reviews criticised this sequence for being little more than a re-tread of a classic moment from the movie, but that was the idea. Creative Assembly put it in the game to give players a first-hand experience of following in the footsteps of the *Nostromo*'s crew, walking the surface of the planetoid, discovering the derelict, and gazing up in awe at the space jockey. Honestly, I can't imagine any *Alien* fan not loving this mission. It's the closest any game has ever come to putting you *in* the film, and it captures the mood perfectly.

Foster mentions searching for a beacon, which is in fact the 'distress signal' the *Nostromo* picked up on the moon, which led to the harrowing events of *Alien*. We know it was actually a warning, but these guys don't. Before the Sevastopol incident, Marlow's ship was falling apart, the crew was close to mutiny, and they hadn't found anything valuable to salvage for months. Which made the discovery of the *Nostromo* flight recorder feel like a stroke of good luck. Marlow illegally accessed the black box's flight data, and that's why we are where we are now, on the surface of this cursed moon.

There are no enemies or complicated objectives in this mission: just following a handheld tracker to locate the source of the beacon. As it was in *Alien*, the visibility on LV-426 is almost non-existent. A storm is raging, but through the haze we can see alien-looking rock formations and geothermal vents spewing steam. In the movie, Ash described the moon as 'primordial', racked by strong winds and with a harsh toxic atmosphere. As we walk across the surface as Marlow, it certainly feels like it. The moon would later be terraformed, settled by humans, and renamed Acheron – becoming the setting for James Cameron's *Aliens* – but at this point it's completely inhospitable.

'You think this could be the big one?' says Meeks as the group plods along the surface, CO_2 venting from the tops of the helmets of their bulky pressure suits. 'No more shitty salvage jobs?' Marlow isn't sure of what lies ahead, but there's a trace of excitement and anticipation in his voice. The path is occasionally blocked by natural rock formations, forcing us to clear a path with explosives, but otherwise this part of the level is just a long, eerie walk.

As a fan of *Alien*'s iconic spacesuit designs, I find that this level provides an excellent opportunity to get a close look at them. While several people contributed to the finished design in the movie, including John Mollo, the basic concept – in particular, those wonderful samurai armour-inspired flourishes – came courtesy of legendary French artist Jean 'Mœbius' Giraud. However, as cool as they looked, the cast of *Alien* hated working in these costumes. They were bulky, clumsy and unbearably hot, so at least the digital actors in *Alien: Isolation* do not have to worry about that. Reflecting this, character movement in this level is slow and cumbersome. Being trapped in that helmet – hearing Marlow's heavy breathing in your ears – gives you an idea of what it must have been like for the actors toiling on that warm soundstage at Shepperton.

Eventually, Marlow and the crew crest a hill and find the source of the beacon: the derelict. This enigmatic-looking starship wreck is the source of all the horror in *Alien*, and was envisioned by Ridley Scott as the sci-fi equivalent of the spooky old haunted house in a slasher movie. The derelict was designed, like all the extraterrestrial elements in *Alien*, by Swiss surrealist H. R. Giger. Chris Foss came up with some concepts, including a strange lobster-shaped spacecraft, but Ridley Scott didn't think they were, well, *alien* enough. 'Foss's ideas were interesting,' he said in an interview with Fantastic Films. 'But they tended to all look alike. Giger's craft was definitely not of this world.'

The looming silhouette of the derelict is even more compelling when viewed from a first-person perspective. This section of the game owes everything to the work of the movie, of course, but *being* there, exploring at your own pace, does bring an extra element of immersion to visiting LV-426. However, before we can get a really good look at the derelict ship – which, if you access a debug camera, you can see is a fully 3D model – the screen fades to black.

Time jumps forward, and suddenly the derelict is right in front of us. H. R. Giger's work is full of provocative psycho-sexual imagery, and getting inside the derelict involves entering some huge, vagina-like openings in its side. The crew of the *Anesidora* find themselves in a dark, twisting bio-mechanical corridor that feels like travelling through the colon of some immense alien beast. After what seems like an eternity of navigating this claustrophobic warren of tunnels, the interior of the ship suddenly opens up and reveals the space jockey in all its glory. This immense alien creature, fossilised and ancient, a strange wound in its chest, is perfectly recreated – but notably expanded in size.

The filmmakers were limited by the size of Shepperton Studios, and by their production budget. To make the space jockey seem bigger, Ridley Scott had child-sized pressure suits made up and got his sons, Luke and Jake, to wear them in the scene where the *Nostromo* crew discovers it. This is especially noticeable on Blu-ray and in 4K transfers, where it's glaringly obvious that it's a couple of very young kids we're looking at. Creative Assembly didn't have to pull any stunts like that, but did make this chamber, and the pilot, way bigger than in the movie. It's a change that makes sense, and if Ridley Scott could have made this set the size it is in the game back in 1979, he would have.

There's a mix of excitement and trepidation among the crew of the *Anesidora*. Meeks, however, is overjoyed. 'Hah, I think we've found our payload!' he shouts, unmoved by the existential questions raised by this long-dead advanced lifeform and the strange surroundings of its crashed spacecraft. Foster calls Marlow over, saying she's found something, which we know is the remains of the *Nostromo*'s previous exploration of the derelict. There's some abandoned equipment with the ship's name stamped on it, and the rope and winch system that Kane used to descend into the egg chamber.

Marlow finds another corridor on the opposite side of the chamber, leading to the source of the signal. This part of the derelict was never shown in *Alien,* meaning some lucky artist(s) at Creative Assembly got to dream up what it might look like. Adding to Giger's design without it feeling out of place is no mean feat, but the developers found a clever way of doing it.

The beacon is an original creation, but its component parts are actually extracted from the space jockey. 'It was important to maintain a feeling of authenticity, building on the forms which are present in the original movie set,' says concept artist Bradley Wright in the official *Alien: Isolation* art book. The art team explored a number of options, including 'various phallic compositions inspired by H. R. Giger's artwork', but settled on a recomposition of existing elements. The result is an extension of the derelict set that feels like Giger himself could have created it, and a chance to witness, for the first time, the mysterious beacon that lured the *Nostromo* to LV-426.

Marlow approaches the beacon, which emits an eerie blue glow inspired by the mist that covered the eggs in the movie – which was, brilliantly, created using stage lasers borrowed from rock band The Who. He disables it, possibly saving the crews of any other ships who might be passing through this region of space. 'Working alongside Fox,' Will Porter says in an interview with AvP Galaxy, 'we were able to build into *Alien* canon that it was Marlow who disabled the beacon, which was really cool.' Writer Dion Lay adds that he was 'really pleased Fox let us put the actual beacon in the level.'

Then we hear Foster's voice. 'Marlow, you've got to see this. It's amazing!' It's not difficult to figure out what she's discovered, especially if you think back to her corpse on the operating table back in San Cristobal with a conspicuous chest wound, and then the sudden appearance of an alien.

Back at the entrance to the egg chamber, Marlow attaches himself to the winch and descends into the heart of darkness. The chamber is stunningly recreated, and seeing hundreds of thousands of xenomorph eggs stretching into the distance really hammers home what a weapon of mass destruction this ship once was, and potentially still is. Marlow reaches the bottom and sees

Foster walking among the eggs, hypnotised by their strangeness in much the same way as Kane was. Naturally, she suffers the same fate.

We switch to a pre-rendered cutscene and see a facehugger emerge from an egg, launching itself at Foster's helmet. Like in the movie, we don't see what happens; just a sudden, shocking cut to black. This is a short level, and barely interactive, but as a mood piece it's exceptional. What a treat to get to experience one of the most memorable moments in cinema history from such an intimate perspective. It doesn't matter that it hits all the same beats as the film. We didn't *need* to see how the alien made it onto Sevastopol, but I'm glad Creative Assembly took the time to fill this part of the story in.

It's just a shame the *Anesidora* and her crew were sidelined by whatever dramatic rewrites the game went through during development. I would have loved to explore the ship itself and get to know these characters more, but such is the merciless, unpredictable business of making games. Every game you've ever loved/will love will have had/will have *masses* of content cut from it. Anyway, that's the end of 'Beacon'. We've had a few short missions in a row, but the next one is longer, harder and scarier than any that have come before – and arguably the most thrilling, dramatic portion of the entire game.

MISSION 10

The Trap
Trust no one.

Back on Sevastopol, Ripley presses Marlow for more information. She wants to know where the *Anesidora* is and whether they can bring it in to dock on auto pilot. He won't play ball unless we get him out of jail, but the conversation is interrupted by Ricardo. 'My board just lit up like a Christmas tree,' he says. 'It's here!' We've enjoyed a break from the xenomorph for a couple of missions now, but it's about to come back in a big way. Waits tells Ricardo that it's time for 'plan B'; Ripley is intrigued, and says she wants to help.

Waits leads us over to a storage room containing a flame-thrower, a favourite weapon of the Ripleys. The design is almost identical to the weapon Parker built in *Alien*, including a distinct-ive front grip and trigger adapted from the pistols used (but barely seen) in the movie. *Alien*'s guns were cobbled together using parts from a Swiss submachine gun called a Rexim-Favor, which was developed in the 1950s. However, the xenomorph's destructive acid blood – and the inherent danger of discharging firearms on a spaceship – meant the *Nostromo* crew wisely never resorted to using them.

'It's an animal,' says Waits as Ripley checks out her new toy. 'Animals are afraid of fire.' The flamethrower is one of the most useful weapons in the game, making the alien retreat into a vent when the flamethrower is used against it. But if you overuse it, the creature's AI will get wise to your play style and begin to keep its distance, making hitting it with the short-range flame difficult.

Early in *Alien: Isolation*'s development, weapon crafting was going to be a major feature. Concept art exists of multiple weap-ons constructed from the same small collection of junk, suggesting Ripley would have been able to jury-rig her arsenal from scav-enged scrap. Creative Assembly also considered not having any purpose-built weapons on Sevastopol at all, but ultimately decided it was logical that the Colonial Marshals would have access to arms.

The weapon-crafting concept was dropped early on, because Ripley being armed to the teeth with a selection of home-made guns would have detracted from the stealth. *Alien: Isolation* isn't a game about feeling empowered; it's a game about being *power-less*. I think they made the right call, because the constant feeling of being on the back foot in this game, of surviving by the skin of your teeth, is so perfectly balanced. A backpack full of guns would have taken away from that feeling and done more harm than good.

The cobbled-together feel of these concept guns was repurposed for the finished game's gadgets, however. Look closely at Ripley's collection of custom-made noisemakers, smoke bombs, Molotovs, EMP mines, pipe bombs and flashbangs and you'll see that they're made up of everyday objects hastily duct-taped together. Crafting was a lot more complex and involved early in the game's development, but it was streamlined to keep the pace of the game up. Ripley does all her crafting through a menu, meaning you have to imagine her ducking into the shadows and slapping these objects together.

Waits has a plan to trap the xenomorph. He tells Ripley to meet Ricardo in the SysTech spire, but before we leave the Marshal Bureau there's an interesting piece of development history to check out here. In the room where Taylor is recovering, there's a suit of body armour that looks like a militarised version of the movie's iconic pressure suit. Early in development, Creative Assembly wanted Ripley to go up against rogue Seegson security guards – a stronger type of human enemy – who would wear this armour. Concept art of these enemies exists, incorporating visual elements from the spacesuits, but the idea was ultimately scrapped. This decoration is all that remains.

But back to business. Ripley heads back to the transit station, receiving a radio message from Waits along the way. Samuels has gone to Android Processing, he says, and when the alien is dead he'll access the APOLLO AI that runs the station and lift the lockdown. We jump on a train and head to the SysTech spire, which seems to be in worse shape than when we left it. Moments after Waits warns us that he's detecting multiple malfunctioning systems, an explosion knocks Ripley unconscious. She wakes up surrounded by flames, and a burning Working Joe marches towards her, unfazed by its fiery predicament.

Ripley activates the fire suppression system and continues onwards, finding herself back in the Lorenz SysTech lobby with the giant starship engines suspended from the ceiling. This kind of backtracking makes Sevastopol feel like a real, connected space rather than just a procession of levels. When you return to somewhere you've already been, there will often be differences in mood, enemy placement or layout to keep you on your toes.

Waits explains his plan as we descend into the depths of the SysTech spire. We're going to block a series of doors and vents, trapping the creature in a makeshift cage. It's at this point you'll hear a sound you haven't for a while: the alien moving noisily through the vents. The big chap (as workers on the *Alien* set often referred to their alien) is back in action, meaning keeping noise to a minimum to avoid attracting attention is a priority once again.

There now follows some incredibly tense close-quarters stealth, locking down doors in a stairwell while the alien stalks the area. Then Ripley moves into the Server Hub to initiate a lockdown. Curiously, there are several Working Joes down here, but they're all white-eyed and non-aggressive. A lot of players, myself included, won't realise this on a first playthrough and pointlessly extend the length of this mission by trying to creep around them.

There's an amusing audio bug in this part of the level, which several gaming news outlets covered, making the bug go briefly viral. A locked and completely innocuous door near the Server Hub makes Ripley cycle through her various screams and gasps – usually triggered by the alien – when approached. There are many hilarious videos on YouTube of players walking towards the door and Ripley shrieking in fear for no good reason. This is now referred to by fans as the *scary door*, and it's worth visiting if you want a quick laugh.

Ripley uses her access tuner to hack into a terminal and trigger the lockdown, which seems to send the alien AI into overdrive. Not only is this dimly lit maze of toppled-over server racks an incredibly confusing, oppressive environment, but the alien seems to pop in and out of vents constantly. Worse still, you have to wait for Ricardo to open the exit to escape, which feels like an eternity with the xenomorph breathing down your neck. The level of tension in this mission is almost unbearable at times, which I suppose is your punishment for enjoying a few relatively calm stretches of gameplay before it.

Ricardo overrides the lockdown, letting us escape. Waits is

pissed. 'We had it locked down and you let it out?!' he yells at Ricardo over the radio, seemingly unmoved by the fact that he did it to save Ripley's life. Waits tells us to move to Gemini Exoplanet Solutions, where there might be one last chance to trap the beast. 'We can't let it escape again,' he says. 'No matter what.'

As if things weren't stressful enough, the path to the Gemini labs is being patrolled by heavily armed, trigger-happy survivors. We dodge them and make our way back to the Lorenz SysTech lobby, taking a newly unlocked elevator to Gemini Exoplanet Solutions – the Sevastopol HQ of a scientific research and development company specialising in mineral extraction.

Gemini were studying KG-348, the gas giant we keep catching glimpses of through the station's windows, extracting valuable minerals and rare elements from it. But at some point, after devastating funding cuts, operations largely ceased and only a skeleton crew was left to run the lab. Using 'irregularities' in the company's accounts as leverage, Seegson executive Ransome (who seems to be desperate to impress someone other than his Seegson bosses) pressured the remaining scientists there to study xenomorph samples he gathered in San Cristobal following the birth of the creature.

But Ripley doesn't care about any of that: she just wants to get the place powered up and locked down, ideally with the alien trapped inside it. She makes her way through the labs, finding an upgrade for the gas torch that transforms it into a plasma torch. This opens up even more of the station, and any plasma-sealed doors you've taken a mental note of can be revisited and cracked open once you get out of here. Backtracking to find the hidden *Nostromo* logs, recorded by some of the original cast of the movie, is worth doing, but not until late in the game when you have a complete collection of tools.

Ripley carefully sneaks through a series of clinical, poorly lit laboratories – whose design is partly extracted from the *Nostromo*'s medical bay set – and activates breakers to bring the dormant facility back to life. Waits explains that while the place has been shut down due to a lack of funding, essential systems are still in place – including security. This is evident in the number of CCTV cameras sweeping the area. Luckily, their field of view is clearly telegraphed with a glowing, grid-patterned light. Stray into the light and an alarm will sound, alerting nearby enemies to your presence. You can also disable some of them using the rewire panels littering the station, which are used to reroute power between different systems and switch them on or off if necessary.

The pacing, claustrophobia and escalating tension in this section is reminiscent of the end of *Alien*, specifically when Ripley is trying desperately to activate the *Nostromo*'s self-destruct with the alien closing in. There are no open spaces here, making it feel like the creature is constantly *around* you as you navigate the maze and activate switches. Eventually, power is restored and Ripley takes a freight elevator to Project KG-348 – a facility dedicated to studying and extracting resources from the gas giant.

This part of the laboratory can be separated from the main station, so if we can trap the creature in it and jettison it into the gas giant, everyone on Sevastopol will be safe. Well, *safer*. The place is still falling apart and full of looters and murderous androids, but one problem at a time. This self-contained lab is even smaller, tighter and more claustrophobic than the previous area, and the tension ratchets up so much that it's almost sadistic. Then an alarm begins to wail – that old trick again – just to make sure you're really freaking out. The alien even seems to be tuned to be more aggressive here.

Ripley reconnects the lab to Sevastopol, so Waits can remotely detach it, and sprints to a nearby escape pod. But just as she reaches the door, it slams shut and the lab is violently separated from the station by a controlled explosive blast. Through the windows we can see the colossal mass of KG-348 spinning past the glass at an alarming rate. The lab is being yanked towards the gas giant by the immense pull of its gravity, and Ripley begins to float as the artificial gravity within the lab is disabled. Surely Waits didn't do this on purpose . . . *right*?

A backup gravity generator kicks in, then it's a race against time to escape into an airlock, strap on a pressure suit with seconds to spare, and get out of the wildly spinning lab before it's consumed by the massive storms raging on KG-348's hellish surface. The airlock opens and Ripley is blown out into space, giving us an incredible, and terrifying, distant view of Sevastopol. It's a neat piece of scene-setting, showing us the station from this perspective, that reminds us of where we've been trapped for the last ten hours.

But before we can admire it, the force unleashed by the lab depressurising throws us violently back towards the station. Ripley manages to grab hold of something before she drifts away (that's the second time this has happened today) and pulls herself safely through an airlock. Well done: you've just finished one of the most intense parts of the game. There's still some gnarly stuff to come, but this is the level that always makes my heart beat the fastest. With the Project KG-348 lab hurtling towards the planet with the xenomorph trapped on it, maybe it's finally gone for good.

MISSION 11

Hazard Containment
Retail therapy.

Ripley stumbles into the airlock, dumps her suit, and contacts Waits on the radio. 'You son of a bitch!' she yells, gasping for air. 'You locked me in. You blew the lab into space and . . .' Waits interrupts, saying he had no choice. He had to get the alien off the station by any means necessary. Ripley is unmoved, her voice shaking with anger. 'Yeah, by using me as bait and leaving me to die!' He's right, though: the creature is gone and we can now enjoy exploring the station without worrying about alerting it. After hours of sneaking around, it's liberating to be able to sprint and use guns freely. There are still Working Joes and looters to worry about, but they're a much more manageable threat.

Ripley calls Waits a heartless bastard and tells him she's heading back to the Marshal Bureau to discuss what just happened.

Leaving the airlock, we find ourselves back in the spaceflight terminal from the beginning of the game. Next to a corpse, Ripley picks up a new toy: the Henjin-Garcia Model 37-12, a pump-action shotgun that will come in very handy in this chapter. The design of the shotgun seems to have been adapted from a late 1970s SWATriplex-18 bullpup shotgun, with some visual elements – specifically the vents on the side of the gun – based on *Aliens'* iconic M41A pulse rifle. All it takes is one well-placed shot to the head with the H-G 37-12 to take down a Working Joe.

Continuing on, Ripley returns to where she met the dearly departed Axel Fielding and encounters the first of many rogue synthetics, making short work of it with a shotgun blast to its rubbery dome. A huge amount of behaviour and dialogue was recorded for the Joes, and they have something to say for pretty much any situation. If one bumps into the alien (which will never attack a synth) they'll stand and stare inquisitively at each other. Sometimes the Joe will say, 'What *are* you?' Very rarely, one will gurgle, 'To sleep, perchance to dream . . .', quoting Shakespeare's *Hamlet*, when you kill it with a firearm. But the cruellest random Working Joe bark has to be when one says, usually when you're in stealth mode and the tension levels are peaking, 'With Seegson *there is someone behind you*, helping you, every step of the way.' This one still makes me jump.

Early in development, the Joes were actually much bigger Shakespeare fans. In an interview with fansite Strange Shapes, *Alien: Isolation* writer Dion Lay says, 'We had all these amazing Shakespearean actors working on the game, so I followed through with that and snuck various ominous, death-heavy lines into recording sessions. The androids would say something along the lines of "initiating vocal routines" and then deliver a malevolently neutral couplet or two. But it was cut, because it felt a bit out of nowhere.'

In *Alien*, when Ash is aboard the *Nostromo* remotely monitoring the crew's exploration of LV-426, he runs on the spot briefly. It's an odd, inscrutable little character moment, and there's a neat reference to it in *Alien: Isolation*. Often, while observing a

Working Joe and waiting for a window of opportunity to slip past it, you'll see it do the very same bizarre little jog as Ash.

In an interview with AvP Galaxy, Dion Lay reveals that the calm, eerie politeness of the Joes' robotic voices was inspired by an infamously sinister 1970s public safety film warning children not to play near water, narrated by actor Donald Pleasence. Check it out on YouTube; it's absolutely *chilling*. All of these elements combine to make Sevastopol's army of Working Joes wonderfully quirky and memorable adversaries. They're every bit as terrifying as the xenomorph, but in a more subtle way – like how they *march* slowly towards you, utterly focused on crushing your skull.

Ripley takes an elevator to Solomons Galleria, which is essentially a shopping mall in space. It's made up of a series of wide concourses, and a large central area containing numerous shuttered stores and restaurants. However, access to this part of the galleria is sealed off and crawling with survivors with itchy trigger fingers – including a few cops in full riot gear. Approach them and they'll tell Ripley to back off, which means we have to find an alternate route. Powering up a friendly-looking robotic vacuum cleaner grants us access to a vent via its charging dock. Emerging into a maintenance corridor, Ricardo warns us that the Working Joes are now not only killing people, but freely venturing into the station's public areas. 'They've left their posts,' he says. 'That's not normal.' Working Joes are supposed to be a silent workforce, running the station from behind the scenes, but now they're *everywhere*. Great.

Exploring the Galleria, Ripley finds a bar lit with neon violet strip lights. The cosy chairs, ambient lighting and fine selection of booze make it seem like this would have been a great place to catch a post-work beer before the incident. Ripley asks Waits why the androids alert level has been raised, and he tells her Samuels will know. It's been a while since we've seen or heard from our Weyland-Yutani android friend, but we'll be reunited soon. Ripley finds a power generator in a utility room and fires it up, opening the security gates blocking access to the main galleria. This is the only way to reach the Marshal Bureau, which is still our objective despite this huge detour.

The central galleria is chaos. Smoke-spewing fires have broken, parts of the mall have collapsed, and there are Working Joes and survivors clad in riot armour to contend with. Over the radio, Waits says the Joes aren't just responding to trespass violations; they're actively *hunting*. 'For who?' Ripley asks. 'For everyone and anyone,' he responds gravely. This is bad news, of course, but also works in your favour. If you lure an android near a group of human enemies, the red-eyed Joes will have no trouble killing them for you. But our top priority now is getting the hell out of here.

This can be a confusing level, because there are shutters every-where and it's never made clear which ones can be opened. Some are just scenery, while others will open automatically when the player approaches – with a slight delay that means you might assume it's locked and move away before it opens. Spotlights shining on the openable doors, or some other visual indicator, would have been helpful here. It's a rare example of poor level design in *Alien: Isolation*. This entire level feels somewhat rushed. It's very different visually and spatially to other parts of Sevas-topol, which is a nice change of pace, but the map doesn't feel as detailed or fleshed out as the rest of the game.

Ripley finally reaches the Marshal Bureau – and the door is locked, of course. She tries to radio Waits to open it remotely, but all we hear is him having the life gruesomely squeezed out of him by a Working Joe. It seems the androids have made their way into the bureau, so maybe it's for the best there's currently no way in. This means we have to make yet another detour.

Returning to the central galleria, Ripley explores the upper levels and finds one of the most unique environments in *Alien: Isolation*: a capsule hotel named Bunkhouse. This is one of many examples, including kanji on signs around the station, that there's a strong Japanese influence on Sevastopol. Ripley finds rows of pods with beds in them, once rented by weary deep-space travel-lers looking for somewhere inexpensive and unfussy to spend the night. The capsule hotel features in some very early concept art, suggesting the idea to feature one in the game came to Creative Assembly's art team during pre-production.

An audio log recorded by Sevastopol resident E. Winters reveals that some of the station's population decided to hide out in the galleria, but as time went on things got rough. 'The people here, they are scared, but they still believe that Marshal Waits will kill the creature,' she says. 'But they forget other dangers. They forget themselves. People are turning on each other for food, for water. I cannot stay here.' This is, perhaps, another piece of in-universe justification for why almost everyone you meet is hostile towards you.

Ripley makes her way through more backrooms, which again are notably lacking in detail compared to other parts of the game. I feel like Creative Assembly probably had bigger plans for the world-building in this section of the station, but were forced to scale things back for time or budget reasons. After squeezing through a few more vents, Ripley finds herself back in the Marshal Bureau we visited earlier – and finds the body of Marshal Waits.

His head has been smashed against a wall by a Working Joe, similar to how Hughes died back in Seegson Communications. A tragic end, no doubt, but it's hard to feel too much sympathy given that he tried to kill us earlier. Ricardo, a haunted look in his eyes, sits defeated in the lobby. He asks Ripley why the androids killed everyone. She doesn't know, but says Samuels will. It's time to reunite with our old pal and find out what's happening.

An audio log on a cluttered desk, recorded by slimy Seegson exec Ransome, reveals something that will be of no surprise to anyone who's ever seen an *Alien* movie or read a spin-off comic or novel. 'What about catching the specimen without killing it?' he asks Waits. 'If we play it smart, we could be set up for life. I have connections. I can set it up.' As is typical in this universe, people like Ransome see the xenomorph as a fast-track ticket to fortune and glory – regardless of who dies in the process. His mysterious 'connections' are also another clue that he's in the pocket of Weyland-Yutani.

Ripley asks Ricardo to hole up in the Marshal Bureau and use the CCTV system to be her eyes and ears while she searches for

Samuels. Understandably, he doesn't like the idea of sticking around – especially with the still-warm body of Marshal Waits lying in a bloody heap nearby. But he relents, and Ripley promises to come back for him. It's time to head to the transit station and take a train back to the SciMed tower. There are a bunch of Working Joes loitering around the Marshal Bureau (presumably the same ones responsible for killing Waits and the others), but you can easily outrun them if you don't want to waste any shotgun shells. Usually, you'd have to watch your sprinting because of the lurking presence of the alien, but the creature is still AWOL.

Ending the level is as simple as grabbing a train, and with that we're done with the Solomons Galleria. I've been fairly negative about this level, but only because its relative weakness only highlights just how great the rest of the game is. I wonder if Creative Assembly bit off more than they could chew, and when it came time to finally build an entire sci-fi shopping mall, they just couldn't dedicate the resources they needed to do it right. This part of the game has always felt very *BioShock*-inspired to me, reminiscent of the shopping mall in Fort Frolic. But that game does a much better job of filling its commercial district with stories, history and interesting environmental storytelling.

MISSION 12

A Synthetic Solution
Under siege.

If we're gonna get off this station, we need to deal with those rampaging androids. Samuels, being a synthetic, should be able to interface with APOLLO – the central AI that controls them – and order them to stand down. Then, with the Working Joes deactivated and the alien dealt with, everything will finally get back to normal. This is what's racing through Ripley's head as she takes an elevator to our next destination, Seegson Synthetics.

There's another reference to *Alien* in the reception area. The body of Smythe, Seegson's head of synthetic development, is slumped on a chair, dead, with a rolled-up magazine jammed into his mouth. You may remember that this is how Ash attempts to kill Ellen Ripley in the movie, which according to Ridley Scott was him expressing a twisted kind of sexual frustration.

'I figured androids had to, if they were really sophisticated, have the urge occasionally,' Scott says on a commentary track recorded for the *Alien Quadrilogy* DVD set. His idea was that Ash wanted to rape Ripley, but didn't have the, uh, *equipment* to do it, so this seemed like a suitable alternative in his malfunctioning synthetic brain. *Alien* is loaded with this kind of violent, provocative sexual imagery; *Alien: Isolation*, not so much.

This doesn't explain why a Working Joe would want to subject Smythe to the same ordeal, but I don't think this macabre tableau is anything deeper than a creepy visual callback to the movie. Ricardo radios Ripley and tells her that the presence of Samuels, a Weyland-Yutani android, has put Seegson Synthetics on high alert. The place is locked down tight, and to reach the upper levels where Samuels is, she's gonna have to climb an elevator shaft.

After a precarious ascent, which ends with an elevator plummeting down the shaft and exploding in a fireball, Ripley reaches Seegson Synthetics' secure upper levels. This area is where broken Working Joes are sent for repair and reprogramming, and they're everywhere: lying cut in pieces on the floor, twitching on hospital gurneys, standing eerily motionless, clumped into heaps. It's dark too, meaning your flashlight is constantly picking out the silhouettes of androids as it cuts through the shadows. After the slightly underwhelming Solomons Galleria, this is *Alien: Isolation*'s level design back to its terrifying best. You feel like you're in a haunted house, waiting on a knife edge for something to leap out at you. There's a great moment where a pile of android bodies begins to stir, and one suddenly emerges from the heap, ready to strike.

Creative Assembly added Working Joes to the game when they realised having the player relentlessly stalked by the alien, and no other type of enemy, would have been too much. But even the Joes, while nowhere near as intelligent as the creature, have an element of unpredictability to them. Some will follow prescribed paths, while others will navigate the level by themselves. Creative Assembly balanced out their superhuman strength, and how hard they are to kill by conventional means, by making them move slowly.

Early in the development of *Alien: Isolation*, the Working Joes had more human-looking faces (along with the rubbery-looking hairpieces mentioned earlier), but Creative Assembly found that play testers would get human and synthetic enemies confused in the heat of the moment. This is what led to their now famous mannequin-like appearance, which was later factored into the storyline as Seegson losing the android tech race to Weyland-Yutani. This change also let the developers use the Joes' eyes as status indicators, turning red to let you know they've become hostile. You can see what the Joes used to look like in leaked footage of an *Alien: Isolation* pre-alpha build. An android body, torn in half, sits in a pool of fluid in Project KG-348, and the face is notably softer and more human than in the final game.

Working Joes have also made appearances in other *Alien* media. In the audiobook version of *Alien: Out of the Shadows* – a story set between the events of *Alien* and *Aliens* – Ellen Ripley says that Ash was 'not just a Working Joe, he was totally flawless, took us in.' This reference doesn't appear in the book itself; it was added to the audiobook following the release of *Alien: Isolation*. In co-op shooter *Aliens: Fireteam Elite*, which brings in elements from all kinds of *Alien* media, Joes appear as enemies wielding maintenance jacks.

On a terminal, Ransome complains that he woke up and found a Working Joe in his apartment. 'When I asked what the hell it was doing, it lunged at me!' he says. 'Send your best technicians to the APOLLO core and find out what's going on.' Ripley crawls through a vent and observes Samuels through a grate. He's talking to a Working Joe, trying to get access to the private APOLLO transit system, which is usually reserved for Seegson executives. 'Biocontainment hazard level omega,' the Joe says. 'All permissions rescinded.' Then, in one of my favourite moments in *Alien: Isolation*, the android tries to stop Samuels, only to find itself being brutally beaten by the much stronger Weyland-Yutani model. It's a stark reminder that, while Samuels is a calm, well-spoken, agreeable kinda guy, he could pop a human's skull like a balloon if he wanted to.

Ripley crawls through a vent and exits into a Working Joe showroom. The only way forward is along a corridor flanked by eight androids frozen in various innocuous-looking poses. I remember the first time I had to walk past these freaky waxworks, convinced one of them was going to jolt to life and grab hold of me. It's a brilliantly unnerving piece of level design. At a nearby desk is the body of Seegson Synthetics receptionist Suzanne Archer, who a terminal log reveals was in a relationship with a fellow employee, Spedding. 'I need you to get to the showroom and shut yourself in,' says Spedding. 'There's a lockdown button near my desk from when these machines were actually worth something. Don't worry about them: they're only display models.'

The developers knew this would make us immediately start worrying about the Joes lined up in the showroom nearby coming to life. *Something* killed Suzanne, and it doesn't look like the xenomorph was responsible. Ripley hits the aforementioned button, lifts the lockdown, and right on cue the display models shudder to life one by one and come for us. Suzanne, it seems, fell victim to the Working Joes. We flee into the next room and the door slams behind us, giving us some time to prepare a counter-attack. The Joes bang on the door menacingly, and will eventually break in, but there are numerous ways to deal with the inevitable flood of synths.

This is one of *Alien: Isolation*'s most entertaining set-pieces, and I wish there were more moments like this in the game. Reminiscent of the splicer assaults in *BioShock 2*, we have to set up traps for the Joes. You can craft and lay down pipe bombs or EMP charges, using them as makeshift proximity mines. There are also heaps of materials in a nearby office, letting you craft Molotovs, and you can even the odds by blowing a gas main and creating a wall of flame over the door where the Joes will enter. There's also another shotgun here, resting on a bloody corpse, in case you missed it in the previous mission.

Eventually, the mob of Working Joes will break through the

door and begin their death march. With all the tools at your disposal, they're fairly easy to deal with, but it's possible for a few to slip through your traps and grab hold of you if you aren't careful. The fire from the busted gas main will damage the androids, but it won't stop them, and seeing them wandering calmly towards you while doused in flames is quite a sight. When the dust settles, Ripley grabs a keycard from one of the destroyed Joes and continues through the level.

She enters the room she saw through the grate earlier, and the android Samuels made mincemeat of is lying in a pool of white fluid. 'Weyland-Yutani synthetic registered,' it gurgles through a distorted voice box. 'Attempted unauthorised access.' Luckily, this Joe is too broken to get up and hassle us, and we can safely activate a nearby generator to power up an elevator that will take us to the next part of the level: Android Orientation.

We're back in the synthetic fluid factory from mission seven, but high above the production line this time. Ripley edges along the rafters, dodging jets of steam. Then, after evading some security cameras and a few more Working Joes, we're finally reunited with Samuels. I've mentioned *BioShock* a few times in the last couple of chapters, and its influence on *Alien: Isolation* is undeniable. The way Samuels speaks to us through a glass window here, and how other characters have done previously, such as Dr Kuhlman, is very *BioShock*.

Samuels explains that only a Seegson synthetic can interact with APOLLO, but he has a plan. He's going to reformat himself, risking his life in the process. When we reach him on the other side of the glass, he slips into an adjoining room and begins the reformatting process, speaking directly to APOLLO. 'Infection has been purged,' he says. 'The creature is no longer on board. The station is safe. Request that all hazard containment operations are suspended.' But the AI ignores the information and tries to forcibly disconnect him. Ripley follows Samuels' instructions and carefully disconnects a series of cables, but it's too late. He's ejected from the reformatting machine and lands in a heap on the ground. With his last breath – or whatever the android equivalent is – he thanks

Ripley for treating him like a person, and tells her the private transit to the APOLLO core is now active. We're on our own now.

'You did that for me?' says an emotional Ripley. 'I wanted Amanda Ripley to have closure,' he replies, echoing the very first moments of the game where he suggested that Ripley might find some closure if she accompanied him to Sevastopol. Back then, we wondered if this was just an empty promise from a Weyland-Yutani stooge; now we know he really meant it. Damn. In a game where death is everywhere, this one hits harder than most.

But back to the job at hand. It's time to visit the APOLLO core and find out what the hell is going on with these androids. Ripley informs Ricardo, who's still locked away in the Marshal Bureau, about Samuels' demise and shares her plan to visit the core and lift the lockdown. We now have to backtrack quite a bit to the APOLLO transit station, but along the way, in the fluid plant, we receive a mysterious update from Ricardo. 'I just found something here,' he says. 'An interview tape. You need to hear it.' Ripley asks him to play it.

It's the voice of Taylor, speaking to Marlow. 'I want data,' she says. 'The location of the planetoid where you found the derelict. All data you have on the origin of that organism.' Marlow agrees, but only if she frees him from his cell in the Marshal Bureau and gets him off the station. It seems Taylor, like Ransome, wants to get hold of the creature for her paymasters – but she may just be following orders. At this point, it's difficult to tell what her motives are, but we can figure that out later. It's time to meet APOLLO.

MISSION 13

Consultation
Order out of chaos.

Ripley is now on the floor above the APOLLO core. (Side note: according to the official *Alien: Isolation* art book, APOLLO is an acronym for Artificial Personality Overseeing Lifestyle and

Logistics Operations.) Seegson security protocols meant Samuels couldn't speak to the central AI remotely, but Ricardo says Ripley will be able to interface with it manually if she can reach the core. A terminal log in a security office reveals that Spedding also ventured down here prior to our arrival, trying to find out what sent the Working Joes into a frenzy.

Then *Alien: Isolation* plays a very mean trick on us. Ripley walks through a metal detector, and her collection of guns triggers a lockdown. 'You have got to be shitting me,' she says as she reluctantly drops her shotgun, revolver and flamethrower onto a conveyor belt. The belt whisks them away, leaving us completely unarmed and about to face the game's toughest non-alien enemies. It's frustrating in the moment, but from a gameplay perspective, this is a clever way of shaking the player out of their comfort zone.

By this point in the game, you will probably have established a play style and routine incorporating Ripley's arsenal. But now you have to adapt and play a different way, relying more on gadgets, scavenging, crafting and manipulating systems than pure brute force. But even though dropping her guns lets her through, accessing the core is a different problem altogether. Normally, a person could just take an elevator straight down to it. But, of course, it's been disabled by the lockdown and we need to find an alternate path.

Ripley consults a schematic of the facility used as part of a VIP tour, spotting a power conduit that links directly to the core. This map is laid out on and lit up by a lightbox-style table, and the way she runs her finger over the schematics is reminiscent of the scene in *Aliens* where her mother and the Colonial Marines study a map of Hadley's Hope on a similar surface. But before we can squeeze into this conduit, we're going to have to shut off the power.

In an audio log recorded by Porter, Sevastopol's chief engineer, we hear about some Working Joes Porter assigned to asset-strip lower Habitation who suddenly stopped working and began babbling about a hazard containment order. If you're a fan of sci-fi comedy *Red Dwarf*, Porter's voice may sound familiar. He's played by Mac McDonald, a veteran American character actor who portrayed Hollister, captain of the titular crimson-coloured mining ship. McDonald also appeared in the extended cut of *Aliens* as Simpson, the administrator of Hadley's Hope, and plays several minor background characters in *Alien: Isolation* too.

A sales sheet on a terminal gives us an idea of what APOLLO actually does, albeit presented in a way designed to lure potential buyers. Its advertised features include 'security through removal of synthetic self-determination', which seems like a bad idea in retrospect. If the Working Joes could make decisions for themselves, maybe they wouldn't be mindlessly killing everyone. 'A true Seegson product,' the pitch ends, which is darkly ironic considering how poorly designed everything this company produces clearly is.

In an interview with AvP Galaxy, writer Will Porter (the namesake of Sevastopol's chief engineer, W. Porter) describes Seegson as 'the masters of corporate double-think.' In a breezy pre-recorded voice, it tells us that everything is okay, that it values its customers and employees, while the executives 'look for their next plum job and syphon off what remains of the company gravy train.' He adds that it's the little guys, 'the real working Joes', that suffer at the hands of these greedy corporate machines: a recurring theme in the *Alien* series. Chances are you've worked for a company like Seegson (I certainly have), which makes this aspect of *Isolation*'s world uncomfortably familiar.

Ripley disables a turbine and has a few tense moments to dash past it before it spins back up again. Then it's time to get through the power conduit, which is the smallest space we've squeezed through yet. To make matters worse, the deeper we go, and the closer we get to the APOLLO core, the fainter our radio signal gets. This means we'll shortly lose contact with Ricardo, our eyes and ears, which is where the *Isolation* part of *Alien: Isolation* really comes to the forefront. This level is especially lonely and claustrophobic, and Ripley's confiscated weapons only adds to our uneasy feeling of vulnerability.

We squeeze out of the conduit and find ourselves in the lower levels of the APOLLO core. Ripley moves through a door and sees an android wearing an orange hazmat suit – a new type of Working Joe that, while moving a lot more slowly than the regular model, is a *lot* tougher to take down. They can absorb a huge amount of damage and their hazard suits make them immune to the stun baton and EMP mines. The safest and most efficient way to deal with these heavy-duty Joes is to sneak around them, which strips *Alien: Isolation*'s stealth down to its core fundamentals. We have to make ample use of the motion tracker to move through these tight spaces without being spotted.

Ripley picks up a new gadget, the gas mask, which we can use to move safely through clouds of toxic gas. There are some gas-filled rooms elsewhere in the station containing optional *Nostromo* logs, but otherwise this mask doesn't get much use. She also finds an intriguing audio log on a terminal, in which Seegson exec Ransome is in unusually high spirits. 'Something crazy just happened,' he says. 'Sevastopol is off the market. We got a buyer.' He also mentions that APOLLO has received a 'packet of new operation rulesets', which may be (read: *is*) responsible for the AI's current bizarre behaviour. Take a mental note that Ransome's log is dated *after* the xenomorph outbreak.

Ripley's next job is activating a series of servers, which involves navigating some incredibly tight, dangerous spaces patrolled by Joes. This is one of the most difficult stealth challenges in the game, and a log recorded by Spedding reveals he had a hard time down here as well. 'I'm in APOLLO,' he says tearily. 'There are androids at the door. Ransome's nowhere to be seen. There are conflicts with the hazard containment breach. Synthetic safety procedures are getting bypassed left and right. Oh God, they're going to get in.'

The lighting in this level is really impressive, particularly in the server farms. Coolant fluid covers the floor, reflecting the glowing lights of the servers and the Working Joes as they splash through it. But there's no time to admire the visuals, because with the servers activated, Ripley can now make her way into the core. She climbs through a tunnel lit eerily by red emergency lights and emerges into a large, dark chamber. Hacking a series of terminals with her access tuner, APOLLO's security perimeter drops and lights clunk on, revealing the core itself: an immense dome with bundles of thick cabling flowing into it.

According to concept artist, Edouard Caplain, in an interview in the official *Alien: Isolation* art book, the initial idea for the design of the APOLLO core was 'inverting the MU-TH-UR 6000 computer from the movie'. This led to the idea of a sphere suspended by cables, 'like an eye connected by its nerves', and a mix of organic and mechanical shapes. It's an impressive and dramatic piece of world design, and there's a nice treat for *Alien* fans inside too.

We hack our way into the core when it begins to vibrate violently, rising up and spewing jets of steam. It feels like we've awakened some great, angry beast. Then, suddenly, a bridge extends and a door opens, letting us inside. The interior of the core is an identical replica of the iconic mainframe room Dallas uses to talk to MU-TH-UR in *Alien*. In J. W. Rinzler's *The Making of Alien*, the author states that this memorable set was modelled after a cathedral chapel. Thousands of individual blinking light bulbs were threaded through the set to create the illusion of a vast, advanced supercomputer – and cinematographer Derek Vanlint shone a 1,000-watt lamp through tracing paper to make it seem like the bulbs were lighting the room. The warm, womb-like ambience of this space was, of course, no accident; the computer *is* called 'mother' after all.

Ripley sits down at the console and attempts to disable the androids, but the computer won't play ball. Words flash on the screen in the same City Light typeface as in the movie: 'NEGATIVE. WY SPECIAL ORDER 939 IN PROGRESS.' Ripley presses APOLLO for more information and learns that, two days after she left for Sevastopol, the Company bought the station. Remember the mystery buyer Ransome mentioned? They're a mystery no more.

In a callback to the famously chilling 'crew expendable' scene from *Alien*, Ripley asks APOLLO to outline special order 939. 'PRIORITY ONE: PROTECT SPECIMEN. MAINTAIN STATION QUARANTINE. DISALLOW COMMUNICA-TIONS. ALL OTHER CONDITIONS SECONDARY.' Ripley tries to tell the computer that the creature is gone, that the quarantine can be lifted, but APOLLO refuses, stating that 'scheduled reactor scans' are 'unverified', whatever that means. We'll have to visit the reactor to find out.

In S. D. Perry's book *Alien: The Weyland-Yutani Report*, a fictional guide to the xenomorph species, it's revealed that the 900 series of special corporate orders was created by Weyland Corp. following the events of the *Prometheus* expedition. It was determined that the actions of human crew members could potentially deny the company lucrative opportunities to secure and back-engineer alien technologies or biological specimens. *Isolation*'s special order 939, and *Alien*'s special order 937, were both a result of this policy, which continued when the corp. became Weyland-Yutani.

So, to recap: thanks to their man on the inside, Ransome, Weyland-Yutani knew all about the outbreak, bought Sevastopol, and sent new orders to APOLLO to lock it down and contain the xenomorph. Once again, a member of the Ripley family has been screwed over by the Company and its obsession with weaponizing and profiting from the alien. But if there's one thing the Ripleys are known for, it's interfering with the immoral scheming of corrupt megacorps. Weyland-Yutani messed with the wrong engineer.

An exit opens up beneath the core, and as Ripley descends a ladder she hears a computerised voice chirp over a speaker: 'Weyland-Yutani. Building better worlds!' The Company never misses an opportunity for a bit of corporate branding, even when secretly buying space stations to capture killer aliens. Ripley activates a cargo elevator and begins her journey down to the reactor to find out what exactly APOLLO's 'unverified' scans are referring to.

MISSION 14

The Descent
Strength in numbers.

Ripley descends into the reactor through a deep ventilation shaft. An immense backlit fan (that old Ridley Scott favourite again) spins above her, casting looming shadows over the walls. She radios Ricardo and updates him on the situation, then heads into the dense, dark, industrial maze of corridors and chambers surrounding the reactor. The design of this part of the map takes visual cues from the *Nostromo*'s hangar set. It's all high ceilings, dangling chains, deep shadows, greasy machinery, and strange vehicles awaiting repair. The ceaseless, thrumming mechanical groan of the reactor, which vibrates through the walls, makes for an oppressive sonic ambience.

After the relative comfort of the Habitation tower, it's a shock to the system finding ourselves back in the dark, cold, metallic underbelly of the station. In the movie, these areas of the ship were made up of parts scavenged from airport graveyards. 'We couldn't afford vacuum moulding or anything like that,' says Ridley Scott on the *Alien Quadrilogy* commentary track for *Alien*. 'So a lot of this stuff had to be found, assembled like a sculpture, then painted and joined together with polystyrene painted to look like plastic.'

A lot of the visual elements in *Alien: Isolation*'s industrial environments – control panels, levers, switches, panels, pipes, ducts and so on – were taken directly from the film, so in a roundabout way Creative Assembly were also building their world from this disused aircraft scrap. It's in these environments, which are very similar to the lower decks of the *Nostromo*, where the game most accurately captures the claustrophobic feel of the movie.

There are more Working Joes to contend with down here, but luckily they're the normal, more easily dispatched kind. On a workbench Ripley finds the final upgrade for her torch, letting her use an ion flame to cut open the strongest vent covers. There now follows an extended trek through the bowels of the reactor facility, where we run into Joes – including the heavy-duty hazmat variety. Ripley still doesn't have her weapons back, but she finds a new one here: the DV-303 bolt gun. Well, weapon isn't quite the right word; this thing is more like an industrial *tool*. However, one well-placed shot to the head of a Working Joe, even the tougher models, is enough to kill them instantly.

In a log we discover that chief engineer Porter was responsible for creating this jury-rigged weapon. 'One of those damn androids nearly took my head off, so I've scavenged enough parts together to make a weapon,' he says. 'It's got enough kick to punch a nice clean hole in one of those bastards.' This is a nice callback to the movie, where engineers Brett and Parker cobbled together various gadgets and weaponry for the crew of the *Nostromo* to use.

After what feels like an eternity trapped in this industrial labyrinth, Ripley finally makes it to an elevator that takes her to the reactor: and what a sight to behold this thing is. Located at the base of the station, underneath the spires, is an impossibly vast chamber. The room is completely dark, save for the brief moments when blue arcs of electricity shoot from the generator and illuminate Ripley's surroundings. This is the biggest part of the station we've seen so far, and after all those narrow corridors and low ceilings, the scale of the place is almost overwhelming.

Our next stop is the central reactor. Whatever is stopping APOLLO from lifting the quarantine is located here. Ripley makes her way across a series of catwalks, introducing her new bolt gun to a few hazmat Joes. It's immensely satisfying charging this thing up and unloading a slug of hot steel into the heads of your former tormentors. Making it safely to the other side of the reactor chamber, Ripley takes an elevator down and the enormity of what has actually been happening on Sevastopol becomes terrifyingly clear.

What was once the central reactor is now an alien hive. The place is covered in the sticky resin secreted by the xenomorph, and there are cocoons suspended from the walls containing bodies. Ripley contacts Ricardo. 'They're all here. Everyone that's missing.

Everyone. They're trapped in some kind of nest. There are eggs. It's like a *farm*.' The contrast of the metallic, industrial station and the creeping organic matter consuming it makes this one of the most visually striking, and unique, parts of the game. There are dozens of slimy, leathery eggs here; the same ones we saw in the derelict on LV-426.

Concept artist Bradley Wright was responsible for visualising the hive and retrofitting it to the reactor core structure. 'I saw that these environments were already very organic and egg-like, with their rounded tanks of coolant,' he explains in an interview in the official *Alien: Isolation* art book. 'I then covered everything in the alien hive material, which gives it the look of some kind of humid, moist tree root, or maybe a massive termite mound.'

Wright twisted and contorted the hive resin around the existing structure of the facility, giving it distinctive growth patterns and multiple layers of writhing organic mass. In early concept paintings, Ripley is seen wearing a pressure suit as she explores the nest. Unused script files dug out of the game's data also seem to suggest that, at one point, Ripley would make a return visit to the hive after her initial discovery. As impactful as this level is, it's pretty short, leading me to believe Creative Assembly perhaps had bigger plans for it.

Listen carefully and you can hear the anguished moans of the people trapped in the cocoons, waiting to be impregnated and . . . *wait a sec*. Eggs means facehuggers. Human hosts means chestbursters. Chestbursters means xenomorphs. Okay, you've probably figured it out by now. Ripley bravely takes it upon herself to destroy the nest and moves deeper into it. Facehuggers occasionally burst from eggs or scurry out of the darkness, and if they latch onto us it's an instant game over. Luckily, someone left a spare flamethrower by the entrance that we can use to toast the scuttling little suckers.

Ripley begins the process of purging the reactor, which would be simple if it wasn't for the fact that the alien is back. Well, not *the* alien. *That* alien – the one we tangled with before Waits' betrayal – will have been burned up in the atmosphere of KG-348 by now. As if it wasn't obvious already, there are multiple aliens on Sevastopol. Dozens of them. Hundreds, maybe. It's impossible to know for sure. Hell, what we assumed was a single creature hunting us earlier in the game could have actually been several of the things.

It's a bold and provocative twist, and not everyone who plays the game loves it, but it's something Creative Assembly always had in mind. In an interview with PC Gamer, *Alien: Isolation* director Alistair Hope explained that the idea was to turn the tables on players who had become confident around the alien. 'We wanted to make things doubly worse for the player, and I wondered what the reaction would be,' he says. 'They're gonna kill me for this, but it was as easy as just placing another alien in the level. But only because they did such a good job creating this creature that can look after itself.'

As for whether the alien we met in the early missions was in fact operating solo, Hope prefers to leave this open to interpretation. 'I'm happy for players to decide that for themselves. No one on Sevastopol knows all the answers. Amanda doesn't, and the player shouldn't either.'

And he's right. A part of what makes *Alien* so special is the sense of mystery that pervades everything. Where did the derelict come from? Is the xenomorph a bioweapon? Who made it? How much does Weyland-Yutani actually know about LV-426? What was Ash doing before he joined the crew of the *Nostromo*? The film raises many tantalising questions, and answers very few of them, which is part of why it's so alluring and compelling. *Alien: Isolation* is similarly opaque, which is another way it captures the spirit of the source material.

However, one mystery *has* been explicitly addressed by the developers: where all those eggs came from. Although you never meet it, there is an alien queen in the depths of the reactor. 'She's down there somewhere, in amongst the cacophony,' says writer Will Porter in an interview with AvP Galaxy. 'But Ripley was lucky enough not to bump into her.' Creative Assembly were also worried that showing glimpses of the queen would make players think a boss battle was imminent. While Ellen Ripley battling the queen in *Aliens* is a great moment, and it would have been cool seeing her daughter having her own run-in with one, this kind of set-piece wouldn't suit the game.

Playing with headphones, a number of strange sounds can be heard in the hive, including heavy, rhythmic breathing and distant screeches. While this could just be the audio designers creating a generally spooky atmosphere to unsettle players, some fans interpret this as sounds being made by the otherwise unseen queen. Some of the sounds *are* similar to those heard in *Aliens* when we meet the queen, but this mystery currently remains unsolved.

As if things in the hive weren't stressful enough, Creative Assembly pulls a devilish trick on the player. We pull up our motion tracker and it picks up multiple signals all around us, under the floors, behind the walls. This place is crawling with facehuggers and xenomorphs, and the cacophony of bleeps emitted by the tracker is deeply unsettling. I know several people who reached this level and, when confronted with all this, plus two aliens stomping around, decided it was too much and never progressed any further.

Ripley makes it out of the hive, back across the catwalks (where more hazmat Joes have appeared), and heads to the reactor control room to initiate the purge. Great surges of electricity run up and down the reactor, unleashing powerful waves of crackling blue energy. This destroys the hive as planned, but a few xenomorphs manage to escape the devastation. They climb out of the reactor and back to the upper levels of the station, which means we'll be running into them again later. But at least all those eggs, and presumably the queen lurking in the depths of the nest, have been permanently dealt with.

Ricardo is relieved to hear Ripley has survived, even if she feels guilty for letting some of the creatures escape. But there's some good news: the reactor purge has reset all of the station's core systems, including outside communications. Weyland-Yutani's APOLLO comms block has been lifted, but who knows for how long. If we can get a message out, maybe someone will come to the rescue. Time to head back to the SciMed tower.

MISSION 15

The Message
Closure.

Moments after arriving at the SciMed tower, Ricardo informs Ripley that APOLLO has already recovered from the reactor purge and external communications are locked down again. But we also learn that Marlow, who has now been released from his cell in the Marshal Bureau, took advantage of the brief comms blackout and sent auto-docking codes to the *Anesidora*. His ship is in a holding pattern around the station, and Ripley decides on her next course of action: taking an emergency shuttle from Medical over to the *Anesidora*.

With our recently acquired ion torch, we can now cut through San Cristobal's front door and stroll right in, rather than having to take another elaborate shortcut. Ripley takes an elevator to the lobby where she had her explosive encounter with the alien – courtesy of Waits's booby trap – back in mission six, which feels like a lifetime ago. A few fires are still burning, but the place is in remarkably good shape considering how big the blast was.

Ripley cuts through another sealed door with the ion torch and heads towards the emergency shuttle bay. Ricardo tells us that Marlow is way ahead of us and has already taken a shuttle over to the *Anesidora*. Hopefully there's another. Hazmat Working Joes are loose all over Medical, and so is the alien. Well, *an* alien. Yes, we're fully back to having to deal with xenomorphs again. No more sprinting around the station firing your guns whenever you feel like it.

Grabbing a level three upgrade for the access tuner, Ripley hacks her way into a shuttle. She sits in the pilot's seat and we see the exterior of Sevastopol through the window as the shuttle launches itself out into space. Early in development, these kinds of shuttles played a much bigger role in the game. Blocky, untextured pre-visualisation footage of an elaborate shuttle launch sequence has been unearthed by data miners. The shuttle folds out of the side of the station, which is a brilliantly nerdy reference to a piece of Ron Cobb concept art for an unused *Nostromo* lifeboat. There are also some very finished-looking CCTV-style loading screens buried in the game's files showing the shuttle moving between the station's towers, which were reportedly part of a cut mission.

Alas, in the finished game, all we get is a fairly underwhelming cutscene, a fade to black, and suddenly we're aboard the *Anesidora*. We don't even get an establishing exterior shot of Marlow's ship, despite the official *Alien: Isolation* artbook revealing that detailed designs were created for it. This whole section feels disappointingly rushed, and it's a bit of an anti-climax just being dumped on the *Anesidora* without any fanfare or scene-setting.

Concept art for the *Anesidora*'s interior shows a shabby, ill-maintained salvage ship with dripping pipes, exposed cabling, and junk littering the corridors. The idea was that, compared to Verlaine's impeccably maintained *Torrens*, the crew of the *Anesidora* didn't really give a shit about their own vessel. There's a beautiful concept painting of the *Anesidora*'s bridge, too, which artist Bradley Wright littered with personal items – including toy dinosaurs, vases stuffed with dead flowers, and cut-out paper skeletons hanging from the ceiling – to reflect the personalities of its crew. But, curiously, none of this made it into the finished game. Visually, there's very little setting the *Anesidora* apart from Sevastopol. It just feels like another part of the station.

But the *Anesidora* isn't a total washout, because it's home to a small but memorable piece of level design that is the work of an evil genius. In a dark room, Ripley's and the player's hearts leap as her flashlight catches the unmistakable silhouette of a xenomorph. Or so we think. Get closer and we realise that it's actually just a piece of unidentifiable sci-fi machinery shaped, very much on purpose, like an alien's head. I don't know who at Creative Assembly was responsible for this prank, but *bravo*.

Ripley restores the ship's power, then hears the voice of Marlow over a speaker. 'Welcome to the *Anesidora*,' he says. 'Maybe you want to join my crew? Plenty of free spots.' Back in mission twelve,

Ricardo played us a recording of Taylor and Marlow making a deal in the Marshal Bureau, but now we learn from Taylor herself – whose voice also crackles over the same speaker – that Marlow didn't hold up his end of the bargain. He promised her he'd give her all the data he had on the alien for the Company in return for being freed; but then he double-crossed her, kidnapped her, and took her with him aboard the *Anesidora*. 'Come find me, Ripley,' he says. 'I've got something for you.'

Ripley searches for Marlow, toasting a facehugger (how did *that* get here?) with her flamethrower along the way. These things are weak and can be killed with any weapon, but everything except the 'thrower leaves you open to being killed yourself. If one latches onto your face, understandably, it's an instant game over. In the movie they – and the xenomorphs they grow into – have highly corrosive acid for blood. 'It's got a wonderful defence mechanism,' says Parker, observing a pen being dissolved by the stuff. 'You don't dare kill it.'

While writing *Alien*, screenwriter Dan O'Bannon insisted that the creature be mortal – but with something stopping the crew from outright killing it. Concept artist Ron Cobb then came up with this idea of it having acid for blood, and the rest is history. To create the illusion of it melting through the *Nostromo*, special effects supervisor Brian Johnson concocted a dangerous mix of chloroform, acetone, cyclohexylamine and acetic acid, then poured it on Styrofoam painted to look like metal. His chemical cocktail ate right through it.

But why no acid blood in *Alien: Isolation*? The game goes to great lengths to accurately recreate the experience of being hunted by, and fighting against, a xenomorph, but Creative Assembly elected to leave this element out of the mix. 'We had some cool ideas around it,' director Alistair Hope says in an interview with PC Gamer. 'But ultimately it felt like we were starting to make an alien simulator, rather than something that would be a fun experience to play.' He adds that having holes appearing in the world 'started steering the game in a weird direction' and so the concept was dropped. However, if you manage to smack a facehugger with the maintenance jack (good luck with that), it does release a splash of blood that saps your health a little.

On a terminal, Ripley finds a message from Marshal Waits sent when the *Anesidora* first arrived at Sevastopol. 'Officially, I should deny your request to dock,' he says. 'However, in light of the property you found, I will allow a small number of your crew to dock via a short-range shuttle.' This 'property' is, of course, the recently recovered *Nostromo* flight recorder.

The mysterious disappearance of the *Nostromo* and her crew is a well-known unsolved mystery, despite Weyland-Yutani's best efforts to sweep it under the rug, which is why Waits was so willing to break the rules to get a hold of the black box. 'I must remind you that Sevastopol is entitled to a cut of any reward for return of said property once it's on the station,' he says, adding himself to the long list of people in the *Alien* universe who are so obsessed with money that they lose any sense of morality and/or common sense.

Ripley explores the *Anesidora* further and hears Marlow's voice again. He has, to his credit, correctly identified the severe existential threat the xenomorph poses to the human race. 'You've got to wipe out every trace. Destroy every clue. Stop this infection from spreading.' Then, deep in the bowels of the ship, Ripley finally finds what she's been desperately searching for: closure. The flight recorder data, recovered by Marlow when he illegally went digging into the device, has been loaded onto a nearby terminal.

Text flashes on the screen alongside Weyland-Yutani's older, pre-*Aliens* winged sun logo: LT. E. RIPLEY. TRANSMISSION RECEIVED. ORIGIN: *NARCISSUS*. The *Narcissus* was the lifeboat Ellen Ripley used to escape the destruction of the *Nostromo* – and where she defeated the xenomorph once and for all at the end of the movie. Then, as a distorted waveform spikes on the screen, we hear the voice of Sigourney Weaver, reprising her role as Ellen Ripley, recording a personal message for her daughter. Weaver settles back into her most iconic role effortlessly, and if you were told this new dialogue was recorded back in 1979, when she was in her late twenties, you'd believe it.

Chronologically, Ellen Ripley is supposed to have recorded this personal message to Amanda following the report she files at the end of *Alien*, just before the credits roll. It's a neat way of fitting new dialogue into the movie in a way that feels organic, and whoever penned it must have been pinching themselves. Weaver hadn't played Ripley since 1997's *Alien Resurrection*, which makes her presence in *Alien: Isolation* all the more special.

She describes the events of *Alien*, but reassures Amanda that she's safe. 'I'm okay, stuck on this lifeboat a long way out,' she says. 'But we had to destroy the *Nostromo*. We just couldn't bring that thing home with us. I hope I see you very soon. I love you, sweetheart.' Then the recording abruptly stops playing and the words MESSAGE END flash coldly on the screen.

The atmospheric visuals in this sequence, featuring the game's trademark VHS distortion and interference, were created by lead UI artist Jon McKellan. 'I genuinely feel humbled to have played any sort of part in this series at all,' he says in a Kotaku interview. 'When I was designing the intro title sequence, and later the final message to Amanda, working with our new Sigourney Weaver dialogue, it was an exhausting, intense, but giddy time.'

Ripley is stunned into silence, but before she gets a chance to process what she's just listened to, Marlow and Taylor enter the scene – protected by yet another *BioShock*-style pane of glass. Marlow has decided to blow the *Anesidora*'s fusion reactor, destroying his ship and the station in the process. He wants to annihilate every trace of the creature, and is determined for the Company not to get its hands on it, because it'll just start the cycle of death and destruction all over again. Admittedly, his logic is sound.

But Ripley doesn't want to die. Moments ago she found out that her mother is still alive. Her mission is only just beginning. Marlow leans over and fiddles with a device that looks a lot like the *Nostromo*'s self-destruct control panel, complete with slowly rising pistons emitting a soft white glow. But while he's distracted, lamenting the death of his wife, Taylor takes advantage of the situation and whacks him over the head with a wrench and knocks him out.

Unused animation files unearthed by data miners reveal that this scene went through several iterations. In one, Marlow enters the scene, shoots Taylor, triggers the reactor overload, then shoots himself. *Alien: Isolation* underwent multiple rewrites during its development, some as close as a year before release. Ripley was originally going to work *with* Marlow to destroy the station, and the game reportedly ended with her escaping on the *Torrens* with a group of survivors as Sevastopol exploded. The finale in the final game is *very* different, and arguably a lot more in line with her character.

But back to reality, and Ripley and Taylor try to work together to disable the rapidly overloading fusion reactor. Alas, it's too late. A violent surge of energy hurls Taylor through the air and into the glass wall separating her from Ripley, killing her instantly. All we can do now is get the hell off the *Anesidora*. Ripley dashes back to the shuttle as emergency lights flash, arcs of electricity shoot out of the walls, and explosions echo through the ship. She makes it, *just*, and the level ends unceremoniously with another anti-climactic fade to black as she sits down at the shuttle's controls and returns to Sevastopol.

MISSION 16

Transmission
Gravity, all nonsense now.

Good news: the *Anesidora*'s fusion reactor overloading didn't destroy Sevastopol. Bad news: the blast took out the station's orbital stabilisers, meaning we're now spinning wildly out of control and will, eventually, crash into KG-348. Worse still, with the *Anesidora* reduced to a pile of scrap, using it to escape is no longer an option. At least we're alive – but for how much longer? This mission brings a sense of impending doom and chaotic urgency to *Alien: Isolation*, which doesn't let up until the credits roll. The end is in sight.

Ricardo radios Ripley and tells her that while the *Torrens* – our last remaining lifeline – remains nearby, external comms are still being blocked by APOLLO and there's no way to communicate with the ship. Then we receive a message from Verlaine. 'Sevastopol, we just saw a ship blow on your starboard side,' she says. 'It took out an entire orbital stabiliser array. We have no place to dock. Please, tell us what's going on in there. We can take survivors.' Well, that's encouraging. Maybe there's a way out of this mess after all. We just need to find a way to send a message back to Verlaine and tell her what's going on.

Back in the familiar surroundings of Seegson Communications, Ripley receives some troubling news from Ricardo. He says Seegson security forces also heard the *Torrens*' broadcast and plan on taking the ship by force. Luckily, they're just as affected by the comms blackout as us, and can't trick Verlaine into docking, but this does mean we now have a bunch of armoured, desperate security officers in riot gear to deal with. There are also frequent, ominous reminders of the station's precarious orbit, with the distant groaning of metal being twisted and torn apart and the screen occasionally shaking. According to an announcement from a computerised voice, the orbital stabilisers are operating at 80 per cent efficiency: a number that is rapidly falling every minute.

Ripley finds herself back where she picked up the motion tracker in mission four. The layout of the level is familiar, but the vibe is very different. A failing lighting system has plunged the facility into darkness, fires are breaking out everywhere, and instead of Working Joes there are nervous shotgun-toting Seegson security guards patrolling the corridors. This section is essentially a remix of our first visit to Seegson Communications, but with much higher stakes.

Then, through another pane of *BioShock* glass, we finally see our old pal Ricardo in the flesh again. He tells us that Marlow is still logged into the terminal he used to auto-dock the *Anesidora* earlier, and if we can find the coordinates for the *Torrens* we can bypass APOLLO and do the same. We just have to take a trip through Comms Control and find a place called the Observatory. Before departing, the computer, ever the harbinger of bad news, reminds us that the stabilisers are now at 60 per cent. Time is not on our side.

In the comms hub, Ripley overhears Seegson goons trying and failing to communicate with 'that ship', meaning the *Torrens*. Ripley swerves them and makes her way into the Observatory: a computer-filled chamber with a large window overlooking a cluster of colossal satellite dishes. To continue, we need to complete a series of simple Jon McKellan-designed minigames built to mimic the aesthetic of *Alien*'s retro-futuristic computers.

Doing so lifts the Observatory higher, rewarding us with a stunning vista of Sevastopol, the comms array and KG-348. But, more importantly, we've also gained access to the *Torrens*' coordinates. However, because nothing is ever simple in *Alien: Isolation*, to actually contact the ship Ripley has to manually align the position of those massive dishes – which means going outside. It's time to strap on another one of those bulky pressure suits.

Ricardo unlocks the airlock remotely and we make our way outside, walking along a catwalk with the deep, dark infinity of space all around us and the swirling storms of KG-348 cresting the metal horizon of the station. After hours of being trapped in Sevastopol's submarine-like warren of industrial tunnels, it's slightly overwhelming being in an environment this vast. The air (well, *vacuum*) is filled with microscopic debris twinkling in the light of the nearby yellow dwarf star; this debris may be all that's left of the *Anesidora*.

Ripley takes a painfully slow elevator to the top of a maintenance platform, releases a lock preventing the dish from being moved, then twists a radio-like tuning dial to enter the *Torrens*' coordinates. The giant dish grinds to life, rotating towards the ship, and for the first time since we arrived on Sevastopol we're able to speak to the outside world. Ripley gets Verlaine up to speed about the alien and requests an urgent extraction, but there's nowhere to dock. The station is tearing itself free from its gravity mooring.

But there might be a way. There's a towing platform at the bottom of Sevastopol, and even though the *Torrens'* umbilical isn't compatible, we might be able to extend the platform manually. But first, a slow march back across those precarious-looking EVA catwalks. If you look *very* closely here, just as you're about to reach the exit, you can see a xenomorph clambering up the side of the station. It won't attack you, but it's an unpleasant reminder that we still have these things to deal with along with everything else.

Ripley shares the good news with Ricardo, but his relieved response is suddenly cut off.

In another example of the game remixing levels we've visited previously, our return trip through the comms hub is made difficult by the presence of an alien. That means, to date, we've encountered Working Joes, humans *and* aliens in this one location. But now the place is in extra bad shape following an explosive decompression. It's completely dark except for the rhythmic, strobe-like sweep of yellow emergency lights, which makes picking out the creature and tracking it visually distressingly difficult.

Ripley successfully evades the creature and makes it back to the office where she met Ricardo earlier, finding out why his transmission was suddenly cut short. He's slumped in a chair with a 'hugger stuck to his face, meaning his journey has finally come to an end. Ripley is distraught, seeing yet another ally succumbing to the dangers of Sevastopol, but she has no choice but to press on and get to the towing platform beneath the spaceflight terminal.

Ricardo's unfortunate demise is very sudden, with little fanfare, but this wasn't always the case. Throughout the game we see the evidence of recently birthed chestbursters, but never see it actually happen in person. 'Early on I was thinking Ricardo could get face-hugged during Ripley's period of radio silence in the APOLLO core,' writer Will Porter tells AvP Galaxy. 'He wouldn't entirely remember or understand what happened, as with Kane in the movie, and would keep his growing fears a secret until the point of chestburst after the comms dish realignment.' But it was ultimately decided that, if the game was being faithful to *Alien*, the gestation period wasn't long enough.

Before you make your way to the towing platform, this is an excellent time to do some backtracking. You now have every gadget and upgrade in the game, meaning you can access all those locked or blocked-off rooms you've been passing that contain extra supplies, *Nostromo* logs and ID tags. You can't return to the Project KG-348 labs or the hive, for obvious reasons, but everywhere else is open to you. If you're a completionist, this is your last and best chance to retrace your steps and gather up all the collectibles you've missed up until this point.

It's also worth stopping by the spaceflight terminal and cracking open a previously sealed door with your ion torch. Inside you'll find the body of Mike Tanaka – the guy I told you about back in the Crew Log chapter – along with some of his drawings pinned to the walls. There's a safe in here too containing some useful supplies, but the code (2931) is never shown anywhere in the game itself. It was posted on Tanaka's in-character Twitter account, as a reward for players who were following his tragic story online.

Also, if you're an *Alien* fan, it's worth seeking out the *Nostromo* logs. They only amount to around five minutes, or 700 words, of dialogue, but hearing some of the original cast reprising their roles from the movie is a real treat. Collect them and you'll hear Captain Dallas (Tom Skerritt) complaining about his usual science officer being replaced at the last minute, Parker (Yaphet Kotto) griping about not being respected by the higher-ups, Brett (Harry Dean Stanton) snubbing a request from Kane (who has no logs of his own, incidentally) and Lambert (Veronica Cartwright) recording and filing a navigation log. The only crew member *not* played by their original actor is Ash (Ian Holm), whose voice is instead mimicked brilliantly by actor Dave B. Mitchell. Why Holm didn't get involved is unknown, but some actors just don't like lending their likeness to these kinds of projects. Notably, John Hurt never agreed to let toy manufacturer NECA use his face for their Kane action figure, a limitation they got around by hiding his face with a facehugger latched onto his pressure suit helmet.

Creative Assembly didn't have long with the cast, many of whom were basically retired from acting. That's why there's only a small amount of new dialogue. The writers were also limited in what they could have these characters say, to avoid clashing with the movie or other *Alien* media. But what *is* in there nicely captures the spirit of the *Nostromo* crew. Tom Skerritt in particular effortlessly slips back into the role of Dallas. The VO directors also had to get some of the actors up to speed, reminding them of certain details about their characters. But come on, this is a job they did *thirty-six years ago.*

Anyway, when you're done exploring every nook and cranny of this cursed station, it's time to get the hell off it. Ripley makes her way back to the Habitation tower's transit system, which will take her back to where it all started: the spaceflight terminal. There's a lot of returning to previously visited locations in the final act of *Alien: Isolation*, but Creative Assembly manages to keep things varied and interesting by mixing up the atmosphere and enemy placement, making them feel both familiar and fresh at the same time.

But for some players and critics, by this point in the game – around the thirteen-hour mark – *Alien: Isolation* outstays its welcome. One of the most debated aspects of the game is its length and pacing, with some claiming it's overlong and too slow. Personally, and perhaps unsurprisingly given my love for the game, I've never agreed with this assessment. Admittedly, when I first started playing it for my PC Gamer review, I worried it might just be one long, gruelling game of hide-and-seek with a scarily powerful xenomorph.

But I was pleased to discover that it constantly mixes things up to keep you engaged: removing or adding parameters to the stealth, mixing up enemy types, and shifting between different or cleverly remixed environments. The alien is a constant threat, but the different layout of each area you face it in, the variety of gadgets you can use to distract or avoid it and its thrillingly dynamic AI means it never feels like you're just going through the motions.

And as for the pacing, well, it's a game based on a film that is itself incredibly slow. Those beautiful, lingering opening shots of the *Nostromo*'s empty corridors before the crew wakes up. The tense, drawn-out sequence with Dallas in the air vents. The fact that you don't see the creature itself for over an hour. This is what makes *Alien* such a powerful horror film, and I think Creative Assembly captured that feeling perfectly. *Isolation* is a game designed to be played, and savoured, at a steady, careful pace. It's a detailed, richly atmospheric world that demands to be absorbed and thoroughly explored.

'We felt like there was a good amount of variety in the game,' says director Alistair Hope in a post-launch interview with PC Gamer. 'We wanted to keep changing things up, so that just as you were getting a bit more confident we'd throw something new at you. We tried to put as much into the player's hands as possible, so the pace of the game can often be determined by your own play style and how confident you're feeling at any given moment.'

But with the end now in sight, *Alien: Isolation*'s pace is about to pick up significantly. Ripley has reconnected with the *Torrens*, and Verlaine is her last hope of escaping Sevastopol before it's consumed by KG-348. There's just the small matter of a horde of xenomorphs and gangs of increasingly desperate, heavily armed Seegson security guards getting in the way.

MISSION 17

Desolation
Homeward bound.

We need to get back to the spaceflight terminal, but the transit system in the Habitation tower has been powered down. 'We can't afford to keep our sanctuary wide open,' says Jake Sinclair, a former Seegson security officer turned desperate survivor, in an audio log. 'All it takes is one creature to get in and all the supplies and weapons we've taken will come to jack shit.'

This means we have to restore power to the transit system, which is no more complicated than interacting with a computer terminal in a server room.

Speaking of logs, *Alien: Isolation*'s writers always made sure the terminals told stories not just about what was currently happening on Sevastopol, but things that happened in the past. According to writer Will Porter in an interview with AvP Galaxy, his job was filling in the details 'around the edges' of the levels. 'Seegson Synthetics, for example, has the overlay of current events – the survivors, the alien, Ripley – but through our work, and that of the art team, you can also gauge what Seegson originally intended the area to be. If we did our job right, you'll always have an idea of where you are, what was intended for that facility, and what happened there as Sevastopol declined.'

Porter also littered his audio and text logs with modern concerns that will 'likely still be a going concern in the next century', to evoke a grounded sense of reality and create a vision of the future that felt convincing. There are references all over these logs, and the station itself, to health insurance, payday loans, gun ownership, home repossession, and other issues that the people of the future could still be debating and wrestling with, even in space.'

A lot of work also went into where and when certain logs would appear. Writer Dion Lay created a massive timeline of Sevastopol's history, and used that to make sure these hundreds of diaries, logs and other pieces of storytelling intersected logically. 'After that it was a case of weeding out any logs that were repetitions, shifting them along the timeline and rewriting when we realised there was a way to tie them closer to another log or story point,' says Lay. 'We then worked with the level designers to figure out where they should be placed, to make sure nothing was revealed too early.'

The sound of the system groaning back to life attracts an alien, leaving us trapped in the transit hub with it until the train arrives. Your first instinct is to duck into a nearby office to hide, but Creative Assembly plays a dirty trick here. Correctly predicting that players will hastily head for this room the moment the alien appears, a level designer thought it would be funny to hide a face-hugger under a stack of boxes. If you're ready for it, a well-timed swing of the maintenance jack will silently kill it. But a more common reaction is panic, flailing, maybe firing a gun and attracting the prowling xeno.

After what feels like an eternity, the train arrives and whisks Ripley away to the upper levels of the Habitation tower. Verlaine's voice crackles over the radio and tells her that the *Torrens* is in position, lining up with the severely decaying orbit of the station, waiting for her to extend the towing platform. 'I don't know how you sweet-talked me into this,' she says, trepidation in her voice, as Ripley presses on, besieged by the most persistent aliens yet.

While the creatures' AI is entirely dynamic, there are parts of the game where Creative Assembly step in and tweak its parameters to reflect the escalating tension of the story, forcing the more advanced behaviour nodes in their brains open. As a result, this is arguably the most stressful mission in the game. Every digital grey cell of the aliens' brains seem to be active and operating at maximum capacity, and on harder difficulty settings, getting through this chapter alive is a brutal test of skill, patience and mental fortitude.

In an interview with PCGamesN, lead designer Gary Napper talks about quietly 'balancing' the creature's behaviour at different points throughout the game. 'Although we do have an alien AI that ultimately utilises its senses and does what it wants when it's hunting, we can tweak the amount it hunts and the amount the player sees it,' he says. 'We have various values for these settings, and we almost have the alien in different flavours. This one's mild, this one's aggressive, this one is moderately intense, and so on.'

So if Creative Assembly decided a level would be better if the alien was in your face constantly – this mission being a prime example – they could ramp the AI up accordingly.

From the outset, the developers didn't want *Alien: Isolation* to be a theme park ride. 'We could have made it very heavily scripted with a lot of jump scares,' design lead Clive Lindop tells Video-Gamer. 'But by building this systemic entity, a creature that is reactive, we put players in a life or death struggle that is never predictable. It was a very risky thing to do, but it's something people always wanted from an *Alien* game.'

Creative Assembly's designers also realised, inspired by the movie, the importance of *not* showing the alien. In an interview with Video Games Uncovered, Gary Napper notes that 'the fear of absence, of *not* seeing the alien, is often a lot scarier than when you can actually see it. We're very specific about when players should see a lot of the alien, and when to instruct it to hold back. When it vanishes into the vents you jump at the shadows, not sure if it's the alien or not. You end up fearing everything around you.'

Ripley takes an elevator to the spaceflight terminal, but it malfunctions and grinds violently to a halt, forcing her to find an alternate route. We make our way along a wide corridor, only for the station to suddenly tilt to one side. 'Orbital stabiliser failure,' says a computerised voice. 'Abandon station.' The Working Joes operating in this part of the station are unconcerned with Sevastopol's imminent destruction and march after Ripley as she detours through a cafeteria, navigates a maze of corridors, dodges the alien and whacks the occasional screeching, lunging facehugger with her maintenance jack.

There are very few objectives in this mission, and even the world-building is stripped back – which is why this is one of the shorter entries in the mission guide so far. By design, it's not a level that tells any interesting stories or fleshes out the setting in any meaningful way: it's just pure, raw stealth.

This is Creative Assembly challenging you to take everything you've learned so far and use it against an alien with its tenacity and ferocity cranked up as far as it can possibly go. It's also a test of your resource management, because if you're low on flamethrower fuel or crafting materials, surviving is significantly tougher. The hoarders among you will be fine, but a less disciplined player might find themselves limping to the end with empty pockets.

Then Verlaine makes a big mistake. She broadcasts a message to the whole station saying the *Torrens* is about to dock at the towing platform and will take any survivors who need help. This is very nice of her, but remember, she has no idea what's been going on aboard Sevastopol all this time. As far as she knows there are innocent people stuck on the crashing station waiting for help – not violent Seegson security guards looking for skulls to crack, bloodthirsty Working Joes, deadly xenomorphs and scuttling facehuggers.

Then, after fifteen nightmarish hours of unspeakable horrors, near-death experiences, EVA mishaps, shootouts with looters and more gruesome deaths than we can count, we've come full circle. Ripley makes it back to the spaceflight terminal and uses her ion torch to cut through a sealed door, revealing the elevator to the towing platform. The end is in sight.

MISSION 18

Tomorrow, Together
Over and out.

Sevastopol is in bad shape. The stricken station is now on a permanent tilt, lending this final chapter a woozy, unsteady feel. As Ripley moves through the disintegrating structure, emergency lights flashing, fires blazing, steam choking the air, you can't help but think of her mother's frantic escape from the *Nostromo* at the end of *Alien*. Our final mission objective flashes up on the HUD, and it's a simple one: ESCAPE SEVASTOPOL. No shit.

Verlaine's voice barks from a speaker, reminding us of the urgency of the situation. 'Ripley, I am waiting for your signal! Do you read? We don't have much time. The station is falling apart!' Way to state the obvious, Diane. But there's something oddly comforting about hearing her voice amidst all this fiery devastation. The friends, acquaintances and uneasy allies Ripley had are all dead. The captain of the *Torrens* is all she has left.

Ripley is now close enough to Verlaine's ship to contact her by radio and lets her saviour know she's still alive. But there's one last engineering job to do: manually extending a pair of cradle clamps to allow the *Torrens* to dock with Sevastopol. They're nearby, but the station has become a mess of collapsed ceilings, exposed electrical wiring, burst pipes and twisted metal. Ripley squeezes past the debris, hacking a couple of terminals to extend the docking clamps. One is powered down, so we have to crawl into a nearby vent, yank a lever to restart a power generator, and bring it back online.

We use a terminal to engage the clamps and Verlaine instructs us to find the upper control room. Quite how the captain of a commercial transport ship knows so much about the functions and layout of a deep-space station is left unexplained, but who knows – maybe she worked on one before she saved up enough credits to buy her own vessel and quit the nine-to-five.

Ripley climbs a staircase and the station is jostled by KG-348's immense gravitational pull, shuddering and convulsing like some great, sick beast. We reach a control room, only to discover that Sevastopol's personnel umbilical – a device that allows passengers to be ferried safely from the station to ships docked with the station – is mysteriously missing. There's no way around it: we're gonna have to slap on *another* pressure suit and get our EVA on, using a maintenance rig to make our way over to the *Torrens*.

We find a log on a terminal from the day Sevastopol officially opened its doors. 'I can now confirm that all of Sevastopol systems are operational and our KG-348 orbit is no longer degenerative,' the anonymous author writes. 'My thanks to the tow team. We're open for business. Good luck, everyone.' There's something haunting about reading this optimistic message, written in happier times, as the station is being torn apart all around us. This terminal also has a record of the aforementioned personnel umbilical being removed as part of the station being decommissioned. Ripley can't catch a break.

Ripley makes a dash for a nearby airlock, and right on cue an alien decides to join Sevastopol's explosive farewell party. Creative Assembly have been holding them back, lulling us into a false sense of security, but now it's time for a last waltz with the perfect organism. The deafening cacophony of the station's destruction dramatically lessens our ability to track the alien by ear, making the motion tracker your best friend in this stretch of gameplay.

Reaching the airlock, Ripley opens a pressure-suit bay and begins to suit up. But subverting the cutscene we've gotten used to by now, something drips on the glass of the visor – a callback to the moment in mission two when the alien's drool dribbled on Axel's arm before it killed him. Ripley looks up, only to see a xenomorph emerge from the darkness of a vent in the ceiling. It grabs her, violently drags her away, and the screen fades to black.

But there's no fade up. Not immediately anyway. All we see is blackness, accompanied by a gross, organic, *squelchy* sound, before Ripley suddenly gasps for air and wakes up from her temporary slumber. We may have destroyed the main alien hive back in mission fourteen, but there's at least one more on Sevastopol, and we're currently cocooned in it. Before us we can see a cluster of leathery facehugger eggs and a corpse with a conspicuous hole in its chest. These xenomorphs aren't going to let a trifling matter like the imminent destruction of the station get in the way of spawning new drones.

Luckily, Ripley manages to break her arms free and drop back to the floor. I'm not sure exactly *how*. Maybe the resin hadn't fully hardened yet. Maybe she was just so determined to reach the *Torrens* she momentarily experienced a surge of strength, like those people who lift cars off others trapped under them.

Anyway, time to get back to that airlock. Only now we have to be careful around the unhatched eggs in the hive in case a facehugger decides to leap from one and give us the universe's deadliest French kiss. Between the encroaching hive and the station being slowly crushed like a giant tin can, this is the worst shape we've seen Sevastopol in yet. A long, smoke-filled corridor lined with the recognisable silhouettes of facehugger eggs is a particularly troubling gauntlet to run, but Ripley has no choice but to flamethrow her way through. At least some kind level designer has left a lot of fuel lying around.

We crawl through a long tunnel of shattered metal and gloopy hive resin, dodging facehuggers as they spring out of the rubble, and our reward is the sudden appearance of *two* aliens. *Alien: Isolation* only pulls this trick a couple of times – typical of the tasteful restraint of the developers – which makes the arrival of this terrible tag team even more impactful.

We make our way through the ruins of Sevastopol's transit system, moving through the burning wrecks of derailed trains and encountering dozens more eggs. Did the queen manage to escape the reactor purge? Or did she lay these before settling down in the main hive, where writer Will Porter confirmed she was lurking? It's hard to say, and honestly, who cares: we gotta get off this doomed scrapheap before KG-348 eats it for breakfast.

Ripley finds a service elevator and steps inside, only for it to snap free from its cables, fall down the shaft, and land with a bone-shuddering thump. We move into a nearby living space, and there's a nice tribute to some of *Alien*'s original creators down here. Pinned next to a bunkbed is a poster of a very seventies-looking singer with a leisure suit and oversized shades, and the name JEAN MOLLO printed beneath him – a reference to concept artist Jean 'Mœbius' Giraud and costume designer John Mollo. A cute detail, but let's not get distracted. Ripley climbs down a ladder and opens a door, getting a shock when an out-of-control transit car screeches past, inches away from her face.

She crosses the tracks, praying another train doesn't come speeding through. At one point we have to duck as one rumbles directly over our head. Then, while climbing down an elevator shaft, the ladder snaps and leaves us in a heap at the bottom. There's a great jump scare here (one of only a handful in the game) where it looks like an elevator is about to shake loose and land on us, before it grinds to a halt just above us. This station is *wrecked*.

Moving through a room dense with thick, lung-filling smoke, Ripley manages to get back in touch with Verlaine. 'Ripley, I thought I'd lost you,' the *Torrens'* incredibly patient captain says. 'We're being dragged down with Sevastopol! The gravitational pull has twisted the rig and we can't get free from the station!' To solve this problem, we're gonna have to get to an airlock, EVA over to a maintenance platform and trigger the emergency release.

We cycle the airlock and step outside, getting a nice look at the *Torrens* and its massive Saturn J-3000 engines, which are glowing white hot and ready to ignite as soon as we can free the ship from the station and, hopefully, get safely aboard. Ripley crosses a catwalk, helmet juddering as the station wrestles hopelessly against KG-348's gravitational might. Ripley takes an elevator over to the platform and begins to prime the release mechanisms. Looking up at the station's towers, we see explosions dancing across the surface like fireworks – and set against the display, the silhouette of a xenomorph.

Ignoring it, Ripley activates the device that will let her blow the emergency release bolts. This is an exact replica of the device Ellen Ripley used to activate the *Nostromo*'s self-destruct. Amanda even runs her finger across the instructions like her mother did. The pistons are just as slow too, and the tension of watching them rise is just as stressful as it is in the movie.

Then the aliens come out to play. A group of them approaches Ripley, but she manages to finish priming the emergency release. Before the creatures can attack, a blast sends us, and them, flying. We're treated to a cutscene showing the station being ripped to shreds, wreathed in flame, as it finally succumbs to the gas giant's gravity. A wide shot of KG-348 shows us a brief, bright blast on its surface, then silence. Goodbye, Sevastopol. You sucked.

Ripley, amazingly, is safe. She managed to grab hold of the freed *Torrens* and pull herself in through an airlock. 'Verlaine,' she says. 'I'm on my way up to the bridge.' No response. We make our way through the familiar corridors of the *Torrens*, remembering when we explored it all the way back in mission one. But our homecoming is cut short when a door opens and a xenomorph creeps out of it, hissing menacingly. We don't hear from Verlaine, but it's highly unlikely she's alive. Ripley backs away from the beast, holds her breath, and slams an airlock override button, jettisoning the alien and herself into space. It's a good thing we kept our pressure suit on when we arrived on the *Torrens*.

The next thing we see is Ripley floating in the darkness of space, an endless starfield surrounding her. She drifts away from the camera, slowly consumed by darkness, until a light suddenly catches the glass of her helmet. It was fifty-seven years before scrappers happened to chance upon Ellen Ripley and Jones in the *Nostromo's Narcissus* shuttle, triggering the events of *Aliens*. But it seems Amanda won't have to wait that long to be rescued.

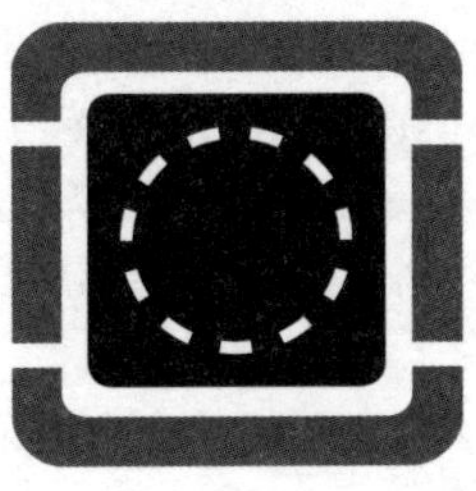

Cut Content

Alien: Isolation *could have been a very different beast.*

Around a year before *Alien: Isolation* was released, the game underwent extensive script rewrites. Entire chunks of story were ripped out, including a sequence set aboard the *Solace* – a small transport ship that had narrowly escaped the horrors unfolding on Sevastopol. In the final game, following the opening cutscene, we're on the *Torrens* briefly and then promptly dumped on Sevastopol. But before the rewrites, Verlaine's ship would pick up a distress call from the *Solace* and Ripley would be sent to investigate.

Ripley would board the ship and find it deserted – like a deep-space *Mary Celeste* – and the place would be frozen, presumably due to the failure of its life-support systems. Some early concept art of the *Solace* exists, created by Bradley Wright, which shows corridors crusted with ice and Ripley finding a frosted-over hypersleep pod with a body visible through broken glass. Exploring the ship, Ripley would discover that it was a floating coffin, full of the corpses of people who were desperately trying to get away from Sevastopol.

With no FTL drive and limited space, the unfortunate souls on the *Solace* planned to use its hypersleep chambers in shifts. But, listening to audio logs recorded by a man named Eisner, Ripley learns that the survivors turned violent. Then the power failed, plunging the ship into chaos. Ripley would then restore power, and the sudden thaw would have started tearing the ship apart, forcing her to make a hasty exit and get back to the safety of the *Torrens*. We would also have caught a glimpse, or seen some evidence, of a xenomorph – an early hint, perhaps, of what was waiting at our next destination.

This sequence sounds wonderfully atmospheric, and the idea of a ghost ship with a sci-fi twist is evocative, but it was reportedly cut for pacing reasons. Creative Assembly wanted to get Ripley on Sevastopol sooner, which makes sense. This detour wouldn't have added much to the story. However, the *Solace* sequence seems to have been repurposed at a later date – minus the frozen element – for Ripley's brief trip to the *Anesidora*. In fact, the *Anesidora*'s map file is still named 'SOLACE' in the finished game, and the *Anesidora* mission shares most of the same beats as the cut *Solace* excursion.

A *lot* was cut from *Alien: Isolation*, but this isn't unusual for a video game. These are massive, expensive creative endeavours – involving hundreds of people and taking years to build – and it's inevitable things are going to be altered, tweaked, re-evaluated or just downright ditched. But as an *Alien: Isolation* obsessive, the things that didn't make it into this particular video game are of special interest to me and other dedicated fans.

Lucky for us, heaps of scrap data were left in the game's files, providing an insight into what could have been. Pre-release footage also gives us an intriguing glimpse of how the game changed during its four-year development cycle. From this wealth of unused animations, script files, audio clips and other data never intended to be seen by players, we can paint a vivid and surprisingly complete picture of a version of *Alien: Isolation* that never existed.

In 2012, Creative Assembly was searching for a networking programmer to join the *Alien: Isolation* project – because, for a brief period, the game was going to feature multiplayer gameplay. However, following a review by Sega after *Aliens: Colonial Marines* had been savaged by critics and players alike, the feature was dropped. But there are still multiple traces of this abandoned multiplayer mode, or perhaps *modes*, in the game's files, including support for client-hosted game sessions and networked player entities with physics support.

Scripting nodes buried in the game's proprietary Cathode engine, discovered by *Alien: Isolation* modders, include 'NumConnectedPlayers', 'AllPlayersReady', SyncOnAllPlayers', and other indicators that this was, for a while, a game we could play alongside other people. Traces of a marking system, allowing players to ping things in the world and use preset communications, were also found, suggesting there may have been a co-op mode. These include phrases such as 'Wait', 'Use That', 'Thanks', 'Hurry Up', and 'Alien Spotted'.

As interesting as this is, I don't think *Alien: Isolation* needed multiplayer. This was a period in the games industry where every game had to have some kind of online component, in part to stop people from finishing the story and immediately trading their disc in. User retention was a big deal in the 2010s, which is how we ended up with multiplayer in games that didn't really fit it at all – *BioShock 2* being a prime example. The servers for these modes would usually be dead, or clinging on for dear life, just a few weeks after launch.

But an online feature I *am* sad to see cut is the so-called Memento Mori system. Inspired by FromSoftware's influential fantasy RPG *Dark Souls*, *Alien: Isolation* players would have, at one point, been able to leave spare items or messages in the world for other people playing the game. All that remains of this system is a backpack (the same one Ripley wears), which would have been a visual representation of these helpful player drops. It's a shame this didn't make it into the finished game, as it would have been a clever, subtle way to add an element of multiplayer cooperation to the experience. But I suppose it could have worked against the 'isolation' part of the game's title.

A side note about Ripley's backpack: an unused texture of Sonic the Hedgehog's head exists in the game data, which is from a keychain that once hung from the bag at some point during development. A 3D render of Amanda posted on ArtStation by 3D artist Ranulf Busby, who worked on *Alien: Isolation* as its lead character artist, gives us a good look at this in situ. But it was cut for whatever reason, which is probably for the best. It's a nice little nod to publisher Sega, but perhaps feels a little out of place in this setting.

Creative Assembly also experimented with a virtual-reality mode for *Alien: Isolation*, a demo for which was shown behind closed doors at various gaming conventions during development. Shortly before the game launched, however, Sega confirmed that the idea had been dumped. Still, an experimental version of it was left in the game's files – and could be easily accessed and played by anyone with an Oculus headset by tweaking a configuration file.

I tried this myself back in 2014, using PC Gamer's Oculus DK1 development kit. With its low-resolution display, high latency and narrow field of view, the first Oculus headset was primitive compared to the much more advanced tech we have now. But even with these technical limitations, and an experimental mode that didn't always work properly, *Alien: Isolation* in VR was still an utterly terrifying experience. If you think that nine-plus-foot tall alien is intimidating on your TV or monitor, imagine it turning and looking *right at you*.

Sega-owned studio HARDlight was reportedly working on *Alien: Isolation*'s VR mode, which would have been included as an extra and focused on a series of tailor-made side missions. But the project was in a state of limbo for a long time and never made it to full production. Even so, the developers at HARDlight had a great time working on the prototype – and from what I hear, got very good at figuring out just the right time to trigger a sound or a jump scare (like a steam pipe suddenly bursting) to really mess with players' heads.

Some unused audio logs have also been discovered, including: Axel suffering a hangover after an underwhelming-sounding decommissioning party; Taylor sending a message to Waits ahead of landing on Sevastopol about the significance of the flight recorder; Marlow sending the auto-dock signal to the *Anesidora*; and Heyst chewing out Meeks for getting drunk and attracting the attention of the Marshals. None of these add anything new or especially meaningful to the story, suggesting they were removed for pacing reasons or because they repeated information relayed elsewhere.

A number of locations didn't make it into the game either – some of which would have been home to important storylines before the script rewrites. Scattered fragments of these have been found in the game's data, and there's also a wealth of concept art (some of which can be found in the official *Alien: Isolation* art book) that gives us a tantalising look at what these unseen parts of Sevastopol, and beyond, might have looked like.

In *Alien*, Brett and Parker stress the importance of getting the *Nostromo* into dry dock so she can undergo major repairs. Well, at one point we were going to get to visit Sevastopol's dry docks, which would have been a large hangar-like structure housing the *Anesidora*. A piece of unused concept art shows the *Anesidora* docked, undergoing repairs and surrounded by power loaders – an iconic piece of hardware from *Aliens* that didn't make it into *Alien: Isolation*. I'm glad, though: they're such an intrinsic part of Cameron's sequel that seeing one in a game based on the original would have felt incongruous.

Ripley would have also visited a cooling plant and a waste management facility, located in the depths of Sevastopol's engineering decks. An early render by 3D concept artist Stefano Tsai shows a vast garbage chute, down which the tonnes of crap disposed of by Sevastopol's residents would have been tossed for recycling or incineration. But there's no solid evidence on why Ripley would have been down here, or what she would have done, leaving these cut locations something of a mystery. Based on scripts left in the game's files, it's likely the cooling plant would have been accessed while Ripley was down in the reactor core. Perhaps deactivating something there would have been an extra objective before purging the reactor and destroying the alien hive.

It's also likely that Creative Assembly intended players to visit Sevastopol's gravity anchors – which, based on the name, likely either generated the station's artificial gravity or kept it in a stable orbit around KG-348. If it's the latter, they were renamed gravity stabilisers in the finished game, probably to make their function clearer to the player. There's a great piece of concept art of this area, created once again by Bradley Wright, which shows an immense, claw-like structure jutting out of the bottom of the station with the gas giant glowing in the background. A complex catwalk system around the comms array has also been discovered in the game's files, with ladders connecting multiple floors, but none of these structures are ever accessed by the player.

Ripley's visit to the *Solace* wasn't the only major story beat removed during development. There's evidence of the existence of a prologue, before Ripley even sets foot on Sevastopol, featuring characters she eventually meets later in the game. Script files reveal that we would have seen Waits and the Marshals ejecting people from the spaceflight terminal; APOLLO tricking Hughes into shutting down outside communications; Kuhlman breaking into San Cristobal to remove a chestburster he'd apparently been impregnated with; Spedding investigating the Working Joes' strange behaviour; and an engineer named Jackson witnessing the alien brutally killing a colleague.

Some of these stories made it into the final game via text logs, audio logs and character dialogue; others were cut entirely. Whether this prologue was a cutscene, a series of playable sequences or something else entirely is currently unknown, but Creative Assembly must have had a very good reason for getting rid of so much *stuff*. One of *Alien: Isolation*'s weakest links story-wise is never really getting to know its characters, but it seems we might have spent a lot more time with some of them before the rewrites were started.

Alien: Isolation contains a few pre-rendered cutscenes, usually reserved for dramatic story beats like the EVA going awry at the beginning of the game, which were produced by British animation studio Axis Animation. But there were originally many more cutscenes, which fell victim, like so many other things in this section, to those script rewrites. Digging through the game data gives clues as to what some of these could have been.

These cutscenes included the crew of the *Torrens* encountering the *Solace*, Ransome forcing Lingard to perform an autopsy on Foster to recover a sample of the xenomorph, various characters speaking to each other via videolink (rather than by radio, which is the most common form of communication in the finished game) and Verlaine attempting to dock with Sevastopol.

It seems there was a time when the narrative would jump around a lot more, showing characters in other parts of the station, or aboard the *Torrens* or *Anesidora*, separate from Ripley's adventures. But it must have been decided, perhaps as a result of the rewrites, that it was better to see everything (not including Marlow's chapter) through Ripley's eyes and leave what was happening elsewhere on Sevastopol more of a mystery. Whether this change was for practical or stylistic reasons, I think it was the right call. Not knowing exactly what's going on while inhabiting the role of Ripley adds immeasurably to the game's sense of isolation, horror and mystery – even if it does leave the story feeling a little thin at times.

There's also a hint buried deep in the game's files that there may have been a third part to Marlow's LV-426 flashback. In the game, we explore the surface of the planetoid then venture into the derelict. These maps are named BSP_LV426_PT01 and BSP_LV426_PT02 respectively, but there's also a reference to an unused (and, sadly, as yet undiscovered) BSP_LV426_PT03. With so much concept art in the official *Alien: Isolation* art book of the interior of the *Anesidora*, it's likely Creative Assembly planned to show us the aftermath of the discovery of the egg chamber; perhaps the crew returning to the ship with a gruesomely face-hugged Foster, and Meeks channelling Ellen Ripley and arguing against breaking quarantine protocols to bring her aboard.

It's also likely a visit to a second, larger hive, was planned. Based on unused script files, it seems Ripley would stumble upon a hive that was considerably bigger than the one that made it into the final game, and with a very different layout. There are some striking pieces of concept art in *The Art of Alien: Isolation* showing a vast hive with enormous, tree trunk-like organic formations snaking around the reactor facility. In the final game the hive is almost entirely composed of tight, resin-clogged corridors, but based on this art, Creative Assembly may have had bigger plans for the aliens' nest. In an unused line of dialogue, Ripley says to Ricardo: 'Can you imagine what would happen if this thing got loose in one of the colonies?' We would, of course, see exactly that in *Aliens*.

A YouTube video titled 'Alien: Isolation – Dialogue Uncut', created by GalaxyTraveler, restores a vast amount of deleted dialogue and cleverly edits it back into the game. With only a folder full of contextless audio files to work with, they had to guess where these lines were supposed to be triggered. But even with this limitation, they did a seriously impressive job of slotting them in pretty much seamlessly. If you've played a lot of *Alien: Isolation*, it's a strange sensation seeing familiar scenes recut with new or alternate dialogue.

Ripley doesn't say much in the final game, but she was originally a *lot* chattier. In a lot of modern AAA games, the protagonist will endlessly talk to themselves, commenting pointlessly on everything they do – and, surprisingly, *Alien: Isolation* was once guilty of this. 'Maintenance panel,' Ripley says when confronted with a blocked door. 'Plasma torch will cut through that.' Then, later, searching for a way out of a level: 'That's gotta be the exit up ahead.' She also has a few more lines when you find the motion tracker, spelling out to the player what it is and how it functions. 'Someone's moving,' she says as a Working Joe creeps up behind her and the tracker bleeps in response, which is one of the finished game's best scares. 'Okay, useful.'

This adds nothing to the moment. In fact, it kinda ruins it. The final scene is much more subtle and chilling when what's going on is left unspoken, and that Joe appears with no fanfare. Luckily, it seems Creative Assembly realised this and *massively* reduced Ripley's monologue at some point during development. Having her constantly muttering to herself, stating the obvious, would have had a negative impact on the game's atmosphere.

Some conversations used to be longer too. When Ripley and

Axel meet a pair of survivors in an elevator, the conversation is bitter and brief. But there were once more lines here. 'I'm Relf,' the woman says. 'Freight coordinator. This is Dinsky, ops and cargo.' The man is annoyed. 'Don't need to give them our damn life stories. Who are you?' To which Axel responds, 'I'm John, this is Paul. George and Ringo are right behind us carrying the fucking drum kit.'

Speaking of Axel, he has a lot more barks relating to how you play, to the point where it's just annoying. 'You're a fucking liability!' he shouts angrily if you sprint. 'I know, I'm beautiful, but you're getting creepy' if you stand too close to him. 'Stop pissing about!' if you move away from the prescribed path. They did us all a favour by shutting him and other characters up. The sparse, minimal dialogue in the finished game is one of its greatest strengths.

It's clear *Alien: Isolation* was on the receiving end of some pretty significant cuts, and it makes you wonder what exactly inspired Creative Assembly and/or Sega to change so much of the game. Could the poor reception of *Aliens: Colonial Marines* have been a factor? If the two projects had any elements in common, maybe the publisher thought *Alien: Isolation* should veer off in a completely different direction to distance itself from Gearbox's maligned shooter. There is a very basic animation test buried in *Isolation*'s files showing an *Aliens*-era Colonial Marine jogging with a pulse rifle, so maybe in one version of the story the grunts were called in to deal with the outbreak on Sevastopol. Or this could have just been a placeholder model used by an animator.

Whatever the case, as an *Alien: Isolation* fan I'm delighted this treasure trove of cut material has been discovered. Who knows, maybe one day someone – using Matt Filer's incredible Open-CAGE modding software, perhaps – will be able to restore some of this cut content and make it playable again. Some of the developers might not be too pleased with people digging up and parading unfinished, unpolished work around. But I'm sure some of them are happy that these abandoned story elements, locations, animations and other ephemera haven't been lost forever. The *Alien: Isolation* fanbase certainly is.

Alien Revisited

Back to the Nostromo.

Early in *Alien: Isolation*'s development, as part of their efforts to back-engineer the aesthetic of the film, Creative Assembly deconstructed the *Nostromo* set and digitally rebuilt it. This involved recreating recognisable sections of the ship, which got them thinking: what if they could let players walk around this iconic location? 'Then you wonder what it'd be like to face the original alien there,' says director Alistair Hope in an interview with PC Gamer. '*Then* you wonder if you can get the original cast together to reprise their roles and play out some of those scenarios again – which we did.'

Sigourney Weaver had been approached many times to star in video games over the years but had always resisted. Ellen Ripley had appeared in video games before, but only in the most rudimentary form – and, crucially, without the involvement of Weaver. Yet Creative Assembly convinced her to not only act in a video game, but also to revisit the most important character of her career. 'This one was different,' she says in a *Guardian* interview. 'It had so much story and so much character. Emotional, but a visceral experience too.'

She was impressed that the game seemed to have some substance to it and wasn't just another shoot-'em-up set in the *Alien* universe. It wasn't just a game about fighting an alien; it had a story to tell too. 'It's taking inspiration from that first, very powerful experience that Ridley Scott put together,' she says in an interview with Yogscast. 'It really puts you in that world.'

Weaver was also won over by Creative Assembly's attention to detail in recreating the movie's sets. 'It was spooky being back there!' she tells the *Guardian*. 'I spent so much time as a young actor in those corridors, and I was constantly wandering around thinking, gosh, they've built all these wonderful sets for us. But yes, the game really took me back there, and I loved seeing Ridley's humorous, bizarre little touches, like all the odd little toys and gizmos lying around the place. It seemed like a real labour of love.'

Ellen Ripley's daughter Amanda being the protagonist was also instrumental in Weaver's decision to be a part of *Alien: Isolation*. Weaver loved the idea of the daughter she'd never get to see again going into space and following in her footsteps. 'It was very touching,' she tells Yogscast. 'I was surprised, actually, by how much that resonated for me.' A scene in *Aliens* revealing the existence of Amanda Ripley was deleted for pacing reasons, and Weaver was reportedly furious that this crucial aspect of her character was lost. So it's not difficult to see why it being revisited in *Isolation* appealed to her.

With each successive *Alien* movie, Ellen Ripley evolved as a character – culminating in a basketball-dunking clone, Ripley 8, in *Alien Resurrection*. But for *Alien: Isolation*, Weaver had to put herself back in the late seventies and channel the original, less experienced version of the character. 'I think I underestimated the connection I had to her,' says Weaver. 'When I sat down in the booth in the sound studio and looked at the text, Ripley just came out. I didn't realise how much she was imprinted in my DNA, lurking in the wings waiting to come out again. Working on the game was a very rich experience.'

But Ellen Ripley was only one member of the *Nostromo* crew, and Creative Assembly managed to convince most of the original cast to revisit characters they played thirty-five years previously. Yaphet Kotto returned as Parker, the *Nostromo*'s chief engineer; Tom Skerritt as captain Dallas; Veronica Cartwright as navigation officer Lambert; and Harry Dean Stanton as technician Brett. John Hurt did not return, sadly, and executive officer Kane doesn't appear in the game at all. Ian Holm lent his likeness to the game for science officer Ash, but not his voice, which was mimicked by Dave B. Mitchell. When Alistair Hope shared the news with the studio that they'd secured recording time with Weaver and the rest of the cast, the office exploded with claps and cheers.

Creative Assembly didn't have long with the actors, and some of them were pretty rusty, so there isn't as much of them in the game as fans might have hoped. Their main contribution was a series of *Nostromo* logs – optional collectibles hidden in the game – as well as a few lines of dialogue, and some more audio logs, in the Crew Expendable and Last Survivor bonus missions, originally released as DLC for the game.

But the real highlight of the cast reunion is undoubtedly Ellen Ripley's heartfelt message to Amanda, which we find at the end of mission fifteen. Sigourney Weaver's performance is superb, and there's something incredibly moving about this mother speaking to her daughter while drifting in a lifeboat in the depths of space, wondering if she'll ever get to hear her message.

This is both a reward for *Alien* fans – the thrill of being reunited with Ellen Ripley after all these years – and the closure Amanda has been so desperately seeking. It's immensely cathartic, and hearing Weaver's voice always has me dreaming of her starring in another *Alien* movie. Whether that will happen remains to be seen, but I'm glad Creative Assembly found a way to reconnect this legendary actor with her most legendary character.

BONUS MISSION 1

Crew Expendable
A cornered beast.

Crew Expendable is the first of two bonus missions set during the events of *Alien*. They loosely follow plot beats from the movie but deviate enough – in the interests of gameplay – to be considered non-canon. Think of them as 'what if' scenarios, giving you a glimpse of how things might have played out differently aboard the *Nostromo*. They're pretty short, only amounting to around forty minutes of new gameplay. But the chance to explore the familiar corridors of that iconic ship, and spend time with members of the original cast, makes the experience something of a dream come true for *Alien* fans.

This mission opens with a recreation of a famous shot from the movie. The camera moves along a curved, padded corridor lit by fluorescent strip lights, then into the *Nostromo*'s hypersleep chamber. Then we cut to the circular table in the lounge area – complete with drinking bird – where Ripley, Lambert, Parker, Ash and Dallas are coming up with a plan to trap the alien and jettison it out of an airlock. Chronologically, this mission seems to be set just after the death of Brett, who we never see alive in these missions.

In 2014, I wrote an article for the PC Gamer website directly comparing the game's depiction of the USCSS *Nostromo* to how it appears in *Alien*. I took close-up screenshots of doors, computer terminals, corridors, pressure suits and so on, then placed them side-by-side with movie screenshots. While I did notice a few small variations – some lights being a different colour, doors being a slightly different shape, and some areas of the ship looking a little too clean – in general, this replica of the *Nostromo* is stunningly well-observed.

'Whatever it was, it was big,' says Yaphet Kotto, stepping back into the role of chief engineer Parker. 'You're sure it took him into the air shaft?' says Tom Skerritt as captain Dallas. 'Disappeared into one of the cooling ducts,' replies Sigourney Weaver as Ellen Ripley, whose voice doesn't seem to have changed at all since 1979. It's surreal hearing these characters speaking to each other decades later. Even though some of their voices sound a little older (thirty-five years will do that to a person), you really do believe you're hanging out with the crew of the *Nostromo* again. Not only that, but you get to *play* as them too.

Dallas decides that if they can get the alien to follow someone through the main air vent, they can lure it to the airlock and blast it out into space. 'Who gets to go into the vent?' asks Lambert, played by Veronica Cartwright, which is when you get to decide who volunteers for this risky job. You can play as Ripley, Parker or Dallas, and while this decision doesn't have any impact on how the mission actually plays out, it does alter the dialogue slightly.

The character select screen gives us a nice close-up look at the character models, and Creative Assembly did an amazing job replicating the movie's costumes. The likenesses of the cast are pretty good too, with an exaggerated, almost caricature-like quality that seems to prioritise capturing the essence of the actor in question rather than making a perfect copy.

Select a character and we get another recreated shot from the movie, of the camera sweeping across the bridge of the *Nostromo*. These shots don't really serve a narrative purpose, and I feel like it's just Creative Assembly showing off how well they recreated the movie's sets. Honestly, fair enough. The fact they can perform almost exactly the same handheld camera movements in these virtual spaces hammers home just how much they nailed it.

Your first job, whoever you decide to play as, is gathering your equipment: a flamethrower, motion tracker, maintenance jack, medkit and flare. Mozart's 'Eine kleine Nachtmusik' warbles from a stereo in the lounge as Lambert sits alone, probably wondering how she ended up in this mess. Ash can be found lurking ominously in the medical bay, with Kane's recently detached facehugger curled up on a table next to him. He notes that the creature stalking the ship is 'extremely adaptable', with a hint of awe in his voice.

It's worth exploring this part of the ship before descending into the lower decks and starting the mission. There are a few audio logs lying around – and elsewhere in the level – letting you hear more from the crew of the *Nostromo*. These are presented as personal logs recorded during the events of the movie, as the characters try to make sense of what they discovered on LV-426, what happened to Kane and what will happen to them next.

'We should never have landed on this damn ball,' says Brett, played by the late, great Harry Dean Stanton. There's a great clip of him in an *Alien: Isolation* promo video, shocked to learn that he first played this character three decades ago.

But one log, recorded by Ash, is of particular note. 'This is an official record in the ship's log of my actions today,' he says. 'A member of the crew was compromised by an unknown creature. I made the decision to allow him back on board without following established quarantine procedure. Looking at the bigger picture, I feel comfortable with this decision.' This is nothing we don't already know from watching the movie, but it's interesting hearing the justification coming directly from Ash, in his own words.

Ash is the last person you see before we climb down a ladder into the bowels of the ship. 'Good luck,' he says. 'I'm closing the hatch behind you.' An innocuous line, but an eerie one for a player who knows his true identity and what he does later in the story. Down in B deck, we have to avoid the roaming alien and seal a series of hatches to guide it towards the main air vent. A nice touch here is the appearance of the motion tracker, which is modelled after the bulkier jury-rigged one seen in the movie, albeit with the more advanced *Aliens*-inspired readouts like from the tracker Amanda finds on Sevastopol.

As we seal the hatches, we see Brett's body slumped against a wall: the only time he physically appears in the DLC. Then, with all escape routes cut off, it's time to lead the alien into the primary air shaft – recreating the famously scary moment in the movie where a flamethrower-toting Dallas is trapped in the ship's ventilation system with the creature. Ash contacts us by radio telling us he can connect to the airlock systems remotely and will flush the alien out of the ship. Well, that's the *plan*. We all know what Ash is up to.

Watching Dallas inching his way cautiously through the vents is one of *Alien*'s most heart-stopping moments, and actually *being* there ramps the tension up even more – to an almost unbearable degree. This is one of those sequences that made me glad the planned VR version of *Alien: Isolation* never saw the light of day. However, in the game we don't die horribly in this steel labyrinth and instead manage to make it to the C deck airlock. This is an example of how these DLC missions take events from the movie and remix them.

We access a terminal and give Ash control of the airlock system. He primes it and tells us to wait for the creature to enter the outer chamber, where we can then close it in and end this nightmare. Yeah, *right*. The moment the alien enters the airlock, an alarm sounds and scares it away. This recreates a deleted scene from the movie where Ash intentionally sets an alarm off to scare the creature away from the airlock, as part of his secret mission to protect the creature for his Weyland-Yutani masters. The alien knocks Parker unconscious as it panics and flees, which is exactly what happens to your character here.

The last thing we see is Ash looming over us. 'Looks like we're back to square one,' he says. 'I need to consult with MU-TH-UR.' The mission ends with another roaming handheld shot, this time of the medical bay, and our android antagonist reciting his famous death speech from the movie. 'You still don't understand what you're dealing with, do you? Perfect organism.'

BONUS MISSION 2

Last Survivor
The final countdown.

This next bonus mission jumps forward in time, following Ripley as she attempts to activate the *Nostromo*'s self-destruct system and get off the ship. The first thing we see is the MU-TH-UR computer interface from the movie, into which Ripley types an inquiry: EVALUATION OF POTENTIAL PROCEDURES TO ESCAPE NOSTROMO. We don't see MU-TH-UR's answer, but after a cut to black, Ripley knows exactly what has to be done. 'We're going to blow up the ship and take our chances in the shuttle,' she says to Parker and Lambert, the only remaining crew.

But before we can do anything, we need to find coolant for the shuttle's air support system. Otherwise it'll be a real short trip.

The mission begins properly with Ripley aboard the docked *Narcissus* shuttle, and the level of detail and accuracy in the design and construction of its interior is some of Creative Assembly's most impressive environmental work. We head towards Parker and Lambert's location to help them find the coolant, but before we reach them, we hear them being brutally killed off-camera by the alien. Their anguished screams are highly unsettling, and kudos to Yaphet Kotto and Veronica Cartwright for shrieking with absolute gusto.

We make our way through the warren-like industrial maze that is C deck, stumbling upon the bloody, freshly eviscerated corpses of our ill-fated crewmates. Ripley is understandably distressed, but there's nothing she can do for them. We need to blow this damn ship up, *fast*, and to do so we need to lift a pesky lockdown that is preventing us from reaching the self-destruct control system. Ripley grabs a keycard from Parker's body and delves deeper into engineering while being actively hunted by the alien.

There are no difficulty options for these DLC missions, which can make them quite tricky for anyone who played through the main game on a lower setting. The alien is especially aggressive and relentless, rarely disappearing into vents to give you a moment of respite. Difficulty-wise, the creature's AI in these missions is equivalent to playing through the story on hard.

Ripley locates a terminal and lifts the lockdown, slips into a vent, and makes her way to the self-destruct console. There are some more audio logs scattered around in this level, which again describe events we see in the movie from the perspective of the *Nostromo* crew. Dallas talks about leaving Ash to decide what to do with the dead facehugger ('anything science is his department'), Parker laments the sorry state of the ship following the sketchy landing on LV-426 ('Dallas made the call to leave before we could finish repairs') and Ash talks about Ripley being close to discovering the truth about Special Order 937: the order to retrieve the xenomorph specimen at all costs.

There's a nice piece of connective tissue with the main game in a log recorded by Ripley. 'Dallas, have you approved my request yet?' she says. 'I haven't seen any movement on it. If we can send out work logs via Sevastopol's relay, surely we can send out a couple of personal messages too? Just take the cost out of my salary. I just want to let my daughter know that I'll be home late. It's important.' She never did get to send that message out, but at least Amanda eventually hears it via the *Nostromo*'s recovered flight recorder in mission fifteen.

The self-destruct system is another wonderfully recreated prop from the movie, accurate down to the instructions – on which, especially when watching *Alien* in 4K, you can actually see brush strokes from where the art team painted it. Mirroring the movie, Ripley goes through the complicated, laborious activation process, giving her just ten minutes to escape the *Nostromo*. Emergency lights flash, sirens wail, and steam bursts from vents, creating a sense of chaos and urgency – a disorientating trick borrowed from the movie that Creative Assembly pulls many, many times in the main game.

In *Alien*, Ripley is not alone. She's carrying a cat carrier designed by Ron Cobb (there's some excellent concept art of this), containing the ship's cat, Jones. Alas, her feline friend is nowhere to be found in this mission. In fact, the only cat we encounter in the entire game is the distant meowing we hear back in mission two of Amanda's adventure. It seems a shame to leave Jones, a survivor in his own right, out of the story. But cats in video games weren't as much of a big deal back in 2014 as they are now. If *Alien: Isolation* was developed now, Jones would definitely be in it. He might even get his own bonus mission.

Ripley makes her way back to the *Narcissus*, the alien hot on her heels. As in the movie, she comforts herself by singing 'You Are My Lucky Star' from *Singin' in the Rain* – which was, reportedly, something Sigourney Weaver came up with while filming the scene. It's a tender human moment, in stark contrast with the ear-piercing sirens assaulting our ears as we dash to the exit.

We make it back to the *Narcissus*, and . . . that's it. In the movie

Ripley has her final showdown with the alien, which tries to smuggle itself aboard the shuttle, but the game skips past this and all we get is a fade to black. Ripley logs her final report and we see a computer screen – data from the *Nostromo* flight recorder – tracking the shuttle as it drifts out of range, finally disappearing into the depths of space. But, as a final bittersweet treat, we get an extra line of dialogue. 'I'll see you soon, Amanda. Be a good girl. I love you.'

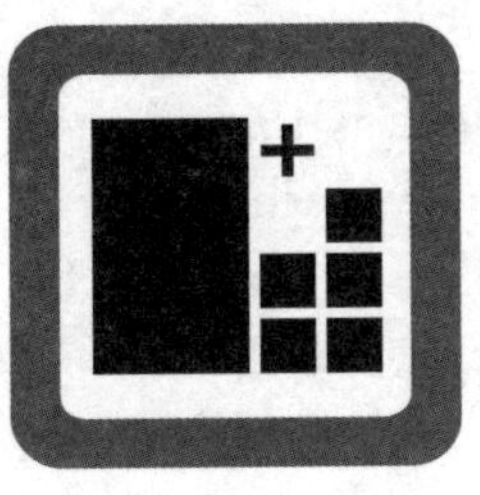

The DLC

Other perspectives on the Sevastopol incident.

As Ripley explores Sevastopol, she encounters a few interesting characters but she only catches fleeting glimpses of their lives. These include Seegson exec Ransome, communications manager Hughes, survivor Axel, chief medical officer Lingard, and deputy Marshal Ricardo – all of whom are playable in *Alien: Isolation*'s somewhat divisive post-launch downloadable content.

Five map packs were released for the game's Survivor mode, a series of competitive single-player challenges with a focus on pure stealth, point scoring and gameplay mastery over atmospheric storytelling.

While it would have been nice to continue the story of Amanda Ripley – especially after *that* cliffhanger – these maps do at least let us explore new parts of Sevastopol and see what other people were getting up to while Amanda was dealing with her own nightmare. Survivor mode is for people who really love the core gameplay of *Alien: Isolation* and want more opportunities to test themselves against the alien. It strips the stealth, action, evasion and distraction aspects of the game down to their most fundamental core and implements a scoring system so you can put a number on your skills.

It also encourages *fast* play, which for me is the antithesis of why I love this game. Start a Survivor map and your score is constantly ticking down, urging you to complete objectives as quickly as possible. You can earn points back by tackling bonus objectives, but even then, speed is key. I'm someone who plays *Alien: Isolation* as slowly and methodically as possible, immersing myself in the world and being very careful around the alien. That's why I've never really enjoyed this mode, and rarely revisit it in repeat playthroughs.

It's almost arcade-like. I know people who really enjoy throwing themselves at the alien in this way and have spent hours honing their skills on these maps. The difficulty is fixed, just like in Crew Expendable and Last Survivor, and the alien's aggression and sensitivity are cranked up pretty high. If you're bad at stealth, or find *Alien: Isolation* too tense, this is not the mode for you. There's no breathing room here, no moments of respite. It's *relentless*.

And the only way to get good at these levels is playing them over and over (and over) again, memorising the layout of the maps, the best places to hide, and escape routes. Making these mental maps involves a lot of trial and error, and even more deaths at the claws of the alien, which means only the most dedicated players will ever finish them or see everything in them.

But for those of us who are in it for the story, setting and characters, it does at least have something to offer. Each map is played through the eyes of the aforementioned Sevastopol residents, and there are some small hits of narrative that come from this shift in perspective. Don't expect to play these levels and be inundated with lots of rich new storytelling that really fleshes out the station and its residents. It's pretty thin, all told. Even so, if you really must squeeze every morsel out of the game, they're worth a shot.

DLC MISSION 1

Corporate Lockdown
Every man for himself.

In this mission we step into the no doubt expensive designer shoes of Ransome, the slimy Seegson suit whose greed, lack of morals and flagrant disregard for human life we learn about in the main game via audio and terminal logs. I like how Creative Assembly lets us play as a character like this in the DLC, because even the biggest assholes on Sevastopol have a story to tell.

The first map, Severance, sees Ransome covering his tracks and deleting any trace of his involvement with the xenomorph outbreak. Ransome, you may remember, was determined to capture a sample of the creature and return it to Weyland-Yutani in order to secure a well-paying job with Seegson's biggest rival. This only escalated the situation on Sevastopol, however, and now he's making sure, with a little help from us, that no one finds out about his evil schemes.

The level starts in Ransome's luxury penthouse, located in the upper levels of the Solomons Habitation Tower. This is an area of the station we don't get to visit in the main game, and it gives us an insight into what life is like there for the privileged and wealthy. In contrast with most of the station, the suite is cosy and spacious, with a big, comfy-looking bed, soft furnishings and a tasteful rug. Life in deep space isn't all bad if you can afford a place like this.

Ransome evades the alien and deals with some lunging facehuggers, deleting server records and disabling security cameras. One of the more striking locations in this part of the level is a cinema, with a big screen – currently broken, flickering and displaying a test card – and rows of armchairs. These rooms feel very different from the areas Amanda visits, and they're so fully formed that I wonder if this map is actually a story level that was cut.

Then it's onto the next map, Scorched Earth, which takes place in the San Cristobal Medical Facility. Ransome steals copies of chief medical officer Lingard's research files and hides evidence that he's been blackmailing people. 'Waits, I think you should read these,' says Lingard in a message to the Marshal Bureau. 'It's an archive of every log I could get my hands on where Ransome has blackmailed or threatened someone. There's evidence here that he stole samples of the incident from my lab. I'm watching people die and all he's thinking about is how to spin a profit.' Ransome reads this, then deletes it.

After an explosion rocks the medical facility – the source of which we'll witness first-hand in the next mission – Ransome escapes to Seegson Communications via an elevator, which is detached from its cables and lands with a crash. But before we leave, there's a bonus objective to save a civilian from a burning room. This seems very out of character for Ransome, but perhaps it's to show that he has *some* trace of humanity still left in him.

Ransome's last objective – in the final map, Loose Ends – is disrupting communications and securing a *Nostromo* log for Weyland-Yutani, recorded by Ellen Ripley. 'There's something loose on this ship,' she says, speaking during the events of *Alien*, shortly after the chestburster incident. 'It came out of Kane. We just ejected his body out into space. I don't know how Ash missed this thing on the medical scans, it would have been visible.' Ransome thinks he can use this log as a bargaining chip to get on the *Torrens* and escape. He steps onto an elevator and the mission ends, leaving his fate a mystery.

It's highly unlikely Ransome survived. Even if he somehow made it into the *Torrens*, the presence of an alien there suggests he would've been killed by it. If not, he would have died when the station plunged into KG-348. However, considering how many deaths he was responsible for, it's hard to feel sympathy. He's the archetypal *Alien* antagonist: a person who values money above all, no matter how many innocent lives are lost in the pursuit of it.

DLC MISSION 2

Trauma
The doctor is in.

This time we're playing as Lingard, Sevastopol's chief medical officer – a character who features heavily in The Outbreak. In that mission, she reveals in an audio log that Ransome had been black-mailing her to gain access to the xenomorph gestating inside Catherine Foster. She attempted to remove the creature surgically, but the chestburster exploded out of Foster's body and fled, eventually growing into one of the drones that stalked Sevastopol.

In Trauma's first map, Reoperation, we learn that Lingard has been camping out in a safe part of the station with a group of survivors, but supplies are running out. She bravely decides to return to the San Cristobal Medical Facility, also hoping to destroy her research into the xenomorph. She's somehow aware that an unknown intruder has been stealing it – which we now know, based on our escapades in the previous DLC mission, was Ransome.

Lingard finds San Cristobal in a sorry, graffiti-strewn state, avoids the alien and gathers boxes of life-saving medical supplies. One of my favourite new locations in this mission is the children's ward, where a spinning night light casts silhouettes of stars, moons and space rockets across the room. This, and the butterflies painted on the walls, give you an evocative sense of what everyday life was like on the station before the outbreak.

Keep your eyes peeled and you'll catch a glimpse of Ransome in the upper levels of the facility looking for her research to steal – a clue that Corporate Lockdown and Trauma both take place simultaneously. Lingard then initiates an emergency hazard cleanse, triggering the explosion we got caught in as Ransome in the previous mission. I do appreciate how Creative Assembly went to the effort of connecting these storylines, when they could easily just have presented us with a bunch of contextless Survivor mode maps.

A terminal log gives us an insight into what life is like in Lingard's survivor camp. 'Everyone is responsible for the safety of the camp,' it reads. 'We have all lost loved ones and colleagues through stupid mistakes and inexperience.' A system of identification involving a manifest and ID tags is then described, to make sure anyone who doesn't belong in the camp doesn't slip in. Paranoia and a general fear of strangers is a major issue on Sevastopol, as Ripley experiences first-hand when most of the people she meets try to kill her.

The next map, Crawl Space, gives us a break from the alien. Lingard takes a detour through an air shaft, thinking it'll keep her safe, only to find a bunch of facehuggers lurking in the ducts. She toasts them with a conveniently placed flamethrower and stumbles upon a hive. Between this, the big one in the reactor core, and the one Ripley gets briefly trapped in towards the end of the main game, it seems there are a lot of nests on Sevastopol.

The final map, Overrun, sees Lingard returning to the camp with the supplies, only to find the inhabitants dead and the place crawling with Working Joes. The camp is located in the Josiah Sigg Executive Apartments: the 'sanctuary' that is mentioned in numerous logs in the main game. These living spaces are modest compared to the lavish, spacious penthouses inhabited by Ransome and the other higher-ups, with simple bunk-style beds and basic amenities. But it's still the height of comfort compared to the rest of the station.

These apartments seem to be named after Josiah Sieg, founder and CEO of the corporation that would eventually become Seegson. But for whatever reason, his name is spelled incorrectly in this level. Perhaps the name was changed at some point during development, and this was just an oversight from the developers. It's strange that no one noticed it – or maybe they did, and they just didn't have time to fix it. Whatever the case, it's a pretty glaring error.

I like the black and orange padded corridors here, which gives the executive apartments a touch of added luxury. It's a visual motif we don't see anywhere else on the station and reinforces the divide between Sevastopol's downtrodden working class and the elite executives who manage them.

Lingard sneaks past the Working Joes – including a few of the tougher, more resilient hazmat suit-wearing variety – and collects the manifest mentioned in the terminal log. She makes her way to an elevator and flees the camp, leaving her fate ambiguous. It's likely she died along with everyone else when the station was destroyed, but who knows: she might have found a way to escape while Ripley was dealing with her own problems.

DLC MISSIONS 3/4

Safe Haven & Lost Contact
Pure survival.

I've bundled these missions together because in terms of storytell-ing and world-building they have very little to offer. The maps were designed with Salvage mode in mind; a twist on Survivor mode that involves completing multiple stages of objectives in the same level. The maps are a lot bigger, and after each stage the player has to return to a safe house.

The difficulty also ramps up gradually as you complete stages, throwing more enemies at you: Working Joes, humans and even-tually the alien itself. Survivor mode and its points system already felt distractingly arcade-like at times, but with enough narrative elements to keep the story-minded player engaged. Salvage mode, however, doesn't make any effort to hide the fact that it's focused purely on gameplay, and it feels a little shallow as a result.

There are no audio logs, no new terminal logs, and nothing in the way of interesting environmental storytelling. It would have been nice to learn more about the ill-fated Hughes, whose head we see being violently bashed against a wall by a Working Joe in mission four, Seegson Communications.

The first Salvage map, Safe Haven, is set before the events of the main game. Communications officer Hughes explores the Bac-chus Apartments and Gemini Exoplanet Solutions, avoiding danger and gathering supplies. The idea is that, as chaos begins to grip the station, Hughes embarks on a mission to stockpile food, ammo and meds in order to protect himself and his family.

Later, Hughes would bravely venture into Seegson Communi-cations, which was crawling with murderous androids, in an attempt to restore external comms with the outside world and send for help. He didn't make it far, though. Ripley witnesses his brutal death and that's the end of his story.

The next Salvage mode map, Lost Contact, stars Axel Fielding – the sarcastic Scottish survivor who teams up with Ripley in mission two, Welcome to Sevastopol. But in terms of narrative, it's even flimsier than Safe Haven. Axel is simply surviving in the station. This does at least give us an insight into what he was up to before he encountered Ripley. In the main game we get the sense that he's a hardened survivor, well versed in the madness of Sevastopol, and I suppose this difficult mission is the evidence of that.

DLC MISSION 5

The Trigger
An explosive revelation.

Thankfully, this collection of Survivor mode maps falls more in line with Corporate Lockdown and Trauma. This time we're playing as the good-hearted deputy Marshal Ricardo, who bent over backwards to help Ripley in the main game – before getting face-hugged off-camera for his efforts. 'Ricardo, I think we have a lock on that thing,' reads a message from Marshal Waits in the mission's barebones description. 'Leave Prisoner Processing ASAP. Secure it if you have time, but getting out is the priority. Waits out.'

But Waits fails to mention that the alien – or *an* alien – is actually in Prisoner Processing, forcing Ricardo into a desperate survival situation. In this first map, Damage Control, you can make escaping your top priority. However, you can earn some bonus points for locking the armoury down before you bolt, keeping the firearms inside safely away from light-fingered survivors.

Other bonus objectives include collecting prisoner ID tags from dead inmates and prisoner registry data, but why Ricardo would care about this stuff with an alien bearing down on him is something of a mystery. Honestly, it doesn't matter *what* you collect in these missions. They're really just arbitrary objectives, into which the designers have tried to inject some narrative context.

In the next map, titled The Package, Waits shares intel with Ricardo about a mysterious package in the possession of someone named Gardiner. 'Ricardo, Gardiner had the package on him, but he hasn't checked in,' says the Marshal. 'His last message came from Synthetic Storage. Waits out.'

Arriving in Seegson Synthetics, Ricardo finds several eviscerated bodies – one of which is the bloody corpse of Gardiner, a former Colonial Marshal. The package, it's revealed, contains powerful explosives which Waits is planning to use against the alien. Ricardo grabs them from Gardiner and heads to the place where the trap will be set. But not before securing an audio log recorded by Taylor: another one of those arbitrary bonus objectives.

The log in question is very similar to one you can find in the Corporate Lockdown Survivor mission, but with the wording, oddly, slightly changed. 'This is a private message for Marshal Waits from Nina Taylor at Weyland-Yutani,' she says. 'The *Nostromo* black box is of primary importance to the Company. I am authorised to offer you financial incentives to guarantee a smooth, safe retrieval. However, if the data held on the device is compromised or shared, in any way, legal ramifications will be severe.'

The elevator to the next map has been powered down, so Ricardo has to take a detour and stealth past some roaming Working Joes to fire up a generator and juice it back up. He also triggers an alarm in an attempt to lure the alien towards his fiery surprise. 'Plant the explosives and get the hell out of there,' says Waits. 'Let's blast that son of a bitch back to where it came from.'

Then it's onto the final map, Blast Seat, which has an interesting connection to the main game. Ricardo plants the explosives, and as the level ends, we hear a distant, muffled explosion, followed by a message from Verlaine. 'This is Verlaine on the *Torrens*,' she says. 'What the hell just happened? Sevastopol? Did any of your EVA team make it onboard? Please respond. We've taken damage in the blast and are pulling out of Sevastopol space.'

That's right: this explosion is the very same one that almost killed Ripley, Taylor and Samuels at the beginning of the game, interrupting their spacewalk from the *Torrens* to Sevastopol. Ricardo didn't know, of course, so he can't be blamed for it. But between this and the trap in mission six, The Outbreak, you have to question the intelligence of Marshal Waits's decision making. Is setting off explosives on a *space station* really a good idea?

And so, *Alien: Isolation*'s DLC missions come to an end. The Trigger is the best of the bunch, and a fine finale for Creative Assembly's work on the game. I love how it ties into Ripley's story and adds further context to the EVA mishap early in the game. Even though I don't enjoy Survivor mode as much as the regular game, I'm glad it was used to tell more stories on Sevastopol. It's just a shame the Salvage missions, Safe Haven and Lost Contact, don't quite stack up with the other map packs in terms of adding further depth to the station and its residents.

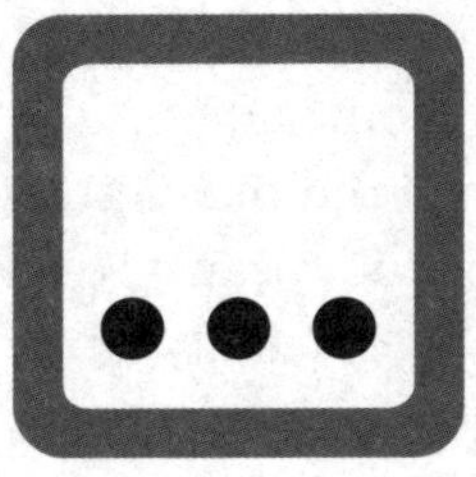

What Ripley Did Next

The continuing adventures of Amanda Ripley.

So what happened to Amanda Ripley? Last we saw her, following the destruction of Sevastopol, she was drifting in space waiting to be rescued. Then, just before the credits roll, a light hits the visor of her pressure suit. Finding out who this light belongs to, and Ripley's next adventure, would have, ideally, been the setup for *Alien: Isolation 2*. No such luck, however. It is, in fact, a mobile spin-off game titled *Alien: Blackout* that gives us our answer.

The game begins with a Weyland-Yutani shuttle, the USCSS *Haldin*, approaching Mendel Station in the remote HIP 51317 system. The shuttle docks and we cut to Amanda Ripley, very much alive, hiding in an air vent. She's flicking between CCTV camera feeds, monitoring the station, and seems relieved when she sees the crew of the *Haldin* coming on board. Amanda gets their attention through an intercom, and one of them introduces herself as Naoko Yutani – who we later discover is a VIP. She's an executive director at Weyland-Yutani and the second cousin of the corporation's CEO.

But before Amanda can respond, we hear the telltale sound of an alien dropping out of a vent. It's the same sound effect used in *Alien: Isolation*, which anyone who's played that game for any length of time will associate with a powerful desire to run and hide. However, moments before it can kill the *Haldin*'s startled crew, Amanda remotely closes a door and blocks its path. Remotely guiding the crew away from danger is *Alien: Blackout*'s central gimmick, but how the hell did our hero end up *here*?

After three days trapped in that pressure suit, drifting into the abyss, Ripley was finally rescued (from 'a bad situation' is as much as she reveals to her rescuers) by the inhabitants of Mendel Station. They took her aboard, but she woke up to find everyone dead and a xenomorph on the loose. She just can't catch a break. Ripley escaped into the station's ventilation system, and it's here we find her as the *Haldin* docks. She's relieved to see these people arrive because the shuttle might just be her ticket to freedom.

Mendel Station is owned and operated by Weyland-Yutani, conducting some kind of mysterious, almost certainly illegal research that is never fully revealed. But the presence of an alien suggests it may well be their field of study. So, after enduring and surviving all that trauma on Sevastopol, she ends up trapped on a Company research station studying xenomorphs. Honestly, it's a bit stupid – and it cheapens her struggles in *Alien: Isolation*. Ripley didn't *need* to be the star of this game, and her presence feels somewhat arbitrary.

Anyway, Ripley saves the crew (how many of them make it depends on your performance in the game), destroys Mendel Station and the xenomorph along with it, then escapes on the *Haldin*, heading back to Earth. 'This is Amanda Ripley, reporting from courier ship *Haldin*,' she says in her final report. 'The Mendel research station has been destroyed. The crew is dead. We are on course for the KOI-125.01 manufacturing colony. We should reach the colony in three days. From there, it is my intention to continue to Earth.'

Three years later, Ripley is home and dealing with the psychological impact of everything she's been through. This is where the comic series *Aliens: Resistance*, written by Brian Wood, picks up. Spending days alone in space in a pressure suit has given her issues with small spaces, and we see her having a panic attack in a cryosleep chamber. She's also seeing a therapist, who she thinks is a Weyland-Yutani plant trying to steer her away from exposing the

Company's involvement in the disappearance of the *Nostromo* and the Sevastopol incident.

This is great stuff, and the kind of thing I would have liked to see explored in an *Alien: Isolation* sequel. But as the story in *Aliens: Resistance* gets going, the fact that it's an *Aliens* comic with an S, not an *Alien* comic, becomes disappointingly clear. Teaming up with Zula Hendricks, a friend and former Colonial Marine, Ripley learns of the existence of a Weyland-Yutani black site being used to experiment on colonists. These experiments, naturally, involve xenomorphs, and the pair blast off into space to expose it.

The comic then descends into the kind of guns-blazing action you'd expect from an *Aliens* comic. I don't have anything against stories like this, but Amanda Ripley deserves better. My main issue with *Aliens: Resistance* is, like *Alien: Blackout*, it cheapens *Alien: Isolation*. It turns the xenomorph into disposable cannon fodder once again, and Ripley's knack for stealth, improvisation, distraction and using her engineering skills to create on-the-fly gadgets – which she honed so brilliantly during the Sevastopol incident – goes completely unused.

By transplanting this character into an *Aliens* story, she becomes just another generic action hero. *Resistance* ends with a heavy serving of explosions and shooting, which is everything *Alien: Isolation* stood against. It's nice to see Ripley still out there, alive and well, fighting the good fight against Weyland-Yutani. But she just doesn't belong in the Cameron-verse. What Amanda Ripley *really* deserves is a direct sequel to *Isolation*, but that seems increasingly unlikely. I don't know what's next for this character, but hopefully it's something more interesting than her shooting aliens with a pulse rifle.

Mods

The fans breathing new life into Alien: Isolation.

For some, *Alien: Isolation* is simply too scary to play. There are people who like the idea of the game, are fans of the movie and would love to spend time in that world. But being trapped in a confined space with a xenomorph? Forget it. However, thanks to the game's small but dedicated PC modding community, it's possible to dull some of the game's sharper edges.

Softcore, a popular mod created by Sgt_Prof, rebalances the game to make it more forgiving. In the vanilla experience, Ripley's carrying capacity is severely limited. This means you can end up with a heap of crafting materials, but no space to make more stuff. *Softcore* deepens your pockets considerably, letting you carry more gadgets. You can also hold more flares and flashlight batteries, making illuminating Sevastopol's corridors less of a resource management issue, and your flamethrower will burn through fuel more slowly.

It even makes your weapons more powerful. But, importantly, it doesn't suddenly make the game a cakewalk. You still have to gather resources, use stealth, outsmart the alien and pay attention to your surroundings. The core gameplay is still there; you just get a slightly easier ride.

If you don't want to be challenged at all, there are mods for that too. *True Story Mode* by TallBear blunts the alien's senses, meaning you have to get really close to it for it to notice you. It spends longer inspecting distractions, and if you scare it away it'll spend more time cowering in the vents. This basically ruins the game, but it's the true definition of a 'story' mode. You really have to go out of your way to die, which is a nice way to experience the game if you've finished it and just want to explore the environments without dying.

But what if you want the game to be harder? Nightmare mode isn't enough for some players. They want to *truly* suffer, which is where mods like JeffCat's *Kitty Isolation* come in. This mod gives players a few minor advantages, like the ability to carry more scrap, the revolver stunning the alien and medkits always restoring 100 per cent of Ripley's health. But these buffs are outweighed massively by the increased brutality, speed and intelligence of the xenomorph.

In *Kitty Isolation*, the alien has hypersensitive vision and hearing, able to spot you from extreme distances. It moves a lot faster – and, in an especially devilish touch, *even faster* if you turn your back on it. Other enemies get an upgrade too: Working Joes will run instead of walk, and armoured human survivors have increased health. Personally, this sounds like a nightmare. But the beauty of PC gaming is that anyone who wants this experience can have it.

There are even mods that add *more* aliens. One named *AlienS: IsolatioN (True Nightmare)*, created by Vyro511, adds a whole suite of difficulty-focused tweaks and alterations, including making hacking harder and increasing the speed, strength and tenacity of Working Joes and humans. But the real reason this mod made headlines in the games press is that installing it means between two and five xenomorphs can appear in a level *simultaneously*. No thanks.

Some modders, unhappy with how the alien behaves in the vanilla game, took it upon themselves to dive into the code and, in their eyes, improve it. *Bay's Alien: Isolation Overhaul*, created by Bay, removes the invisible 'tether' that keeps the alien leashed to the player, making it more unpredictable. It can feel like the alien is always right behind you, nipping at your heels, which this mod seeks to remedy. There's also a version that removes the beast's heavy, thumping footsteps, making tracking it by ear much more difficult.

Reshade mods are also popular. These use colour grading, simulated grain and lighting/shadow adjustments to alter the appearance of the game. *Alien Domination: 1979* by Claudia attempts to replicate the look of the movie more closely than the finished game, with muted colours, a desaturated image and deeper shadows that make the dark parts of Sevastopol *really* dark.

Alien Collection by Loo adds six reshade presets based on the *Alien* movies, from the original all the way through to *Alien: Covenant*. It also includes a bonus preset called *The Lost Tape* that applies various filters to create the illusion of playing the game through a handheld eighties camcorder. I'm generally against these kinds of visual mods because I like to respect the work of the original artists. But for a replay, I admit, some of these are pretty cool.

There are some ultra-specific mods too. One of my favourites, created by NotPork, replaces the standard 20th Century Fox logo with the variant from *Alien 3* – in which the iconic Fox fanfare suddenly mutates into an eerie, shrieking blast of strings. (For the record: I love *Alien 3*, and I'd love to see an *Isolation*-style *Alien* game set on Fury 161.) *Poorly Translated Sevastopol* by TheOneJeff takes all the game's terminal logs, runs them through several Bing and Google translation tools, then feeds them back into the game. Why? I really have no idea, but the resulting gibberish is quite amusing.

But it's impossible to talk about *Alien: Isolation* and modding without mentioning Matt Filer's *OpenCAGE*. This tool lets modders delve into the game's systems, editing almost every aspect of them. You can tweak the alien's behaviour and senses, environmental lighting, how Ripley moves, in-game graphics settings, ammo consumption and much, much more. You can also use its script editor to set custom objectives, trigger visual effects, write your own Sevastolink logs and spawn existing or new custom characters.

Filer has also found a way to import custom maps and meshes into the game, illustrated hilariously by a video in which Ripley battles the alien in Dust II, an iconic map from first-person shooter *Counter-Strike*. *OpenCAGE* is the basis for some of the best *Alien: Isolation* mods (including a few mentioned above), and people have even found ways to create their own basic levels.

It's the efforts of passionate fans like these that is keeping the *Alien: Isolation* dream alive, giving us new ways to experience Creative Assembly's masterpiece years after release – and, hopefully, for more years to come.

Legacy

Reflecting on Alien: Isolation.

Alien: Isolation has won its fair share of awards. PC Gamer, Kotaku Australia, the *New Statesman* and the *Daily Telegraph* all awarded it 2014's game of the year. I was a features editor on PC Gamer at the time, and the team didn't need much convincing from me that *Isolation* deserved the top spot. GamesRadar and Rock Paper Shotgun voted it the best horror game of 2014, and it placed second in *Time* and *Empire*'s list of best games of the year. In 2015, it was nominated for six BAFTAs, including Best Game, winning one for audio. Today, look at any list of the best horror games and *Alien: Isolation* will be on it.

The reviews were largely positive, but with most scores lingering in the 8/10 region. It was only me and a handful of other critics who (correctly, wisely, sagely) nudged it into the upper echelons. The Escapist described it as 'terrifying in a near-perfect way' and said that it made the xenomorph 'scarier than it's been since Ridley Scott first showed it to the world.'

USgamer said it did 'an amazing job of capturing the essence of a classic film and recasting it as a video game' and declared it 'one of the finest film-to-game adaptations ever, and a fantastic stealth adventure in its own right.' Game Informer said it 'delivers the thrill of being in the *Alien* universe, something fans like us have waited a long time to properly experience.'

But it had its detractors too, including two massive, influential American gaming websites. GameSpot, scoring it 6/10, said it was 'four hours' worth of a great idea stretched into 14-plus hours of messy stealth gameplay.' While IGN, in a somewhat infamous 5.9/10 review, said 'someday, someone is going to make an incredible *Alien* video game, but this is not it.'

Unsurprisingly, I disagree with the power of a thousand exploding suns. Of course I do: I'm writing a whole damn book about the game. But I was more bothered by the fact that these reviews, from outlets with such an immense reach, would make people think twice about buying or even trying the game. Maybe it would have sold more, and we'd have a sequel by now, if those critics were kinder to it. Maybe not. I'd rather not think about it.

Dive into the comments sections of both reviews today and you'll see a decade's worth of debate, which is frankly exhausting to read. It's still raging to this day and will for as long as these websites keep their archives up. But this is just more proof that *Alien: Isolation* is a profoundly interesting video game, and one that is still worth talking about – whatever you think of it. See, I could have contributed to the GameSpot/IGN pile-on, but I've been very adult and diplomatic about it. Still, though. *Five point nine*. Oof.

In 2015, Sega revealed that the game had sold 2.5 million copies: a number that will have risen significantly, especially with the game frequently going on sale on digital distribution platforms like Steam and the PlayStation Store. A roaring success by anyone's standards, but seemingly not enough to warrant a sequel. No, *Alien: Blackout* doesn't count.

Bizarrely, cutscenes and edited gameplay from *Alien: Isolation* were recycled and stitched together – along with a few new pre-rendered scenes – to create a web series that was posted on *IGN* in 2019. This retelling of Amanda's story, titled simply (and confusingly) *Alien: Isolation*, was intended to prep players for the impending release of *Blackout*. But low production values, inconsistent animation quality, and a sense that these seven ten-minute episodes added nothing of value to the story we'd already been told back in 2014 meant it was received poorly. Fans were desperate for more *Alien: Isolation*, but not like this.

It's a shame, because *Alien: Isolation* could have been the beginning of a series of horror-focused *Alien* games – and there's a lot a sequel could expand on. I'd like to see a new setting: perhaps a colony like Hadley's Hope, letting Ripley (or whoever the hero might be) venture outside. A deeper crafting system, truer to Creative Assembly's original vision, letting you build your own weapons and tools from a large selection of component parts. The ability to have meaningful conversations and varied interactions with other survivors.

But even if Sega did greenlight a sequel, a lot of the people who made the game – including some of the leads – have since moved on to other studios. That's not to say Creative Assembly couldn't make another great *Alien* game. They definitely could. It would just be *different*. But as I write this, the two highest profile *Alien* video game releases since *Isolation* – *Fireteam Elite* and *Dark Descent* – have both been based on *Aliens*. It feels like the series is back to square one in terms of exploring the rich possibilities of games set in this universe. Yeah, Colonial Marines and pulse rifles are cool, but *c'mon*.

However, the strangest thing about *Alien: Isolation*'s legacy is how little impact it seems to have had. A horror game with a dynamic, reactive antagonist that can learn your weaknesses and take advantage of them was revolutionary stuff. But a decade later, no one has attempted anything even remotely similar. I thought Creative Assembly were leading the charge for a new era of horror games, but no one has taken what they did in *Alien: Isolation* and put their own spin on it.

I would have loved to see other movies given the *Isolation* treatment. Imagine being hunted through the jungle by an intelligent Predator, stripped of your weapons, using primitive, improvised traps to outsmart it. Or a game with the energy of the scene in *Jurassic Park* where Tim and Lex are being stalked by a pack of velociraptors. John Carpenter's *The Thing*, *The Terminator* – the list goes on.

The problem is that the big AAA publishers essentially abandoned horror. Now it belongs to the indies, who are creating some of the most provocative, interesting and thrillingly experimental games in the history of the genre. Being freed from the need to appeal to a wide audience allows independent creators to explore themes, settings and ideas that would be too niche for a mainstream release.

You need millions of dollars and large development teams to make something as complex and lavishly produced as *Alien: Isolation*, which may explain why no serious contender to its throne has emerged. Maybe if AAA falls back in love with horror we'll see a sudden surge of *Isolation*-alikes, but right now, in 2023, I'm not holding my breath. Maybe that will have changed by the time you read this.

Sega have at least continued to release *Alien: Isolation* on different platforms, preventing it from becoming one of those games that is increasingly impractical or awkward to play as the years roll on and hardware becomes obsolete. Originally released on PlayStation 3, PlayStation 4, Xbox 360, Xbox One and PC, the game has since appeared on MacOS, iOS, Android and Switch.

These ports were developed by British developer/publisher Feral Interactive, and they're all superb – especially the Switch version. Surprisingly, despite the relatively low specs of Nintendo's hybrid console, *Alien: Isolation* looks better on it than on the much more powerful PlayStation 4 and Xbox One. Every other version of the game, due to the method of anti-aliasing used, suffers from jaggies: distracting visual artifacts that appear along the edges of objects and scenery.

But the Switch version uses a better form of anti-aliasing, making for a much more stable, smooth image. Combine this with the beautiful Switch OLED display, which makes the shadows in the game look deliciously deep and black, and you have one of the best ways to play *Alien: Isolation* on console. The only downside is a slight controller lag not present in other versions, but for me this is an acceptable trade-off for such a significant boost in image quality and stability.

Logically, the PC version of *Alien: Isolation* should be the best-looking. But while it is possible to play the game at incredibly high resolutions, I think the lo-fi, grainy art style actually loses something when it's rendered too crisply. This is a game that actually benefits from the slight fuzz of a lower pixel count. That said, if you simply must play at the highest possible fidelity, there are mods for the PC version that let you increase reflection quality, shadow resolution, draw distance, and many more variables. There are even fan-made anti-aliasing solutions to help eliminate the aforementioned jaggies.

But honestly, it really doesn't matter *what* you play *Alien: Isolation* on. The strength of the art direction, world-building and gameplay transcends how many pixels are on the screen. Play *Alien: Isolation* on anything – as long as you *play* it. That's the important thing. Hopefully Sega will continue to release it for future platforms. This is a game that deserves to be passed down through the generations. If I ever feel like it's slipping away, I'll do everything in my power to keep it in the conversation and ensure people can still play it. It's like a classic movie; people should be able to appreciate it forever.

Perfect Organism is a part of this preservation effort. Now that I've committed these words to paper, I feel like I've helped in some small way to immortalise the game. Now that you've read it, maybe you'll tell people about it. Then perhaps they'll play the game for the first time and tell a friend about it.

Everything I've said and written about this game over the past decade – in magazines, newspapers, podcasts, radio shows, talks, social media posts, videos or just bending someone's ear about it in a bar or over dinner – has been me carrying the torch for what I think is one of the greatest and most important video games ever made. But honestly, I've said everything I have to say about it now. It's time for you to grab the torch. My work here is done.

Further Reading

Further Reading/Viewing/Listening

BOOKS

Alien: The Archive – The Ultimate Guide to the Classic Movies, Titan Books, 2014

Decandido, Keith R. A., *Alien: Isolation*, Titan Books, London, 2019

McVittie, Andy, *The Art of Alien: Isolation*, Titan Books, London, 2014

Nathan, Ian, *Alien Vault: The Definitive Story Behind the Film*, Aurum Press, London, 2011

Perry, S. D., *Alien: The Weyland-Yutani Report*, Insight Editions, California, 2016

Rinzler, J. W., *The Making of Alien*, Titan Books, London, 2019

Scanlon, Paul, *The Book of Alien*, Simon & Schuster, New York, 1979

Wood, Brian, *Aliens: Defiance*, Dark Horse Comics, Oregon, 2016

Wood, Brian, *Aliens: Rescue*, Dark Horse Comics, Oregon, 2019

Wood, Brian, *Aliens: Resistance*, Dark Horse Comics, Oregon, 2019

ARTICLES

'*Alien: Isolation*: Interview with Dion Lay and Will Porter', *Strange Shapes*, 2015. Also available at alienseries.wordpress.com/2015/05/06/alien-isolation-interview-with-dion-lay-and-will-porter

'Interview with *Alien: Isolation* Writers Will Porter and Dion Lay', *AvP Galaxy*, 2015. Also available at www.avpgalaxy.net/website/interviews/interview-alien-isolation-writers-will-porter-dion-lay

'Interview with Kezia Burrows (Amanda Ripley)', *Perfect Organism: The Alien Saga Podcast*, 2015. Also available at perfectorganism-podcast.tumblr.com/post/114893849645/interview-with-kezia-burrows-amanda-ripley

Bradley, Lee, '*Alien: Isolation* Interview – The Creative Assembly Talks Horror', *Xbox Achievements*, 2014. Also available at www.xboxachievements.com/news/news-17151-alien-isolation-interview-the-creative-assembly-talks-terror.html

Gapper, Michael, '*Alien: Isolation*: The sci-fi masterpiece finally gets the game it deserves', *Edge #263*, Future, 2014

Hogarty, Steve, 'How Creative Assembly designed *Alien: Isolation*'s terrifyingly clever xenomorph', *PCGamesN*, 2020. Also available at www.pcgamesn.com/interview-creative-assembly-alien-isolations-terrifying-alien-ai

Hughes, Sam, '*Alien: Isolation* audio interview with Sam Cooper & Byron Bullock!', *The Sound Architect*, 2014. Also available at www.thesoundarchitect.co.uk/alienisolation

Iwaniuk, Phil, '*Alien: Isolation*: Behind the screams of PS4's scariest game,' *Official PlayStation Magazine*, #92, 2014

Jenkins, David, 'Sigourney Weaver *Alien: Isolation* interview – "It was exciting for me to have a flamethrower"', *Metro*, 2014. Also available at metro.co.uk/2014/07/30/sigourney-weaver-alien-isolation-interview-it-was-exciting-for-me-to-have-a-flamethrower-4814875

Kelly, Andy, 'Addressing criticisms of *Alien: Isolation*', *PC Gamer*, 2014. Also available at www.pcgamer.com/addressing-criticisms-of-alien-isolation

Kelly, Andy, 'Alien: Isolation review', PC Gamer, 2014. Also available at www.pcgamer.com/alien-isolation-review

Kelly, Andy, 'Alien: Isolation review – Giger's creature gets the game it deserves', Guardian, 2014. Also available at www.theguardian.com/technology/2014/oct/03/alien-isolation-review-giger-game-ridley-scott

Kelly, Andy, 'The making of Alien: Isolation', PC Gamer, 2015. Also available at www.pcgamer.com/the-making-of-alien-isolation

Kelly, Andy, 'The Making of horror masterpiece Alien: Isolation: "It was a giddy, exhausting, intense time"', PC Gamer, 2022. Also available at www.pcgamer.com/the-making-of-horror-masterpiece-alien-isolation-it-was-a-giddy-exhausting-intense-time

Rothman, Lily, 'Sigourney Weaver: Why I Signed On for Alien: Isolation', Time, 2014. Also available at time.com/3453689/sigourney-weaver-alien-isolation

Semel, Paul, 'Exclusive Interview: Alien: Isolation Author Keith R. A. Decandido', 2019. Also available at paulsemel.com/exclusive-interview-alien-isolation-author-keith-r-a-decandido

Stuart, Keith, 'Sigourney Weaver on Alien: Isolation – "It's going to be wild"', Guardian, 2014. Also available at www.theguardian.com/technology/2014/jul/24/sigourney-weaver-alien-isolation-video-game

Thompson, Tommy, 'The Perfect Organism: The AI of Alien: Isolation', Game Developer, 2017. Also available at www.gamedeveloper.com/design/the-perfect-organism-the-ai-of-alien-isolation

Thursten, Chris, 'Alien: Isolation: Inside Creative Assembly's revolutionary survival horror', PC Gamer, #262, 2014

Weedon, Paul, 'The Flight interview: Alien: Isolation, composing for video games', Den of Geek, 2015. Also available at www.denofgeek.com/games/the-flight-interview-alien-isolation-composing-for-video-games/

VIDEOS

'*Alien: Isolation* in Close Review', *YouTube Noah Caldwell-Gervais*, 2014, youtu.be/IbsMebWrhDI?si=4TyPvwI--mAspPBY

'How *Alien: Isolation* Survived its Difficult Development | Noclip', *YouTube Noclip*, 2020, www.youtube.com/watch?v=wNIfQz AOKT4

'Revisiting the AI of *Alien: Isolation* | AI and Games #15', *YouTube AI and Games*, 2020, www.youtu.be/P7d5lF6UoeQ?si= K3hi-ud9NvgB_aOk

'Sigourney Weaver and *Alien: Isolation* – YOGSKIM INTERVIEW', *YouTube YOGSCAST Kim*, 2014, www.youtube. com/watch?v=azzZzetXUWo

'The AI of *Alien: Isolation* | AI and Games #15', *YouTube AI and Games*, 2016, www.youtube.com/watch?v=Nt1XmiDwxhY

'The History of Creative Assembly (Total War / *Alien: Isolation*) – Documentary', *YouTube Noclip*, 2020, www.youtube.com/ watch?v=Q2dFl3YFCoo

'The Making of BAFTA-winning game *Alien: Isolation* | The Creators', *YouTube BAFTA Guru*, 2017, www.youtube.com/ watch?v=_ZbV--8J4uA

'Video Game Sound Design with Mark Angus | Sound Makers', *YouTube Sound of Life*, 2022, www.youtube.com/watch?v=No XRtR3c_7A

PODCASTS

'*Alien: Isolation* with Andy Kelly', *Eye of the Duck*, 2021, podcasts.apple.com/au/podcast/alien-isolation-2014-with-andy-kelly-pc-gamer/id15

'Cane and Rinse No. 242 – *Alien: Isolation* with Andy Kelly', *Cane and Rinse*, 2016, caneandrinse.com/242-alien-isolation/

'Episode 80: Top 5 Dreamcast games (with Andy Kelly)', *The Back Page*, 2022, open.spotify.com/episode/6HGVWoLJrZmS ELUcFUBjUB?nd=1&dlsi=e6d39f0c17224d70

'Interviewing Andy Kelly, author of *Perfect Organism: An* Alien: Isolation *Companion*', *Perfect Organism: The Alien Saga Podcast*, 2022, www.perfectorganism.com/home/2022/7/19/196-interviewing-andy-kelly-author-of-perfect-organism-an-alien-isolation-companion

Index

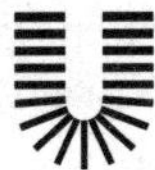

Unbound is the world's first crowdfunding publisher, established in 2011.

We believe that wonderful things can happen when you clear a path for people who share a passion. That's why we've built a platform that brings together readers and authors to crowdfund books they believe in – and give fresh ideas that don't fit the traditional mould the chance they deserve.

This book is in your hands because readers made it possible. Everyone who pledged their support is listed below. Join them by visiting unbound.com and supporting a book today.

Magnus Aadnöy
Lee Abrahams
Stuart Adair
Basha Ahmed-
   Courchesne
Nick Akerman
Bruno Alberton
Chris Aldis
Matt Allcock
Benjamin Allen
Chris Allen
K Allmond

Zachary Allred
Ahmad Alsalem
Harry Alston
Adam Altman
Majid Alzarouni
Dan Amos
Andrian
Richard Anstead
Austin Appleby
Steven Appleman
Rene Aquarius
Brian Arbor

Joe Asercion
Helen Ashcroft
Shane Ask
Spencer Aston
Tony Atkins
Paul Audino
Matthew Austin
Cody Avery
Elliott George Ayling
Jane B
Samuel B.
Duncan Bailey

Martin Baillie
Tom Baker
Lotty Balfour
Björn Balg
Ryan Bamsey
David Baptiste
Daniel Baranski
Tony Barnett
Mark Barrow
basket568903
 basket568903
Samuel Bass
Richard Batten
Dan Bauza
Charlotte Bayes
Nick Beale
Autumn Beauchesne
Gaz Beirne
Kay Beißert
George Bell
Tom Bennett
Christine Bernhardt
Julien Berry
Paolo Marco Bertoldi
Alexander Bickham
Jan Bielecki
Ian Birnbaum
Stephan Bischoff
David Bjorne
David Blatt
Matthew Bloch
Amanda Blok
John A. Blue
Marius Bogaciu
Neil Bolt
Tony Bolton
Franky Bonfanti
Manuel Borges

Ian Boudreau
Jonathan Boulton
Ryan Bousfield
Gareth Bowen
Simon Bower
Simon Bowie
Alec Bowling
Brandon Boyer &
 Sophie Mallinson
Zachary Brackin
Jon Brady
Nathan Brady-
 Eastham
Tom Bramwell
Guus Bremer
Rob Brennan
Sjut Brethauer
Samael Bretondragon
Mike Chuck Bretzlaff
Marc Bright
Jake Brinkly
Jamie Brittain
Steven Broadhurst
Rowan Brocklesby
Paul Broden
Stuart Bromfield
Martin Brookes
Richard Brookes
Anthony Brown
Eric Brown
Ryan Brown
Darren Browne
Paul Browne
James Browning
Chris Brownsell
Alex Bruce
Jonathan Bruce
John Bruins

Ian Brumby
Florian Brusius
Rowan Buchanan
Phil Buckley
Ernest Bueno, Lisa
 Lopez
Mies Buisman
Chris Buñag
Andrew Burger
Jim Burgot
Maria Burke
Leigh Burne
Eric Burns
Marc Burrage
David James Burrows
Courtney Button
Ceri Bythesea
Jack Cahill
Brendan Caldwell
Shelley Calvert
James Cameron
Adam Cammack
Christopher
 Campbell
Lyall Campbell
Paul Canavan
Jeremy Canceko
David Cane
Patrick Cann
Elion Caplan
Cario
Mike Carlson
Brian Carter
John Carter
Alex Cartwright
Mark Case
Dieter Casier
Scott Caslow

Matthew Castle
John Castle-
Anderson
Tom Cawley
Selen Ceri
Gary Chadwick
Jason Chandler
Michael Channell
Chris Chapman
Jonathan Chapple
Aswad Charles
Killian Charles
Rory Charman
Dennis Chauvey
Guy Chetwynd-
Appleton
Gabriel 'Gabgrave'
Chew
Christopher Chinn
Vikas Chowdhary,
Greg Carter
Andrew Christian
Calum Chrystal
Matt Chung
Omer Cinar
Adrian Clabburn
Jacob Clark
Jonathan Clark
Matthew Clark
Tris Clark
Dan Clarke
James Clarkson
Kelly Claxton
Conall Clements
Malachy Clendenning
Alexander Clifford
Palmer Cloud
Patricia Cody

Scott Coello
Rob Coenye
David Cohen
Andrew Coleman
Ben Coleman
Sam Coleman
James Collins
Benjamin Comans
Bob Commane
Christopher-Patrick
Connaughton
Lee Connor
Danielle Consoletti
Paul Conway
Mike Cook
Ashley Cooper
John Cooper
Wil Cornish
Chris Cornwell
Correni
Peter Corrigan
John Craig
Alexander Cranshaw
Helen Cranston
Mark Craven
Mike Cripps
Iain Critien
James Crone
Stephen Croome
Glen Cruickshank
Greg Cummings
Joe Curtin
Daniel Curtis
Darrell Curtis
Andy Cutler
Keith Cyphers
Ian Cyr
Nitin Dahyabhai

Nathaniel Dalby
Anh Dam
Amulya Datla
James Davenport
Michael Davidson
Barry Davies
Chris Davies
Ian Davies
Simon Davis
Niel de Wet
Andy De Wilde
James Dean
Jon Mark Deane
Alex Decker
Nathalie Dekeyser
Alex Delamaire,
Etienne 'Boulon'
Rouzet
Owen Delaney
Thomas Demenat
Yigit Demirag
Kristen Dennis
Anthony Denny
Ash Denton
David Denyer
Kieran Derrick
Stephen M.
Desjardins
John Devine
Lilly Devon
Joe Dillon
Marc Dimbleby
Laura Dines
Brent Disbrow
Mike Diver
Michael Dixon
Patrick Dixon
Leigh Dodds

Michael Dolan
Darren Doll
Joe Donnelly
Daniel Donohue
Dan Douglas
Scott Douglass
Archie Downey
Michael Downie
Jonathan Downin
Connor Doyle
Grant Doyle
Ken Doyle
Kiel Doyle, Courtenay
   Matthews
Nikki Duarte
Lindsay Duff
Chris Duffy
Jerry Duffy
Armando Dugall
Alasdair Duncan
Hamish Duncan
Henry Duncomb
Hannah Dunne
Jesse Duran
Rob Dwiar
Stefan Dziewanowski
Ryan Eastwick
Bryan Eberle
Bradford Eckhart
Mark Eckstein
Robert Eddie
Aaron Edwards
Deryk Egan
Pim Ehrelind
Matthew Eilbeck
Nathan Ellingsworth
Matt Elliott
Kenneth Ellis

DJ Elmer
Andrew Elmore
Matt Elms
Matt Elton
Connor Elward-
   Hopkin
Garrett Erwin
Chris Evans
Elwyn Gruffydd
   Evans
Jon Evans
Ted Everett
evilnoob
Harley Faggetter
Shane Fairhead
Owen Fairnie
Nicolas Fajardo
Su-Yina Farmer
Elizabeth Farmer,
   Katie Farmer
Andi Farr
Andy Farrant
Matt Farthing
Robert Farthing
Jeff Farver
Michelle Fassbender
Jennifer
   Faulconbridge
Cameron Faulkner
Sarah Faust
Jamie Ferguson
Bob Ferry
Matt Filer
Alessandro Fillari
Elliott Finn
Timothy Finn
Jamie Firth, Lucy
   Roslyn

Amanda Fisher
Ben Fisher
Lee Fitzgerald
Hannah Fletcher
Mark Fletcher
James Fleury
Robert Florence
David Folting
Parias Four'Kay
Mercedes Fowler
Ian Fox
Bella Foxx
Robert Foyle
   Hunwick
Matthew Francis
Vieko Franetovic
Alexander Franken
David Fraser
Jean-Noel
   Frederiks
Dean Freeman
Alex French
Dominik Freyer
Daniel Frödtert
James Furlong
John G
Kieran Galaxia
Richard Gale
Bohdan Ganický
Patrick Gardner
Joshua George
Liam Geraghty
Georg Gerleigner
Tom Gilchrist
Paul Gildea
Craig Gilmore
James Gilmour
Jonathan Ginn

Paddy Glenn
John Paul Glennon
Kenneth
   Godberson III
David Godbey
Rik Godwin
David Gogel
Darren Gold
Rob Gonzalez
Terry Goodwin
Patrick T. Gorman
Neil Gorton
Aymeric Goutain
Ben Graham
Ross Graham
Christopher Grainger
Benjamin Grandis
Rob Grant
Pascal Graßhoff
Ashton Gray
Kenneth Gray
Simon Gray
Pete Graylish
David Green
James Green
Joe Green
Patrick Greene
Callum Greenwell
Sam Greer
Pardeep Grewal
Geist Greywolf
Melissa A. Griffith
Miles Griffiths
Keith Grimes
John Grimminck
Kristian Grinsill
Ashley Gunn
Jason Guth

Joseph Guy
Stephen Guyott
Javy Gwaltney
Jake Hadley
Victoria Alice
   Eugenia
   Hainsworth
Chris Halliday
Euan Hamill
Glenn Hamilton
Adrian Hamm
Stephen Hampshire
Ross Hand
Andrew Hanks
Chris Hannan
Edd Hannay
James Hannett
Dan Hansen
Niels Hansen
James Haran
Nikhil Hariharan
Toby Harraway
Peter Harries
Brandon Harris
John Harris
Nick Harris
Colin Harvey
Joel Harvey
Liam Harvey
Elliot Harvey-Massey
George Hasapidis
Matthew Haselton
Tad Hashimoto
Steve Haske
Grant Hatch
Ezekiel Hauge
Carsten Haupka
Connor Hawkes

Stewart Hawkes
Martin Hawkins
Gary Hayman
Luke Hayward
Calvin Hazelhurst
Ashley Head
James Heath
Patric Hediger
Stephen Hegarty
Michael Heilemann
Jeffery Hein
Martin Helmut
   Fieber
Brad Hemming
James Hemming
Alastair Hendry
Sean Hennefer
Christophe Henry
Joe Henson
William Hepburn
Daniel Herbert
Tomas Hermoso
Matt Hernandez
Pepe Hernández
Lee Herron
Rhys Herron
Lea Hess
Paul Hess
Dan Hett
Matt Hewitson,
   Simon Hewitson
Simon Hewitt
Patrick Hey
Michael Hickey
Matthias Hidot
John-Paul Higgerson
David Hiles
Matt Hill

Jörg Hillebrand
Edward Hines-
   Lindo
Tony Hipwell
Matthew Hirst
Hitch
Honor Hiteman
Christian Hobbs
Michael Hobson
Kyle Hoekstra
Alex Hoffman
D Hoffman
Sebastian Hofmann
Steve Hogarty
Jared Holdcroft
Jay Holding
George Holland
Michael Holt
Mike Holton-Jeffreys
Matt Honeycombe-
   Foster
Alistair Hope
DC Hopkins
Benjamin Horlitz
Phillip Hornshaw
Peter Hoskin
David Houghton
Christopher Houk
Philip Howlett
Tóra Hoydal
Richard Hoyle
Richard Hua
Alan Hubbard
Nathan Hughes
Judson Humphrey
Marie Humphrey
Alex Hunt
Dan Hunter

Cameron Hunter-
   Spokes
Martin Huntford
Charlie R Hutchings
Stefan Isberg
Geronimo J
Dwayne Jackson
Kenneth Jackson
Luke Jackson
Michael Jackson
Thomas Jager
Chris Janes
Ollie Janman
Janne
Janneke Janssen
Duncan Jarrett
Ryan Jarvis
AJ Jefferies
Ronni Jensen
Jiminy
Joannawanna
Joedmin
Mikael Johansson
Steven John
Ashley Johnson
Ben Johnson
Connor Johnson
Kurt Johnson
Luke Johnson
Don Johnston
Danny Jones
Gareth Jones
Harriet Jones
Paul Jones
Robert Jones
Ryan Jones
Peter Jordan
Seth Jordan

Nicolai Nebel
   Jørgensen
Aaron Kaczmarczyk
Matthew Kairys
Mike 'Neolun'
   Kammer
Thomas Joseph
   Kane II
Adam Kankowski
Allan Keddie
Philip Keddle
Jarad Keid
Darren Kelley
Jared N. Kellogg
Adam Kelly
John Kelly
John Kent
Rik Kershaw-Moore
Tony Kew
Basil Khan
David Kidd
Ludwig Kietzmann
David Killoughy
Matt Kimmich
Emily King
Matthew King
Roam Kingsbury
Graham Kinniburgh
Jerad Kirk
Sloan Kirkenslager
Iain Kitching
Tobias Kleanthous
Lewis Knight
Garrett Knights
Cody Konior
Corey Koppelow
Aleksei Kosozhikhin
Chris Kotschy

Marcin Kotz
Ryan Kozimor
Tyler Kozimor
kraftcheese
Tomaz Kragelj
Matt Kremer
Jón Kristján
    Kristinsson
Henry Kropf
Leni Krsova
Konstantin Krupp
Daniel Krzeczkowski
John Krzeminski
Kevin Kugler
Christina Kutscher
Stian Lægreid
Anthony LaFauce
Corey Lafferty
Taylor Laird
Phil Lamb
Steve Lambert
Allison Lane
Owen Larkin
David Lasby
Seth Lassing
Roberto Henriquez
    Laurent
Craig Laycock
Julie Le Baron
Thomas Le Puloc'h
Joseff Lea
Michael Leber
Dave Leddington
Warren Leigh
Damien Lejeune
Roman Levin
Swan Levitt
Anthony Lewis

Fridtjof Lexberg
James Lidster
Chris Limb
Eliot Lindsell
Kevin Lingenfelser
Zach Lipman
Ian Littlewood
Artur Litvak
Matthew Lloyd
Martyn Locker
Gavin Logan
Jerry Logan
David Lomax
Dennis Looyen
Jon Cato Lorentzen
Murray Lothian
Ayden Lotter
Ronan Loup
Simon Lovell
Ruby Lucero
Daniel Lucic
Joseph Luhn
David Lusby
Dominic Luxton
Seán Lynch
Thomas Lynch
Aaron M
James M
Michael M
R M
Grace M.
Joshua M.C.
Christopher
    Macdonald
Ripley Mace, Tyler
    Mace
Alastair Macgregor
Ryan Mack

Rob MacMahon
Thomas Mahoney
Will Maiden
Neal Maidment
Julien Maingon
Joshua Maitoza
Jacek Maj
Brett Makedonski
Bryan Maki
John Maloney
Gearóid Manley
Jem Manley-Buser
Stephen Marks
Emily Theodore
    Marlow
Zak Marsh
Alexander Marshall
Brian Marshall
Garry Marshall
James Marshall
Liam Marshall
Stephanie Marson
Alexander Martin
David Martin
Elliot Martin
Don Mase
Charlie Maslen
Graeme Mason
Tom Masters
Stu Mather
Jesse Mathews
Tim Mathie
Lewis Maton
Richard Matthias
George Mattson,
    Waldo
Krzysztof Matuliński
Christian Matzke

Julien Maudoux
Chris Maura
Holiday McAllister
Ciaran McCarthy
Sandra McCaul
Ross McClure
Sam McConville,
 James Thompson
Adam McCorry
Matthew McCoy
Ross McCready
Jake McDaniel721
Morgan McDermott
Andy McDonald
Danny McDonald
Gene McDonald
R. McFarland
Kathleen McGee
David McGilloway-
 Penfold
Cillian McGillycuddy
Evan McGowan
Khayla McGowan
James McGregor
Liam McGuigan
Timothy McInnis
Kirk McKeand
Stuart Mckechnie
Jon McKellan
Chris McMullen
Ian McNertney
Conor McParland
John McPhail
Kris McQuage-
 Loukas
Collin McRae
Ben McSkelly
Ben Meakin
Lee Medcalf
Robin Meijer
Stephan Meijerhof,
 Raphaël Sfeir
Steven Melis
Ian Mellis
JT Mengel
Hannah 'Little Bird'
 Meurer
Karl Meyer
Anthony Micari
Paul Middleton
Anita Miller
Finlay Milligan
Briana Ashley Mills
Robert Mills
Terence Minerbrook
Shawn Minisall
Stefan
 Mir-Mackiewicz
Harry Mitchell
Tim Mitchell
Ben Mitchinson
Scott Modlin
Drew Moffatt
Jason Mogavero
Jack Monaghan
Adolfo Montero
Shaun Mooney
Alex Moore
Olivier Morin
Chris Morris
Daniel Morris
Jess Morrison
James Morton
Andrew Morwood
Jean Moschetta
Keith Moss
Noah Mr.
Gary Mulcahy
Steve Mumford
Jonathan Munday
Bernat Muñoz
Gav Murphy
Jake Murphy
Fraser Murray
Gary Myers
Thomas Myhill
Stephen Napoles
Patrick Naramore
Octavi Navarro
Carlo Navato
Ewelina Nawrocka
Colin Neal
Tim Neale
Maxwell Neely-
 Cohen
Antony Neill
Richard Nelson
Ben Newcombe
Conor Newman
Edwin Ng
Linh Nguyen
Gabriel Nicholson
John Nicholson
Christopher Nicol
Henry Nicol, Robert
 Robear-Burbil
 Thomson
Gavin Niebel
James Niekirk
Vince Noce
Rob Nolan
Timmy Nolan
Keith Noordzy
Martin Noras

Nigel Norman
Todd Norman
Alexander Norris
Gareth Noyce
Joseph O'Donnell
Brandon O'Hara
Jack O'Neill
David O'Reilly
PJ O'Reilly
Leanne O'Hara
Ossian Olausson
Beth Oliver
Tamás Orosz
Adam Orth
Simeon Osborn
Max Osta
Jeff Otis
Kevin Ott
Jamie Owen
Neil Owen
Daniel Owens
Luis Pabon
Jeremy Pack
Lewis Packwood
Josiah Paez
Charlie Park Laws
Chris Parker
John Parker
Simon Parkin
Tom Parkinson
Tony Parmenter
James Partridge
Robbie Paterson
Chris Patrick
Chris Pawlak
Nick Peake
Fabrizio Pedrazzini
Matthew Pellett

Meg Pelliccio
Aaron Percival
Fabian Perez
Paul Perrins
Jayson Perriott
Alexander Peterhans
Jay Petronis
Matthew Pfeiffer
Charlie Phair
Gilles Philippart
Leigh Picard
Badass John
    Pickering
Ashley Pickin
Massimiliano Piepoli
Dan Pietersen
Adrian Pilkington
J. Kyle Pittman
Richard Plant
Ryan Plasch
Charlotte Platt
Sander Pompe
James Poplar
Will Porter
Mark Portnoy
Ben Potter
Jay Pounsett
Jon Powell
Luke Pratt
Marc Price
Wil Price
Rivven Prink
Hereward L. M.
    Proops
Nathaniel Quarrie
Norman Quarrinton
Sean R
Mark Radcliffe

Thomas Ragsdale
Marco Ramirez
Alexandre Ramos
    Coelho
Dan Ramsden
Craig Rathbone
Raxter (Lars)
John Read
Stewart Reaney
Mark Reel
Jordan Rees
Steve Reilly
Dakota Reinhart
Douglas Reinholtz
Travis Reitter
Brian Renwick
Marco Resendiz
RetroGreene
Lauren Reynolds
Matthew Reynolds
Michael Reynolds
Phil Reynolds
John Rice
Myles Rich
Matt Richards
MD Richards
Liam Richardson
Luke Richardson
Keith Richie
David Rickard
Simon Ridge
Matthew Ritter
William Robbie
Keresztesi,
    NODIKA' Róbert
Max Roberts
Samuel Roberts
Trevor Roberts

Craig Robertson
Murray Robertson
Kenneth Robinson
Andrew Robinson
 Hodges
Kai Rochester
Jacob Roden
Carlos Rodriguez
Dillon Rogers
Rosie Rogerson
Dannyorker &
 Carlotus Rojas
Autumn Rolling
James Romanski
Andrey Romanyuk
Logan Romney
Seb Ronson
Neale Rooney
Christin Roper
Shaun Rosado
Rachael Rose
Josh & Jenn
 Rosenberg
Craig Ross
James Rossignol
Joseph Rozner
Kyle Ruiz
Michael Rundle
David Rupp
Bradley Russell
Alex Ruth
Andrew Ryan
FL S
Raunak S
Christian Sadler
Jordi Roquer
 Sanagustin
Sherwin Santos

Jason Sarpolis
Michael Sauers
Loucas Savvides
David Scarborough
Leonhard Schading
Josh Scherping
Chris Schilling
Keith Schlichter
Stefan Schmidt
Katie Schneider
MJ 'jello' Schoerbel
Daniel Schwabe
Samuel Schwager
Jonathan Schwartz
Filip Schwarz
Graham Scott
Robert Christopher
 Scott
Michael Scudieri
Chris Scullion
Jamie Sefton
NJ Sellars, Andrea
 Schicktanz
Adrian Sellers
Elina Sellgren
Kristian Sevilhaug
Rory Shafto
Amadu Shaw
Craig Shaw
John Shea, James
 Smith
Ben Sheppard
James Shields
Robbie Shirley Jr,
 Wesley Shirley
Richie Shoemaker
Maksym Shomodi
Thomas Siddons

Rainer Sigl, Eugen
 Pfister
Gregory Sigston
Scott Sikes
Andy Simcock
Jen Simpkins
Donald Sinclair
Martin Sjøholt
Ben Sledge
Richard Smeeton
A. C. Smingleigh
Michael Smit
Ben Smith
Clayton Smith
Elliott Smith
Erik Smith
John Smith
Liam Smith
Matthew Smith
Michael Smith
Olly Smith
Rebecca Smith
Steve Smith
Chris Smyth
Dayann Soares Froes
Werner Sohm
Rory Solley
Chris Sorrell
Mayo Soto
Eric Soulvie
Will Southeard
Andrew Southern
Rune Spaans
Philip Sparks, Paul
 Robertson
Ashley Spencer
Stephen Spires
Aaron Spratt

Richard Stanton
Charlotte Stark
Zachary Staszewski
Ian Stephen
Krist Stevens
Paul Stevens
Michael Stewart
Graham Stock
James Stockings
James Stocks
Dan Stott
Tim Stride
Christopher Stroker
Mike Subelsky
Mark Sullivan
Michael Fournier
Andy Summers
Sean Sumner
Tim Suter
James Sutherland
Tim Sutton Coulson
Daniel Switzer
Eric Switzer
Lawrence Symes
Sarah Szell
Ripley Olivia
   Rowena Taberer
   Peters
Rowan Tafler
Adam Tait
Pat Tapia
Chris Tarrant
Jack Taylor
Martin Taylor
Travis Taylor
Drop Bear Bytes,
   Leanne
   Taylor-Giles

Kris Telford
@theadmiral
Jay Tholen
Aled Thomas
Ryan Thomas
Daniel Thompson
John Thompson
Joshua Thompson
Nolan Thompson
Tommy Thompson
Max Thompson-
   Walker
Keith Thorburn
Leonie Thorpe
David Thurkettle,
   Ben Thompson
Alex Timperley
Jörg Tittel
Jim Toal
TobyLooksLike
Richard Tock
Michael Todd
Matt Toliusis
Barry Topping
Christophe Torne
Emily Tough
Vivien Troadec
Joel Troughton
Christopher Troutt
Joannes Truyens
James Tuck, Mark
   Riley
Jake Tucker
Charles Turck
Dave Turner
Matt Turner
Frederic
   Turner-Hanquart

Ričardas Tvaskūnas
Christopher Tynan
Paul Tysall
Hunter Urann
Andrew Utting
Tim V
Henno van Arkel
Issy van der Velde
Evert van Houten
Davy Van Obbergen
Russell Varley
Vijay Varman
Michael Vaughn
   Green
Matthew Vayda
Elliott Verbiest
Matthew Verran
Ash Versus
Gregory Verzumo
Harmony Vianne
Daniel Vickers
Leandro Villanueva
Graeme Virtue,
   Christopher
   Cameron
Gernot Vlcek
Vincent Vogt
Ben Vokes
James Vokes
Kristian Volsing
Carson Vowles
Andreas Wagner
Wai-hong & Sandra
Thora Waldmann
Kieran Walsh
Eliott Walton
William Walton
Graham Ward

Matthew Ward
Grant Watmuff
Michael Watson
Ben Webster
Paul Weedon
William Wells
Grayson Wendell
Jennifer Wepierre
Gerrit Wessendorf
Jonathan West
Michael Westbom
Joseph Whalen
Eoin Whelan
Jonel Whitcomb
Andrew White
Braden White
Cormac White
Edward White
Jason White
Peter White
Scott Craig White
Lyle Whitehead
Alexander Whiteside
Colin Whiteside
Tom Whithorn
Alexander Whittam
Will Whitty-Ryan
Brock Wilbur
Alec Wilby
Jon Wilcox
Dominic Wilkinson
Samuel Willetts
Owen Williams
Richard Williams
Stephen Williams
Sam 'Mr Tooltip'
   Williamson
Ronan Wills
Carl Wilson
Iain 'Troph' Wilson
Nick Wilson
Lyndal
   Wilson-Bishop
Alex Wiltshire
Joe Wintergreen
Owen Wolahan
Jason Wolf
J. Morgan Wolff
Stephen Wolters
Joshua Wood
Marcus Wood
Ryan Woodward
Richard Woolf
Ken Worsley
Admiral Wren
Adam Wright
Jonathan Wright
Reese Wright
Sebastian Wuepper
Jamie Wyatt
David Wykes
Xalatar
yarsikula
Ross Yost
Agnes Young
Austin Young
Rob Zacny
Daniella Zelli-Lim
Solh Zendeh
Joakim Ziegler
Tena Zigmundovac
Янош Бан